A Preacher's Guide to
Lectionary Sermon Series

A Preacher's Guide to Lectionary Sermon Series

THEMATIC PLANS FOR YEARS A, B, AND C

Compiled by Jessica Miller Kelley

WESTMINSTER
JOHN KNOX PRESS
LOUISVILLE · KENTUCKY

© 2016 Westminster John Knox Press

First edition
Published by Westminster John Knox Press
Louisville, Kentucky

16 17 18 19 20 21 22 23 24 25—10 9 8 7 6 5 4 3 2 1

Book design by Drew Stevens
Cover design by Lisa Buckley Design

Library of Congress Cataloging-in-Publication Data

Names: Kelley, Jessica Miller, editor.
Title: The preacher's guide to lectionary sermon series : thematic plans for
  Years A, B, and C / [edited by] Jessica Miller Kelley.
Description: First edition. | Louisville, Kentucky : Westminster John Knox
  Press, 2016.
Identifiers: LCCN 2015051049 (print) | LCCN 2016005048 (ebook) | ISBN
  9780664261191 (alk. paper) | ISBN 9781611646658 ()
Subjects: LCSH: Lectionary preaching.
Classification: LCC BV4235.L43 P74 2016 (print) | LCC BV4235.L43 (ebook) |
  DDC 251/.6—dc23
LC record available at http://lccn.loc.gov/2015051049

Most Westminster John Knox Press books are available at special quantity discounts
when purchased in bulk by corporations, organizations, and special-interest groups.
For more information, please e-mail SpecialSales@wjkbooks.com.

Contents

YEAR B

Foreword

When I was engaged in discerning my first call to lead a congregation, I remember being consumed with thoughts about how to answer the committee's interview questions, reading bylaws and constitutions, researching appropriate compensation for a change in cost of living, and thinking about how my family would adjust to a new location and congregation.

What I do not recall—not at all—is thinking about preaching. Sermons. The activity I would engage in almost every single week of the year, the vehicle by which my new congregation would come to know my perspective and trust my leadership, the most effective vehicle for teaching and leading a congregation.

Why this was, I don't really know, except to say that in my previous experience as an associate pastor, preaching was an occasional task, usually assigned for the weeks after Easter and Christmas and the least-attended Sunday of the year, most often sometime toward the beginning of August.

I also remember the feeling of panic—OK, dread—that settled over me about three weeks into that first pastorate. I said to a friend, "I just can't believe they expect me to get up there and say something *every single week*! I already said everything I learned in Sunday school, vacation Bible school, and seminary!"

She answered, "That's what the text is for."

What she meant, of course, was the Bible. Even most mediocre preachers know that the sermon every Sunday is not meant to showcase what you know; it's meant to delve deeply into Holy Scripture, to engage a text that has guided people of faith for centuries, and to bring the deep and eternal truths of that text to bear on the realities of our lives and our world. But how?

I'm now engaged in round four of preaching the three-year cycle of texts assigned by the Revised Common Lectionary. This cycle of assigned texts is used by much of the Christian world to guide the rhythm of the church year and in planning worship. Naturally, the possibility for coherence, synergy, and unity is enhanced when the preacher jumps on the bandwagon too.

I chose to use the lectionary to guide my first few years of preaching for the reason I mentioned above: every week I found myself at a loss about where to even begin crafting a sermon. What I've discovered in the years since that initial decision are other, powerful reasons—both for myself as a preacher and for the congregations I've served—to continue this conversation with the passages of the Revised Common Lectionary.

The first is the truth effective preachers struggle to remember: preaching is not about me. Were I to choose topics reflecting my current interest or passages I randomly prefer, I'd soon veer from the challenging discipline of engaging an assigned text and discerning its resonance for the context I serve. Second, while some might find a tedium in the cycle back to the same texts every three years, this experience has taught me in practice a very real truth of our Holy Scripture: there are depths to be mined, the richness of which I will never fully explore in my lifetime.

Connection with colleagues in both practical and spiritual ways has been a third gift of lectionary preaching. Every year for the past twelve years I've gathered with the same five colleagues to plan preaching for the year ahead. Through our shared conversation and planning we develop the kind of deep relationship that can remind us each of our faith and our calling, and support us through the difficult work of leading God's people.

Leading God's people in the local church is not a task, as we know, for the faint of heart. Local congregations constantly face the challenge of moving beyond immediate conflict, concern, and maintenance to think about the work of the church in the world. The rhythm of the lectionary cycle broadens our understanding of ourselves to include the church universal, congregations of Christians all over the world who gather the same exact Sunday to read the same texts and to explore their relevance for the context in which they live.

I've heard colleagues explain why they prefer to avoid the lectionary: people respond better to thematic preaching, sermon series on a particular topic. Folks don't want a homiletical study on the book of Job, friends will say. They want "Five Steps to a Happy Marriage." They have to surrender the rich experience of preaching the lectionary, they argue, in order to give people what they want.

This reasoning is problematic for me, fundamentally because of the dangerous theological assumption that church is about giving people what they want. It's not. But this argument also assumes that lectionary preaching and series preaching are incompatible. And that's just not true, either.

In fact, though I am a dedicated lectionary preacher, I have experienced what my colleagues have told me to be true: people like series—in fact, more than like. People in the pews engage at a deeper level with a "handle" to hang onto. If the pastor can shape the common worship life of the people in ways that the congregation can engage, the corporate experience of worship and the larger life of the church are richer and more resonant.

Like most things in life, there's no exclusive dichotomy between preaching the lectionary and building thematic arcs into the worshiping life of the congregation. A good preacher should do both. I have found that when we consider assigned texts with an eye toward the rhythm and life of the individual communities we serve, the pressing concerns of the world around us, *and* the deep, universal truths of Christian faith, themes begin to emerge with a clarity one might not have imagined possible.

At one congregation I served, the anticipation of these three- or four-week themes became a source of joy and community building for all of us. We'd work together to find a visual expression of the theme; we'd build discipleship and mission opportunities in conjunction with the theme; and at the end of the year we'd take our logos and themes and create a piece of art to reflect that year of life together.

Preaching the lectionary thematically may be a whole new way of homiletical expression, an outside-the-box invitation for a largely unchurched crowd to learn the rhythms and richness of the lectionary and explore the many ways the ancient text intersects our modern lives. With this innovative use of the lectionary in preaching, we've discovered once again new possibilities for engaging the ancient text in ways that build mature disciples and rich, transformational community.

Amy K. Butler
Senior Minister, The Riverside Church, New York
September 2015

Using This Resource

Some church leaders love the Revised Common Lectionary for the consistency it brings to proclamation and education across congregations and denominations. Others consider lectionary preaching boring and limiting.

Some church leaders prefer to preach in topical series, crafting sermons that explore a book of the Bible, a meaty section of Scripture, or a significant theme in Christian living over a period of weeks or even months. Others say series preaching is hokey or contrived, and that choosing one's own texts biases a preacher toward his or her favorite passages.

A Preacher's Guide to Lectionary Sermon Series is designed to offer the best of both worlds with this comprehensive manual of sermon series ideas designed to frame consecutive weeks of lectionary texts into seasonal and short-term series. Taking into consideration both the liturgical calendar and the secular calendar, this resource, using the Revised Common Lectionary, includes plans for twenty-six thematic sermon series that celebrate holy days and seasons *and* respond to typical patterns of church attendance, maximizing visitor retention and member engagement.

Twelve experienced preachers from five denominations—some dedicated lectionary preachers, others accustomed to topical series—accepted the creative challenge of developing these thematic series plans using the assigned readings of the lectionary. You will find here series studying specific books of the Bible and significant biblical figures, as well as lessons for discipleship from across the Bible's sections and genres. You may wish to use these outlines as they are, adapt for your congregation's needs, or get inspired to design your own thematic series from the lectionary.

What's Included Each of the twenty-six series plans includes:

- A series overview, introducing the overall message of the series
- A chart outlining the sermon title and focus Scripture for each week of the series, along with a very brief description of each sermon's theme
- Tips and ideas for the series, with suggestions for worship elements, visuals, fellowship activities, and outreach efforts that enhance the congregation's engagement with the series topic
- Sermon starters for each Sunday, to summarize the week's message, prompt your research and writing process, and offer illustrations to enhance your preaching

In the back of this volume, you will find a calendar listing the Sundays for Years A, B, and C for three lectionary cycles, from the 2016–17 liturgical year (Year A) all the way to 2024–25 (Year C). This nine-year calendar enables you to plan your preaching schedule to make use of all the series plans this book has to offer, regardless of when you begin to use it.

You will also find that not every Sunday is included in a series. There are breaks between some series, allowing for quirks in the liturgical calendar (years when there are seven or more Sundays between Epiphany and Ash Wednesday, for example) and for weeks you may wish to have a guest preacher, special service, or other stand-alone sermon.

While this resource respects the liturgical calendar, and the lections designed to accompany them, a few exceptions are made for floating holy days like Trinity Sunday and special days that may fall on weekdays but be observed on a Sunday (Epiphany and All Saints' Day, for example). In those cases, the assigned lections for the special day may be substituted for the regularly scheduled Proper lections, or vice versa.

Making the Most of a Series Exploring a theme or book of the Bible across several weeks (as short as three weeks and as long as twelve, in this resource) gives congregants and visitors a memorable handle to latch onto from week to week. Knowing what is being preached on the following week keeps people engaged, coming back, and telling friends. Like a television show or miniseries, preaching in series can create a "don't want to miss it" desire to be there for each week of worship.

To maximize the impact of each series:

- *Use consistent visuals.* Even without a dedicated graphic design person in your church, you can create one image or typographic treatment for the series that can be used on your printed materials (bulletins, flyers, etc.) and digital media (website, Facebook page, or worship screen if you use one). Some of the "tips and ideas" sections of series plans include ideas for altar displays and other visual elements to enhance the worship space.
- *Go beyond the sermon.* We all know that worship and spiritual growth do not hinge entirely on the sermon. Incorporate the theme when planning music and special moments in the service like testimonies or dramas. Plan special events at which congregants can discuss or put into practice the ideas being preached on in the series. Many "tips and ideas" sections have suggestions for such events.
- *Spread the word.* Visitors may be more likely to give your church a try if they know an upcoming service will be addressing a topic or question they have wondered about. Promotion of the series can be done through church newsletters, posters, special mailings, and social media. The week before the series begins, send a special email about the series to all members, encouraging them to attend and asking them to forward the email to family, friends, neighbors, and coworkers.

Year A

Advent/Christmas Series: A Geography of Salvation

Six Parts: First Sunday of Advent through
First Sunday of Christmas, including Christmas Eve

The path to Bethlehem with landmarks from the book of Isaiah.

KATHERINE WILLIS PERSHEY

Series Overview The Scriptures that help us prepare for the birth of Jesus Christ are filled with *places*—holy places, hard places, and the pathways in between. Together, these places present a "geography of salvation"—a map of the heights and depths our good God will go to bring us home. Throughout the weeks of Advent, we will "visit" some of these sacred locales. Along the way we'll learn that we can meet God on the

	Sermon Title	Focus Scripture	Theme
Advent 1	A Pending Invitation	Isa. 2:1–5; Rom. 13:11–14	We await our invitation to celebrate when the house of the Lord is established.
Advent 2	A Tangible Hope	Isa. 11:1–10; Rom. 15:4–13	Even in the midst of a broken creation, signs of hope emerge.
Advent 3	A Desert in Bloom	Isa. 35:1–10; James 5:7–10	Advent isn't only about God's movement toward us. Advent is also about our movement toward God.
Advent 4	Somewhere between Heaven and Hell	Isa. 7:10–16; Rom. 1:1–7	Emmanuel, God-with-us, is here.
Christmas Eve[1]	A Feast of Light	Isa. 9:2–7; Luke 2:1–14, (15–20)	Although we still walk in places of darkness, the Christ light shines.
Christmas 1	When God Walks the Earth	Isa. 63:7–9; Matt. 2:13–23	God is here—and this changes nothing, and everything.

1. If Christmas Eve falls on a Sunday, Advent 4 can be used in the morning and this sermon used for evening candlelight services or a Christmas Day service.

mountaintop—but that God also draws near to wherever it is we find ourselves.

Tips and Ideas for This Series Use vintage-looking maps in your bulletin or screen design, and perhaps as part of an altar display. Or create a hypothetical treasure map with icons of a mountain, stump, desert, and so on along the path to Bethlehem. If you have space and desire for more involved visuals, consider creating and adding to a landscape around the front or perimeter of your worship space: a mountain for the first week; a stump and bare branch in the second; a desert, roadside shanty; and so forth.

Advent 1: A Pending Invitation
Isaiah 2:1–5; Romans 13:11–14

In days to come the mountain of the Lord's house shall be established as the highest of the mountains, and shall be raised above the hills; all the nations shall stream to it. Many peoples shall come and say, "Come, let us go up to the mountain of the Lord, to the house of the God of Jacob; that he may teach us his ways and that we may walk in his paths." (Isaiah 2:2–3a)

As we enter the season of Advent—a time of preparation and anticipation for the coming of Christ—Isaiah reminds us that our excitement is well founded. God will go to extraordinary lengths to dismantle and repair God's broken creation. It is good to recall the breadth and depth and—particularly in this week's reading from the Hebrew Bible—the *height* of what we are called to await.

The invitation is in the mail, so to speak. The word is out; construction has begun. God is establishing a house on a hilltop, a mountaintop villa with a view to die for (*spoiler alert!*). The good news is that there's going to be a housewarming party, and we're invited—or, at least, we *will* be. This passage from Isaiah is one of those classic "already but not yet" theological scenarios. The house of the Lord—the place where God's kingdom is fully realized—is described in lush detail, in a tone of certainty. These promises will be fulfilled. God will reign over a peaceable realm bereft of warfare and gilded with righteousness.

Our Advent invitation—our Advent dare—is to look toward that realm with joyful expectancy. However, one thing is abundantly clear: we are not yet on God's holy mountain. Rather, we are in a spiritual diaspora. Some of us are stuck in deep valleys of sorrow and loss; others wend their way along windy paths beset by anxiety for the unknown ahead. Some of us are lost and know it; others walk in circles without ever realizing that we aren't going anywhere we haven't already been. No matter where we find ourselves, it is easy to give up hope. We can be so focused on our immediate surroundings that we lose sight of the promised land. Yet Paul writes that "salvation is nearer to us now than when we became believers." This is true for us no matter where we are.

Although the invitation to celebrate the establishment of the house of the Lord has not yet been issued, another invitation has: "O house of Jacob, come, let us walk in the light of the LORD!" No matter where we are on our journeys, our feet can trod in the light of the Lord. The light of the Lord falls anywhere and everywhere. The armor of light of which Paul speaks is ours to take upon our shoulders. We don't have to be anywhere special or holy; with God illuminating our way, every place is special. Every place is holy.

Advent 2: A Tangible Hope
Isaiah 11:1–10; Romans 15:4–13

A shoot shall come out from the stump of Jesse, and a branch shall grow out of his roots. The spirit of the Lord shall rest on him, the spirit of wisdom and understanding, the spirit of counsel and might, the spirit of knowledge and the fear of the Lord. (Isaiah 11:1–2)

Isaiah's remarkable litany of promises begins humbly. Look at the ground, he seems to say—for where else would we find a stump? A stump presumed dead but impossibly bursting with new life? Look down at the ground—but know that the ground beneath our feet in this passage is God's holy mountain, a realm of peace and justice that is dependent on the advent of a leader. Isaiah's portrayal of this leader born of David's lineage explains why it is reasonable to hope: the very Spirit of God rests on his shoulders. He is infused with God's own understanding, counsel, and might. He does not lead with the faltering, fallible wisdom of an ordinary man. He embodies and brings about divine justice. Under his watch, the poor and meek are lifted up. There is no room for evil and oppression; on this mountain, even the predators are peaceable.

Isaiah paints an idyllic picture, but it is no mere fantasy. This is not about pie in the sky, a vision of some otherworldly realm. This is about the redemption of creation. This is about the earth that is beneath our feet even now, an earth that will be "full of the knowledge of the LORD as the waters cover the sea." A remarkable thought in a world that often seems to be drowning in something more like *igno-rance* of God's peaceable ways.

This Scripture belongs first to the Jewish people. In a sermon on the text, Rabbi Margaret Wenig identified places where God fulfilled this promise in Jewish history. One of her stories is especially moving. She tells of a group of Austrian Jews who had survived the horrors of the concentration camp in Buchenwald. While they were imprisoned in that living hell, they dreamed of settling in Palestine and starting a kibbutz, a religious commune centered on farming, family, and worship. And they did. They founded a peaceful community that still exists, sustaining yet another generation of families that might not have been. The name of the kibbutz is Netzer, which means "twig"—as in "A twig shall sprout from the stump of Jesse." Their life is a witness to Isaiah's prophecy, a sign of God's faithfulness to his promises.

Signposts pointing to transformation are sprouting up like—well, like shoots from the stump of Jesse. As we await the advent of God's peaceable kingdom, we can find and nurture the twigs of promise God brings forth every day. Perhaps the wolf does not yet lie down with the lamb, but glimmers of peace do surface, even in the midst of danger and despair. Sometimes irreconcilable relationships are reconciled. Sometimes unforgivable sinners are transformed by grace. Sometimes survivors thrive in new life beyond the pain of the past. In these times, God's kingdom breaks into the present, revealing blessed glimpses of the glory yet to come. Our task is to trust that through the Holy Spirit these sacred shoots will arise and to give God thanks and praise for every sign of healing, every signal of hope, every gesture of peace.

Advent 3: A Desert in Bloom
Isaiah 35:1–10; James 5:7–10

A highway shall be there, and it shall be called the Holy Way; the unclean shall not travel on it, but it shall be for God's people; no traveler, not even fools, shall go astray. No lion shall be there, nor shall any ravenous beast come up on it; they shall not be found there, but the redeemed shall walk there. (Isaiah 35:8–9)

I'll never forget the first time I experienced the desert. I was on a church camping trip in Anza Borrego State Park. The views were breathtaking, but I can't quite say it was beautiful. It was certainly unlike any place I had ever encountered. I grew up with deciduous trees and meadows strewn with dandelions; I had no frame of reference for the vast, expansive, seemingly lifeless badlands east of San

Diego. The scenery unnerved me so deeply I learned a new appreciation for the biblical wilderness narratives. Wandering out there for forty days—let alone forty years!—is utterly unthinkable to me.

I confessed to a native Californian on the trip that Anza Borrego made me desperately homesick for the Midwest. She told me that I should refrain from passing judgment on the desert until I'd seen it after rain showers had coaxed it into full bloom. I couldn't begin to imagine what she described to me—fields of purple wildflowers, cactuses crowned with blossoms of gold. I still haven't seen the desert in bloom in person, and if it weren't for the magic of Google Images, I still might not believe that such a parched landscape could really erupt into a brilliant display of life. But it does.

As we ponder the places of Advent, we find ourselves in a desert that should be arid yet is bursting with verdant joy, as though the arms of the saguaros are raised in worship and thanksgiving. The implausibility of streams in the desert and the absurdity of burning sand cooled by pools of life-giving water—this is the wild promise of redemption. And a rejoicing desert is only one of a whole host of impossible promises that will be fulfilled: the blind ones see, the deaf ones hear, the lame ones dance, the silent ones speak.

This is not a stationary celebration. As Isaiah says, there shall be a highway there in the blooming desert. Not a path; a *highway*. Just as my time in California gave me a notion of deserts as bleak and unforgiving places, life in Los Angeles County also gave me some particular ideas about highways. (A seminary professor claimed that there was always a couch somewhere on the Santa Monica Freeway.) But this is unlike any highway we've ever driven. This is the Holy Way. This is a parade route of praise, upon which the redeemed joyfully travel to our final destination. This is a safe road; you can't get lost again, once you have joined the procession to Zion.

Advent isn't only about God's movement toward us, like a heaven-sent rain that can make even the bleakest landscape blossom. Advent is also about our movement toward God. When you find the Holy Way, start walking and keep walking, trusting that the pathway that has been carved for you will take you where need to go.

Advent 4: Somewhere between Heaven and Hell
Isaiah 7:10–16; Romans 1:1–7

Again the LORD spoke to Ahaz, saying, Ask a sign of the LORD your God; let it be deep as Sheol or high as heaven. But Ahaz said, I will not ask, and I will not put the Lord to the test. Then Isaiah said: "Hear then, O house of David! Is it too little for you to weary mortals, that you weary my God also? Therefore the Lord himself will give you a sign. Look, the young woman is with child and shall bear a son, and shall name him Immanuel. (Isaiah 7:10–14)

God offers another sign. The sign can be as deep as Sheol or as high as heaven—unimaginable places, really, for a human being who is situated smack dab in the middle of the biblical three-story universe. One is higher than we could hope to reach; the other, lower than we'd ever dare to venture. At first Ahaz demurs. God insists. God makes a promise that reverberates with meaning—not only for the Hebrew people but also for the Christians who have, for millennia, reinterpreted these words to refer directly to the birth of the Christ child.

Like the shoot from a dry stump and the blossoming of a desert, God says through Isaiah that a young (perhaps unwed, perhaps unprepared) woman will bear a child. And so it is that the sign ends up inhabiting neither the heavenly sphere nor the realm of Sheol. The sign lands in a place somewhere between heaven and hell, a place that is, like the human being, smack dab in the middle: *here*. Or more precisely, in Bethlehem—as Christians tell the story.

A few years ago, the leaders of a small congregation prayed their way into a serious question: *Where would the Christ child be born today?* They recognized that the nativity of Christ emerged from a scene of desolation. So when they set out to build a nativity scene to inhabit the nave of their sanctuary, they borrowed imagery from the newspaper. They constructed a shanty covered with a blue tarp and surrounded it with rubble: cinderblocks, an abandoned shopping cart, empty cans, sleeping bags. Their Advent wreath was an upturned oil drum, on which the candles of hope and peace and joy and love smoldered.

That scene was painful, not pretty. It preached a powerful message that our carols have long proclaimed: the Christ child was "born to ransom captive Israel"; "with the poor, the scorned, the lowly, lived on earth our Savior holy." The hopes and fears met by the Christ child were on display, a silent witness to the depth of our need for the God who saves us by being with us.

My friend who served that congregation confessed that the crèche challenged her to keep her eyes open to God's beloved world. Not all of the members of her church responded that way. Many worshipers didn't want to be confronted by the same pain that was relentlessly broadcast on the news when they gathered to praise God.

My friend is a great pastor who cared deeply about the members of her flock. The nativity scene was meant to be a testimony to how Christ is born to save a suffering world, not to be a cause of suffering. Yet even as she recognized that her people needed comfort, she lamented: "Even if we do clean up the sanctuary, the world remains broken."

The church found a way to rejoice on Christmas Eve. Some of the symbols were taken away, and the light of Christ filled the space they left behind. But that challenging nativity scene was deconstructed because human beings couldn't bear it, not because God couldn't bear it. The hope of the original nativity in Bethlehem, and the hope of every other nook and cranny in creation, is that God can and does bear our suffering.

God can and does show up, in this world somewhere between heaven and hell.

Christmas Eve: A Feast of Light
Isaiah 9:2–7; Luke 2:1–14, (15–20)

The people who walked in darkness have seen a great light; those who lived in a land of deep darkness—on them light has shined. You have multiplied the nation, you have increased its joy; they rejoice before you as with joy at the harvest, as people exult when dividing plunder. (Isaiah 9:2–3)

Christmastime is a delight for the senses. There are the sounds of children giggling as they shred the paper that stands between them and the package from Grandma. There are the jangling bells, the sticky peppermint canes, the itchy warmth of new socks. Christmastime is a feast of rejoicing, a banquet of good cheer that rends the dreariness of the darkest nights of the year.

In the midst of this, there is a child. The child is born into painfully spare circumstances, into the darkest of all nights. The delicate membrane that segregates heaven from earth is torn asunder, pierced by an infant's cry.

The angels are singing, reminding us that this baby is God's response to our hope, that this is the child promised to frustrate the darkness with divine light. The shepherds are on their way, sprinting toward the star. The angels convert their terror into jubilation, with a message of good news that never fails to quicken the pulse of believers: this child is God enfleshed, the Holy of Holies born as a human child. The Prince of Peace, born in a land at war. The only hope for a hopeless people.

We cannot forget why God transgressed the boundary between heaven and earth to show up in the person of Jesus. God loves us so ardently that God startles the universe by showing up cradled in a feeding trough.

We know that the work begun in that manger is not yet complete. Christmas is, for the time being, a feast of light juxtaposed with darkness. We brighten our sanctuaries with candles, but the night persists beyond these walls. Though we wipe our tears away to join in the yuletide celebration, we are still a people who mourn. Though we have seen the light of God's love and been utterly transformed by it, we are still a people who walk in darkness. Heaven and nature sing, but God's beloved creation is still ravaged by violence and death.

Mary has suffered her last contractions and rallied for one final push, but the final cadence of our redemption has not yet been delivered. The Son of God came to earth, preaching of an everlasting kingdom, and all creation is still groaning in labor for the nativity of that peaceable realm. The promise of incarnation—the gift of Christmas—is the assurance that, soon and very soon, God's will shall be done on earth as it is done in heaven.

Our Christmas merriment—with all its joyful visions and melodies and aromas—is but a hint of the feast we will experience.

Christmas 1: When God Walks the Earth
Isaiah 63:7–9; Matthew 2:13–23

I will recount the gracious deeds of the Lord, *the praiseworthy acts of the* Lord, *because of all that the* Lord, *has done for us, and the great favor to the house of Israel that he has shown them according to his mercy, according to the abundance of his steadfast love. For he said, "Surely they are my people, children who will not deal falsely"; and he became their savior in all their distress. It was no messenger or angel but his presence that saved them; in his love and in his pity he redeemed them; he lifted them up and carried them all the days of old. (Isaiah 63:7–9)*

It is tempting to steer a wide course around the Gospel for the first Sunday of Christmas in the Year A lectionary cycle. The sanctuary is still decked out with Christmas finery, and the relatives haven't yet departed for home. People come to church hoping for a little more holiday joy, perhaps even to sing their favorite carols one more time. Or they don't come to church at all—the Sunday after Christmas being one of the more lightly attended days of the year. So it is the few and faithful who are called to worship, and their fidelity is rewarded with a profoundly disheartening and disturbing story.

As we've explored the geography of salvation—with terrain such as God's holy mountain, a highway to Zion that cuts through a desert florid with new life, and the city of Bethlehem—we've dared to hope that the advent of Christ will bring not only joy but safety.

Protection—even peace. So, as we face the unthinkable turn of events that unfolded immediately following the nativity of our Lord, we might feel every bit as tricked as Herod. Was all that joyful anticipation for naught? How else can we reconcile that the birth of Jesus was immediately followed by the fulfilment of a grisly, terrible biblical prophecy: a mother weeping for her lost children in Ramah.

More than any other text in this series, this passage is filled with places—places with profound significance. Ramah. Egypt. Bethlehem. Israel. Judea. Nazareth. We need a geography lesson, a well-drawn map, and a refresher in biblical history to keep up.

This is what happens when God becomes human. This is what happens when God walks the earth—or, as is the case in this story, when God is wrapped in swaddling blankets and smuggled off to the relative safety of Egypt by his frantic, desperate parents. This is not merely about prophecies fulfilled; this is about feet treading—and blood spilling—in particular places.

The horror of the slaughter of the innocents is not to be taken lightly. Our bewilderment at the swell of violence that follows the birth of Christ is not to be shrugged off. The maternal cry that reverberates through the streets of Ramah is agonizing to hear. In Christ we don't find a God who is "strong enough" to overthrow powers and principalities by force. In Christ we find a God who is strong enough to practice radical solidarity. In Christ, God suffers.

We might, for a fleeting moment or a lifetime, prefer the god who is inviolable and indestructible. The one who, from a safe distance, runs a tight ship in which babies aren't subject to the violent whims of insecure monarchs. Instead we have Emmanuel, God-with-us: in Ramah and Jerusalem and Egypt, but also in the cities and towns in which our own lives unfold.

Ultimately, the geography of salvation is about a God who shows up *right here*.

Epiphany Series:
New Year, Same Promises

Six Parts: First Sunday after Epiphany through the
Sixth Sunday after Epiphany

Our resolutions fade, but God's promises last forever.

KATHERINE WILLIS PERSHEY

Series Overview   "New Year, new you": this is the message we get from pop culture, year after year. We vow to make changes to our diet, exercise habits, or lifestyle, but in spite of those resolutions, most things stay the same. This may be cause for disappointment, but there is some consistency we can celebrate. God's promises to us do not change with the calendar or the latest fitness trend. Rather than focusing our energy and attention on making (and in all likelihood breaking) promises to ourselves, let's spend the first part of the new year appreciating God's unbreakable promises.

	Sermon Title	Focus Scripture	Theme
First Sunday after Epiphany (Baptism of the Lord)	God's Promise of New Life	Ps. 29; Matt. 3:13–17	Through the waters of baptism, we are given new life.
Second Sunday after Epiphany	God's Promise of Faithfulness	Ps. 40:1–11; 1 Cor. 1:1–9	God is faithful, even when we are not.
Third Sunday after Epiphany	God's Promise of Ministry	Ps. 27:1, 4–9 Matt. 4:12–23	God calls and equips us to serve the kingdom.
Fourth Sunday after Epiphany	God's Promise of Blessing	Ps. 15; Matt. 5:1–12	The promise of the Beatitudes is for something good to emerge from the dust of something not good.
Fifth Sunday after Epiphany	God's Promise of Guidance	Ps. 112:1–10; Matt. 5:13–20	How do we live in response to the gift of grace?
Sixth Sunday after Epiphany	God's Promise of Freedom	Deut. 30:15–20; Ps. 119:1–8	The choice is ours: life or death?

This is a high-potential time of year, as Christmas visitors may respond to invitations to visit again in the new year, and others may commit to more regular church attendance as part of a New Year's resolution. Keep these newcomers in mind as you prepare by making plain the messages of God's good promises. Consider offering a special class or casual discussion time where people can get to know one another and explore these basic—but often very deep and personal—faith issues.

First Sunday after Epiphany: God's Promise of New Life
Psalm 29; Matthew 3:13–17

And when Jesus had been baptized, just as he came up from the water, suddenly the heavens were opened to him and he saw the Spirit of God descending like a dove and alighting on him. And a voice from heaven said, "This is my Son, the Beloved, with whom I am well pleased." (Matthew 3:16–17)

There, on the front page of the newspaper, was a photo of a young man who had died. He was only nineteen years old. But despite the fact that Charlie died so young, his death was far from tragic. In fact, it was *triumphant*. For though he died to self as he succumbed to the waters of baptism, as he rose out of the Pacific Ocean on Easter Sunday, guided by the hands of his pastor, he was raised into new life in Christ. Through a lens splashed with saltwater, the joy was palpable. Charlie's hands were raised in exaltation as the frigid water clung to his body.

God whispered to Charlie over the crashing of the tide: *you are beloved.*

But make no mistake: the old Charlie died in those waters, just as the new Charlie was born. That is what baptism is, and it is a much bigger paradox than humans can whip up on our own.

Before the Spirit of God moved upon the face of the waters at the time of creation, the darkness was upon the face of the deep. When you go beneath the surface of the deep, it's dark and cold and eerie. There may very well be sea monsters lurking mere inches from your toes. You cannot breathe there.

We are creatures who are 100 percent dependent on breathing. We inhale, and all that good oxygen fills our lungs and, like magic, feeds and cleans all the cells in our bodies. Respiration keeps us alive by keeping all our cells alive.

That's just the physical dimension of breath. We imagine God giving humankind life by breathing into Adam's nostrils. When you make the decision to repent and be baptized, you agree to go to a place where you cannot breathe. Which is to say, you journey to the heart of the thing we humans collectively fear the most: dying.

Of course you don't literally drown. But the life you are lifted into is not the same. Paul says it best: "I have been crucified with Christ, and it is no longer I who live, but it is Christ who lives in me."

At the turning of the calendar year we are inundated with messages pressuring us to remake ourselves, to resolve to improve our health or kick bad habits. And there's nothing inherently wrong with this impulse; if a resolution to quit smoking sticks, praise the Lord and pass the chewing gum. But God's promises are quite a bit weightier than our own; God's promises are trustworthy and true and never—ever—broken.

Charlie no longer lives, but Christ lives in him. And when Christ lives in us, when we have died to self—no matter how old we were or the volume of water in the font—we receive God's promise of new life through the waters of baptism.

Second Sunday after Epiphany: God's Promise of Faithfulness
Psalm 40:1–11; 1 Corinthians 1:1–9

I have not hidden your saving help within my heart, I have spoken of your faithfulness and your salvation; I have not concealed your steadfast love and your faithfulness from the great congregation. Do not, O LORD, withhold your mercy from me; let your steadfast love and your faithfulness keep me safe forever. (Psalm 40:10–11)

Miss Cornelia is one of the characters who vividly populates the Anne of Green Gables novels. She is a churchgoing lady, a devout Christian. One morning she asks Miss Susan about the health of a mutual friend. Miss Susan replies, "Oh, I'm afraid she's going to have to rely on the Lord now." Miss Cornelia responds with horror. "Oh no! Surely it isn't as bad as all that!" To be sure, to believe that God is faithful is not to believe that our every prayer will be answered just so. But for all her piety, entrusting her friend to God feels like a lost cause, a last resort.

We must remember the biblical promise: God is faithful. The first time I encountered the concept of God's faithfulness, I didn't have the foggiest idea what it meant. Faithfulness was something I ascribed to humans, not God. God was the object of faithfulness, not its subject. Yet the Scriptures bear witness, implicitly and explicitly, to the faithfulness of God. God remembers the covenant. God does not abandon God's people. God does not break God's word. God does not withhold forgiveness. God does not hide God's face. God is profoundly faithful.

All of this—despite the fact that we do often forget the covenant. We abandon God. We break our word. We withhold confession. We turn our faces away from God's. In a word, we are often faithless. But God? *Never.* A persistent and pernicious lie pops up frequently in Christian hearts—and in Christian pulpits. The lie proclaims that being a good Christian—perhaps even being a Christian at all—is all up to you. To be saved, you must be faithful—*very* faithful. Doubt, weakness, and (heaven forbid!) good old-fashioned sinning—are all signs of faithlessness, disqualifying you from the kingdom and making you unworthy of God's love. This lie essentially reverses the beautiful definition of grace Frederick Buechner offers, that there's "Nothing *you* have to do, nothing you *have* to do, nothing you have to *do.*"

The lie infects Christianity with perfectionism and gracelessness. The common antidote is to double down on the profound significance of grace. We must be reminded that we do not save ourselves. But we may also need a reminder that we alone are not charged to be faithful—and we are not charged to be faithful alone.

We are saved by faith, not works—but ultimately it is not even our own faith that saves us, but God's. Likewise, the gifts we have are just that—gifts from a faithful God, not emblems of our own goodness. We who long to be the protagonists of our own story are invariably humbled by the biblical narrative. Our role is to receive and respond to God's love, God's grace, and God's faithfulness.

Third Sunday after Epiphany: God's Promise of Ministry
Psalm 27:1, 4–9; Matthew 4:12–23

As he walked by the Sea of Galilee, he saw two brothers, Simon, who is called Peter, and Andrew his brother, casting a net into the sea—for they were fishermen. And he said to them, "Follow me, and I will make you fish for people." Immediately they left their nets and followed him. (Matthew 4:18–20)

The psalmist craves security: *"The LORD is my light and my salvation. The LORD is the stronghold of my life."* He longs to live in the house of the Lord, to be comforted by God's beauty, welcome in God's temple, hidden in God's shelter, concealed in God's tent. He wants God to place him out of reach of his enemies, on a metaphorical (and perhaps even literal) rock.

I resonate with the psalmist's desires. I long to be safe, to let my fears be disintegrated by the sacred solvents of God's love and God's power.

But the Gospel of Matthew does not let us play it safe. When Jesus encounters the fishermen who would become his disciples, he challenges them to follow him. This means sacrificing economic security and social standing. This means entering a wholly unknown future, entirely at the mercy of—well, at the mercy of *God*.

Jesus does not say, *"Follow me and I will make sure nothing bad happens to you,"* no matter how badly we might wish for this to be the message.

To be clear, to follow Jesus is to follow the Lord who is our light and salvation. To follow Jesus is to choose well a stronghold for life. But to follow Jesus is not to receive absolute security. To follow Jesus is to receive that odd yet inspiring promise: *"I will make you fish for people."*

Jesus will show us the path to reconciliation with our God, but he will also give us a purpose along the way. If we entrust ourselves to Jesus, Jesus entrusts us with the holy work of building the sacred community that gathers in his name, giving us the tools to share this good news with all people.

What does it mean to receive this particular promise? It seems a promise *non gratis* to many Christians. At the heart of the assurance that Jesus will turn these catchers-of-fish into catchers-of-people is a challenge to reach out to others in the name of Christ. It helps me to remember that the fishers of ancient Palestine did not fish with hooks that puncture and injure but with nets that surround and gather. I once saw a man fall out of a tree and fracture several bones. Those of us who from the safety of the ground witnessed that fall would have done anything to have a net to catch him before he hit the sidewalk.

People are falling. People are lonely, depressed, hungry, and desperate. People are nursing injuries incurred by bad experiences of organized religion. People need forgiveness and repentance. People are falling, and Jesus promises to equip us to catch them. The net he provides us with is woven of the good news of God, a strong rope made of love, forgiveness, hope, and justice.

The net is not a trap. The net is not a trick. The net is the complex gift of God's grace and healing, given to a creation that is given to spills, a creation that has broken a million bones against the hard cement of sin. When men and women are caught by that net, they are given something beyond security. They are given new life.

Follow me, and I will make you fish for people.

Fourth Sunday after Epiphany: God's Promise of Blessing
Psalm 15; Matthew 5:1–12

"Blessed are the poor in spirit, for theirs is the kingdom of heaven. Blessed are those who mourn, for they will be comforted. Blessed are the meek, for they will inherit the earth. Blessed are those who hunger and thirst for righteousness, for they will be filled. Blessed are the merciful, for they will receive mercy. Blessed are the pure in heart, for they will see God. Blessed are the peacemakers, for they will be called children of God." (Matthew 5:3–9)

The Beatitudes present a laundry list of promises, but frankly, most of them are not the promises we would prefer. Rather than hearing, "Blessed are those who mourn, for they will be comforted," we would rather hear, "You won't mourn." Rather than hearing, "Blessed are those who are persecuted for righteousness sake, for theirs is the kingdom of heaven," we would rather hear, "You shan't be persecuted."

What are these odd blessings, and whatever do they mean?

In Eugene Peterson's first draft of *The Message*, his ambitious one-man biblical translation, the Beatitudes did not speak of blessing. They spoke of luck. His editors nixed the bold move; they couldn't swallow the idea that the poor and meek are lucky (and, apparently, some Christian communities associate "luck" with "Lucifer"). I've always wondered if the editors were right. Luck has strong connotations, few of which point to anything explicitly holy. Gamblers rely on it; fate rests on it. Someone who isn't quite comfortable sending a loved one off with the words "God bless!" might toss out a casual "Good luck." But do they really mean the same thing?

Other translations of the Beatitudes use the word "happy." This translation certainly magnifies the paradoxical nature of these pronouncements. In the *Good News Bible* Jesus seems awfully cheerful as he promises, "Happy are those who mourn, for God will comfort them!"

Then there's the French edition of the *New Jerusalem Bible*, which famously translates the Greek *makarioi* as "debonair." When I consider the beatitude "debonair are the peacemakers," I picture Cary Grant at an antiwar protest, wearing a bowtie as he hoists a placard overhead. The French term we define as "suave" or "stylish," however, really just means *de bon aire*, "of good disposition." Perhaps we might call it "contented."

The original Greek can also be translated as "honored" or "favored." We will always wrestle with what this does and does not entail. If given a choice, wouldn't the grieving mother opt to have her child returned to her rather than receive God's comfort? What good is it to her, to be favored by God, if her arms are still empty of the flesh of her flesh? Yet can she dare hope? In the fullness of time, when Christ reigns and the kingdom of heaven is finally realized, what might God's comfort contain for her? Shall her tears of mourning be transposed into tears of joy?

Lucky. Happy. Debonair (!). Honored. Favored. *Blessed*. No matter how you say it, the promise of the Beatitudes is for something good to emerge from the dust of something *not* good. Perhaps not in the way we would prefer, but nonetheless, can we entrust ourselves to a God who speaks special promises for the small, the suffering, the shy, the sorrowful?

Fifth Sunday after Epiphany: God's Promise of Guidance
Psalm 112:1–10; Matthew 5:13–20

"Do not think that I have come to abolish the law or the prophets; I have come not to abolish but to fulfill. For truly I tell you, until heaven and earth pass away, not one letter, not one stroke of a letter, will pass from the law until all is accomplished." (Matthew 5:17–18)

There is a tug-of-war throughout the New Testament and throughout the whole of Christian history: *does grace get us off the hook*? The apostle Paul is exasperated at one point; though he is a great promoter of the saving power of the grace of God, in his letter to the Romans he writes, "Should we continue in sin in order that grace may abound? By no means!" The epistle attributed to James emphasizes the importance of good works to such a degree that grace-loving Martin Luther longed to strike it from the canon. Christians have long pondered their relationship with the law, and most are content to ignore it— even though in this Gospel passage, Jesus unequivocally states that he comes "not to abolish but to fulfill" the law and the prophets.

In a nutshell, we are saved by grace—and yet, what next? How do we live in response to this extraordinary gift?

That word—"response"—is key. Our actions do not save our lives; God's action does. After that, the ball is back in our court, so to speak. We can choose to live in a way that honors the incredible gift we have been given—a way that embodies the love and justice of Jesus Christ—or we can choose to live in a way that denies it.

The promise we consider today is this: God does not leave us without direction. As we craft our response to God's grace, we are promised a path forward. We are not left to sort it out alone. We have the prophets' cries for righteousness and repentance, from Isaiah to John the Baptist. We have the law as it is expressed in the Hebrew Bible, and as it was fulfilled in the life of Jesus Christ. We have his teachings, those invaluable (if sometimes seemingly impossible) pearls of wisdom.

The promise of these life-giving mandates does not compromise our freedom. Benedict, founder of the Benedictines, crafted for his burgeoning community a "rule of life." There is a beautiful tension between obedience and freedom: once vows have been made, monks and oblates are bound to order their lives according to the rule of life. But each member submits to this rule only through his or her own agency.

The rule doesn't save a Benedictine any more than the law saves the sinner. But the rule, the law, the commandments—the way—is itself a form of grace. We need a map. We need markers reminding us to pursue justice and love kindness as we walk humbly with our God.

There is a promise-within-the-promise here. Remember the psalmist's words: "Happy are those who fear the LORD, who greatly delight in his commandments." To put it as plainly as possible: we are better off when our response to the grace of God is to honor God with our lives—with our obedience. We are happier when we are truly the salt that we were redeemed to be, and we will surely know sorrow and regret if we lose our saltiness.

Sixth Sunday after Epiphany: God's Promise of Freedom
Deuteronomy 30:15–20; Psalm 119:1–8

See, I have set before you today life and prosperity, death and adversity. If you obey the commandments of the LORD your God that I am commanding you today, by loving the LORD your God, walking in his ways, and observing his commandments, decrees, and ordinances, then you shall live and become numerous, and the LORD your God will bless you in the land that you are entering to possess. (Deuteronomy 30:15–16)

I know someone faced with a terrible choice. It feels like a life-or-death decision, except that from his perspective, both options are fatal. He could stay where he is, knowing that his current circumstances cause him to experience soul-crushing unhappiness. He could venture out into the unknown, but that's a terrific risk. Who's to say that the unknown will be better? Yet it's hard to imagine that it could possibly be worse.

Sometimes he wishes that he didn't even have this choice—that some external force would decide for him. As stuck as he feels, it's the burden of his freedom that terrifies him the most. He doesn't want to make the wrong decision.

This is freedom. It's painful, messy, ambiguous, frightening—so much so that it's easy to comprehend why many people seem willing to exchange freedom for fate. If I believe that I am fulfilling a destiny as I journey through life, I don't bear the same responsibility for my life. It's out of my hands.

And it's true: a lot of life is out of our hands. We are free—but so is everyone else. We are free—but forces beyond us nevertheless act upon us. Our freedom is not absolute, and we certainly aren't guaranteed the wisdom and foresight to be good stewards of the freedom we do have.

In Deuteronomy, God addresses God's people: "See, I have set before you today life and prosperity, death and adversity." There is nothing we can do to elude this weighty freedom. The choice is ours. Do we turn to God, or do we turn away from God?

Reading this passage from the comfort of our armchairs (or the discomfort of our pews, as the case may be), it's easy to imagine that this is an easy decision. Of course we choose well. Who would choose death over life? Who prefers curses to blessings? Not I. Not ever.

Yet the choice that God sets before the Israelites "today" echoes in our lives every day. It's a choice we must continue making, a path we make—as the parable goes—by walking. And it isn't always clear which choice is life and which choice is death.

We cannot elude this choice—these choices. We have been promised freedom, and we have been furthermore promised consequences according to how we spend that freedom.

Freedom is a gift, but like so many of the gifts we receive from God, it doesn't always seem like it. Still—do we trust God?

We can grasp our terrible, wondrous freedom by the reins and courageously ride into the land of the living.

We can choose life.

Lenten Series: Boot Camp for the Soul

Six Parts: First Sunday in Lent
through Palm Sunday

Lent as preparation for a greater challenge still to come.

WINNIE VARGHESE

Series Overview We approach the Lenten season with an emphasis on interiority, personal investigation, and contrition—the intentional work of seeking a change of heart or actions. Reflection and change take work, hard work. Lent can be like a boot camp for the soul, a restart in a focused area. We walk this season together, demanding the best of ourselves, ready to support one another, and prepared to see truths that shatter our self-understanding.

The range of the readings in this season is the full breadth of lived human experience from creation to death and new life. The preacher

	Sermon Title	Focus Scripture	Theme
Lent 1	The Need for Change	Ps. 32; Matt. 4:1–11	We face temptation as we discern what God really wants for us.
Lent 2	Reset	Gen. 12:1–4a; John 3:1–17	Spiritual rebirth means a new start.
Lent 3	Hydrate	Exod. 17:1–7; John 4:5–42	Living water sustains us on our journey.
Lent 4	Redefined	1 Sam. 16:1–13; John 9:1–41	We are more than we appear to be.
Lent 5	Dead End	Ezek. 37:1–14; John 11:1–45	When all hope seems lost, God revives.
Palm Sunday	Celebrate and Wait	Ps. 118:1–2, 19–29; Matt. 21:1–11	Rejoice at the end of the journey, but know challenges lie ahead.

has the opportunity to place the foundational Christian narrative on the significant life events of the community in this season, paralleling the false choices of temptation with the conditions of suffering in the world today.

Tips and Ideas for This Series

We get the term "boot camp" from the military, but one encounters boot camps in various areas of life: a particularly rigorous exercise regimen, a period of training before a new job, or even an intensive retreat for personal or marital transformation. Consider featuring testimonies in worship from individuals who have experienced these various kinds of intense training. Connect such experiences to the way Lenten disciplines we adopt are intended to make the season "hard" in the way a boot camp can be, pushing us beyond what we think our limits are in ways that strengthen us.

Lent 1: The Need for Change
Psalm 32; Matthew 4:1–11

Then I acknowledged my sin to you,
*   and I did not hide my iniquity;*
I said, "I will confess my transgressions to the LORD,"
*   and you forgave the guilt of my sin. Selah*
Therefore let all who are faithful
*   offer prayer to you;*
at a time of distress, the rush of mighty waters
*   shall not reach them.*
You are a hiding place for me;
*   you preserve me from trouble;*
*   you surround me with glad cries of deliverance. Selah*
*   (Psalm 32:5–7)*

Boot camp is all about making necessary changes through hard work. In Lent, the church invites people to a similar season of introspection, a time of discernment of sin and all that separates us from the knowledge of the love of God for us, and a time for repentance and renewal of life in preparation for Easter.

We begin the season with a reminder of the power of temptation, that which leads us to sin. These days "temptation" is a word we use primarily with regard to personal choices, many of them susceptible to outside influences. We are vulnerable to choices, offered often through media, that cause us to desire things or experiences that are not essential and might even be harmful. We feel tempted by the choice to be different than we are and the difference between what is healthy or harmful varies greatly depending on our context. Personally, how do you discern which choice is a temptation and which is encouragement? What draws us closer to the knowledge of God's love for us?

We could busy ourselves in endless reflection on where we draw the line in our personal lives, but that might be a temptation in itself. Can we enter this demanding season faithfully and yet not become ultimately self-absorbed, losing sight of the big picture in light of our daily efforts to resist gossip or gluttony? If Lent is like a boot camp for the soul, what is the hard work that can be done in this limited, intensive time?

One helpful framework is to consider the larger context in which we live. What are our temptations as a people, in this nation, or in our community? Where do we act collectively in ways that deny the goodness of those whose daily lives are defined by exclusion or suffering? Social context is a powerful framing of our personal struggles.

In the Gospel, the devil offers Jesus power over others, and he denies it for a kingdom greater than this world. What power are we tempted to seek, and how might we instead work for a kingdom-level justice that might seem impossible in this world? What social norms are we called to defy in favor of God's vision for us?

Let us consider these temptations that Jesus faced—how we acquire our daily bread, how we understand what it means to live, and how we impact the world around us. As we begin the journey of Lent, let us consider these very essentials of living, freed from the tempter and the bondage of sin; for, as the psalmist reminds us, we are forgiven.

Lent 2: Reset
Genesis 12:1–4a; John 3:1–17

Nicodemus said to him, "How can anyone be born after having grown old? Can one enter a second time into the mother's womb and be born?" (John 3:4)

Is it possible to begin again? Apparently the answer is "Yes!"

Well not quite, but sort of. To paraphrase T. S. Eliot, we hear of endings that are not endings and beginnings that are not beginnings.

At the end of his life, Abram is called by God to pick up everything and follow to a new place. As Christians our path includes this difficult truth. The journey of living is long and can be hard, and yet, we say, what we can see is not all that there is, and our end is no real end.

Our spiritual ancestor Abram lives this out quite literally. At the end of his life, God calls on him to begin again, and it is not an easy journey once it begins. We too are called to the journey anew at times. Nicodemus similarly seeks out Jesus to ask questions whose implications are life changing. Can a person begin again, he asks?

The change boot camp brings means leaving some of our old habits, prejudices, and weaknesses behind. The gospel calls this kind of fresh start being born again. Can we crawl back into a place of innocence and openness where we are ultimately vulnerable and dependent and try to see the world anew? Can we be re-formed, re-ordered, or re-built to love more, forgive more, and demand more? Are there wildernesses to step out into with little more than faith?

Jesus today says, yes, this is the journey. He says we speak only of what we have already seen, but that must have been little comfort to Nicodemus, trying to work out exactly what he means.

There is a sweet story told of an imagined conversation among twins in utero speculating on what happens after birth. One twin is convinced birth is the end. The other twin argues that it is a new beginning. They are both correct. Life as we know it ends, and new life begins, sometimes with no awareness on our part of the change, because we are in the midst of living. You might recall welcoming a child into your family or a move of home or work. There might be a story related to increased or decreased health or a change in your body that feels like new life. Rebirth is like those changes in which how we experience the world or how the world experiences us is fundamentally changed. These are just a small taste of the rebirth we are talking about today, in which we align ourselves more closely to God's understanding of us.

Abram goes off alone into the unknown and becomes the great patriarch. Jesus tells us we will be reborn, maybe endlessly, as we move closer and closer to knowing ourselves in relationship to the One who has made us and finds us lovable without condition.

When have you or your community faced an end and found a new beginning? Are there truths you know from your experience that are hard for others to believe? What new beginnings is God urging you toward today?

Lent 3: Hydrate
Exodus 17:1–7; John 4:5–42

"But those who drink of the water that I will give them will never be thirsty. The water that I will give will become in them a spring of water gushing up to eternal life." The woman said to him, "Sir, give me this water, so that I may never be thirsty or have to keep coming here to draw water." (John 4:14, 15)

I was sitting next to a young woman in a worship service a few weeks ago. As the reading was announced and began, she popped the top of her water bottle and took what seemed to me to be a rather loud glug, maybe to illustrate the refreshment about to be offered from Scripture. Where I live and work, people are carrying and drinking water constantly. Maybe we have taken seriously the stories of thirst we read today and conclude we should always have a source of hydration on hand, but I suspect this phenomenon has more to do with attempts at weight loss and the infamous doctor's recommendation to drink eight 8-ounce glasses of water each day.

We live in a time when the lack of clean water is becoming a crisis. Parts of the country are rationing water, and it seems clear that farming will look different in the next decade, as the demand for water for the extraction of fossil fuels and large-scale farming begins to severely restrict the water available for people to acquire and use for daily living. Access to water defines what property has value, and in some societies makes women and children vulnerable to attack as they venture far to acquire their daily water. Would that there were stones today we could break for streams of living water! In other parts of the world, the water rises to dangerous levels, and people seek shelter from dangerous flooding.

Water comforts and cleanses, as well as destroys by its abundance or scarcity. We are utterly dependent on water, and we illustrate that dependence as we carry it around in plastic, sucking on it for dear life. Particularly when engaging in rigorous physical training or exertion, we need to stay hydrated, lest our efforts at transformation be compromised by a lack of essential fluid.

This Sunday of Lent, we particularly note how spiritual hydration is essential for the transformation we seek. In today's readings the people and then Jesus are simply thirsty. In response to their thirst, they ask for water. It seems reasonable to me. New life is offered to the Samaritan woman in this ancient site where she and Jesus share common origins, Jacob's well, and all the people of her town are invited to know Jesus through her good news. The Hebrew people point out that they need water, which invites Moses into a conversation with God that creates from his despair water from a stone.

So many stories of the Bible are stories of water. From creation to the river of life in the end time, we are a people whose spirituality is framed in the cleansing and life-giving qualities of water. Where are our rocks and wells today? Have our sources of spiritual hydration seemed to run dry? How can we seek and experience the living water God wants to provide for us today?

Lent 4: Redefined
1 Samuel 16:1–13; John 9:1–41

They brought to the Pharisees the man who had formerly been blind. Now it was a sabbath day when Jesus made the mud and opened his eyes. Then the Pharisees also began to ask him how he had received his sight. He said to them, "He put mud on my eyes. Then I washed, and now I see." Some of the Pharisees said, "This man is not from God, for he does not observe the sabbath." But others said, "How can a man who is a sinner perform such signs?" And they were divided. So they said again to the blind man, "What do you say about him? It was your eyes he opened." He said, "He is a prophet." (John 9:13–17)

In the news, when someone is described primarily with a physical aspect, it implies there is nothing more to be said about a person. For example, someone might be described as beautiful, as opposed to intelligent or insightful; or by a physical condition like blindness as opposed to hardworking or talented.

In today's readings, we see men of miraculous power, king makers and sight givers, literally changing the destiny of two other men and possibly the Hebrew people. Samuel goes to Bethlehem to anoint a king, one who doesn't seem to have much going for him except pretty eyes. Samuel goes to Bethlehem on God's orders, the story tells us, and the people of Bethlehem are terrified when the man of power comes among them. Rejecting Jesse's older, stronger sons, Samuel anoints a shepherd boy with pretty eyes as the one who will be their king. It is not clear how that is to be, but this is the story we have, as though David himself is an afterthought in the illustration of the power of God.

The blind man also begins as an illustration in a conversation between Jesus and his disciples. The disciples ask Jesus about the effects of sin across generations. Jesus responds that sin had nothing to do with the man's blindness but "that God's works might be revealed in him."

Who defines normal, respectable, well, or whole today?

Are there categories of clean and unclean, sinner or innocent victim, rioter or high-spirited youth, criminal or citizen? Do you ever feel defined by one label or characteristic?

The blind man is defined as a sinner in his very being, because he is blind. Whether he contests this identity or not, we do not know. It seems as though the category of blindness was intractable in that time and place, attached to a set of assumptions that unquestionably defined a human being, like disability, race, or gender in our time. Once Jesus has empowered him to transcend that label, who is he?

We can ask the same of ourselves. When we undergo an extreme transformation, we shed old definitions of ourselves—those, perhaps, that have been thrust upon us by others—and claim a new identity, defined by the power of God working in us.

Lent 5: Dead Ends
Ezekiel 37:1–14; John 11:1–45

Then he said to me, "Prophesy to these bones, and say to them: O dry bones, hear the word of the LORD. Thus says the Lord GOD to these bones: I will cause breath to enter you, and you shall live. I will lay sinews on you, and will cause flesh to come upon you, and cover you with skin, and put breath in you, and you shall live; and you shall know that I am the LORD." So I prophesied as I had been commanded; and as I prophesied, suddenly there was a noise, a rattling, and the bones came together, bone to its bone. I looked, and there were sinews on them, and flesh had come upon them, and skin had covered them; but there was no breath in them. Then he said to me, "Prophesy to the breath, prophesy, mortal, and say to the breath: Thus says the Lord GOD: Come from the four winds, O breath, and breathe upon these slain, that they may live." I prophesied as he commanded me, and the breath came into them, and they lived, and stood on their feet, a vast multitude. (Ezekiel 37:4–10)

There comes a point in every trial when it seems difficult to go on, as if death is imminent. To someone lying facedown near the end of a muddy obstacle course or crying out in emotional agony, there seems to be no hope of relief or revival. Human beings have come over time to understand death and what happens to bodies after death in great detail. In various ways our ancestors have artfully or brutally found places to put the bodies and sometimes actively engaged the decomposing body to facilitate a complete end. Whether in caves, in holes, in fires, or on towers, the body decayed and people understood well how it happened. Death was a one-way street.

Today's stories challenge everything we know about life and death, literally and metaphorically. It is not a healing or feeding, not sustaining water from a rock. No. Every possibility for living has ended.

Life is over; only the stench and decay remain. There is no reason to be emotionally invested or newly concerned. Wondering what could have been or what had been promised would be like being mired in a long-ago past. Hope is dead, appropriately, and into this valley of death God drags the prophet Ezekiel, and Jesus drags his disciples. The prophet and the family and friends of Lazarus know that life is no more. Before their eyes, however, that reality is defied. Life returns to the lifeless.

Today we stand in the stench, sorrow, and maybe even blame of death, and God acts to revive us again. We have a foreshadowing of what is to come next week, a little encouragement as we prepare for the hardest week of the liturgical year. We also have a reminder that our brutal, death-filled world can be flooded in the reality-shattering light of God again.

We will soon see that death is not the end. There is no ultimate separation from the love of God. The breath of the prophet enlivens the bones that have given up all flesh. If this is so, then what power can death have over us? What limit is there to God's love for this creation?

Palm Sunday: Celebrate and Wait
Psalm 118:1–2, 19–29; Matthew 21:1–11

"Tell the daughter of Zion, Look, your king is coming to you, humble, and mounted on a donkey, and on a colt, the foal of a donkey." The disciples went and did as Jesus had directed them; they brought the donkey and the colt, and put their cloaks on them, and he sat on them. A very large crowd spread their cloaks on the road, and others cut branches from the trees and spread them on the road. The crowds that went ahead of him and that followed were shouting, "Hosanna to the Son of David! Blessed is the one who comes in the name of the Lord! Hosanna in the highest heaven!" (Matthew 21:5–9)

The story of Jesus' triumphal entry into Jerusalem is usually done before the procession with palms and in many liturgies is followed by the full passion reading, a preemptive move anticipating poor attendance at later Holy Week services. If you choose to observe the Liturgy of the Passion as well as the Liturgy of the Palms on this day, consider splitting the liturgy and reading the passion narrative at the end of the service, setting the stage for all that is to come.

If this service can be solely focused on the triumphal entry, the preacher has an opportunity to reflect on the celebratory procession, which many scholars have contrasted to the imperial Roman procession, as one that points to Jesus' popularity in his time. The anti-Semitism that has historically and violently emerged, ironically, in Holy Week, in response to the passion narratives, can be addressed and challenged by resting in this scene of humble and risk-taking celebration.

The challenges of boot camp typically culminate in celebration. The hard work and self-examination experienced along the way come to an end with a sigh of relief and a hoot of satisfaction, with high fives all around for the group that has taken this journey together. All four Gospels state clearly and repetitively that crowds followed Jesus, at times to his own frustration. It follows that in his final return to Jerusalem the same crowds would gather and welcome him, potentially becoming the riotous and revolutionary mob that Rome worried about at Jewish festivals. It is exactly this scene that the disciples wanted to avoid, what Thomas meant when he said, "Let us go with him to Jerusalem to die."

The people, the rabble that Jesus loved, loved him back. They did not have the power to protect him, but they could proclaim their love much like those at a rally you might see today. This is what we model in our processions, a mocking of the processions of domination and military power, also known as the ways of the world, and an enactment of our devotion to the king of love. In the flurry of celebration, Jesus' followers may forget that the journey is not really over, that darker days remain before Jesus' final victory. The betrayal at night and the quick trial are to keep the power of the crowds at bay and to frighten them. Their biggest challenge still lies ahead.

Boot camp, after all, is not an end unto itself. It is preparation for the challenges still to come.

Easter Series: Closer and Closer

Seven Parts: Easter Sunday through the Six Sundays of Easter

The resurrection means deeper relationships with God and one another.

WINNIE VARGHESE

Series Overview   At Easter, we celebrate Jesus' resurrection from the dead; but this is no ghostly apparition. Jesus returns in the flesh to be close once again with his friends and to bring them closer with one another. There is tenderness and physicality highlighted in the resurrection narratives, people coming together to hear and respond to this amazing news. Before Jesus' followers become the heroic saints of the church, they are simply a group of friends hearing and telling one another a story

	Sermon Title	Focus Scripture	Theme
Easter Sunday	The Stories Women Tell	John 20:1–18	We hear and trust Mary's story, and the stories we all have to tell.
Easter 2	Reach Out and Touch	1 Pet. 1:3–9; John 20:19–31	Jesus welcomes Thomas to touch him, to get as close as he needs.
Easter 3	Walking with Jesus	Luke 24:13–35	We know Jesus and one another in the breaking of bread and the sharing of stories.
Easter 4	Someone to Watch over You	John 10:1–10	We take the necessary risk to trust the Good Shepherd and one another.
Easter 5	Living Stones	1 Pet. 2:2–10	With Jesus as our cornerstone, we work together to build the kingdom.
Easter 6	The Air We Breathe	Acts 17:22–28; John 14:15–21	We live, move, and have our being in God's freedom.
Easter 7	Bearing Witness	Acts 1:6–14	We are commanded to share the stories of what we've seen.

for which they can barely find words. Like bedtime stories and old family lore, we share our stories in relationships close and safe so that we will be equipped to boldly share the story of Jesus in the world.

Tips and Ideas for This Series

Show Easter visitors the real power of Jesus' resurrection to draw people together with an emphasis on relationships and true connection. Plan events during the series to encourage Easter visitors and infrequent attendees to connect more deeply with the life of the congregation: for example, a storytelling night with food and fellowship, a ministry fair to showcase opportunities for involvement, or a sign-up initiative for new small groups to form, meeting in homes and building deeper relationships.

Easter Sunday: The Stories Women Tell
John 20:1–18

Mary Magdalene went and announced to the disciples, "I have seen the Lord"; and she told them that he had said these things to her. (John 20:18)

Like Mary, we are charged with telling the story of resurrection as though we, like her, have encountered an impossible truth. As preachers on Easter Sunday, we might be speaking to people who will hear very few other words of challenge or comfort from a church this year.

The resurrected Jesus appears to Mary first. Not enough can be made of this simple point, in light of not just the ancient world, but the world we live in today. Christianity relies on this one woman telling the others what she has seen. It is a ridiculous story to have to tell, and she tells it. That the first witnesses and those who first tell the story of Jesus' resurrection are women is confirmed in all the Gospels and is considered reliable, because, in short, who would make up such a thing? If the Gospel writers were trying to deceive readers, they would make a man their primary messenger, not a woman. The testimony of a woman was considered untrustworthy, and yet it is to women that Jesus entrusted this key element of his story to be told.

Clearly women today have more rights than in the first century, but the place of women in private and public life is still debated in ways often degrading of the dignity and worth of women. Violence against women is still commonplace. Health care as it relates to women's bodies is marginalized and debated. And the stories women tell about their own experiences and own needs are often dismissed as irrational, overly emotional, or simply untrue.

The story of Jesus the Christ might have quite literally ended if Mary had not spoken, and if the others had not believed her. That they trusted her word is almost as miraculous as the resurrection itself—almost but not quite. In his resurrection story, Jesus shows us not just that life can conquer death but that even those whom society would deem low can be raised to places of prominence. Those we might be tempted to distrust can become our closest friends. Jesus erases these boundaries so that we can know one another as he knows us. Whose stories might we be missing today because we fail to see all people as Jesus did?

The resurrection is central to our faith, but it is not a mere theological tenet. It is the key to how we live in a broken world. We live in hope, not despair; in community, not isolation; in truth, not in silence. We are the heirs of the apostles, charged with telling that same story told long ago by the women, and then by the men, and then in every language and place. Death is conquered. We are free. How do you tell this story today?

Easter 2: Reach Out and Touch
1 Peter 1:3–9; John 20:19–31

But Thomas (who was called the Twin), one of the twelve, was not with them when Jesus came. So the other disciples told him, "We have seen the Lord." But he said to them, "Unless I see the mark of the nails in his hands, and put my finger in the mark of the nails and my hand in his side, I will not believe."

A week later his disciples were again in the house, and Thomas was with them. Although the doors were shut, Jesus came and stood among them and said, "Peace be with you." Then he said to Thomas, "Put your finger here and see my hands. Reach out your hand and put it in my side. Do not doubt but believe." Thomas answered him, "My Lord and my God!" (John 20:24–28)

Thomas will not be content to believe the stories of his friends, and in return for his disbelief he is invited to touch the body of the resurrected Lord. In a twist of irony, the legend is that it is Thomas who takes the message to far-away India, where one has to wonder what words he found to convince people in such a different context that he had been witness to this miraculous act of power, and that its implications should be compelling for them.

Thomas's is the story for the ones who make their own way, those who cannot inherit religion but who will struggle to figure out what is true for themselves. Many of us that remain on this journey have had a personal encounter with the holy that is at the heart of our journey as Christians. Faith, even if lifelong and the tradition of our ancestors, is realized in each of us through some personal experience, mystical or ordinary. Thomas illustrates this truth. Although many of us do rely on the teachings and experience of church tradition, we are all dependent on a personal, deep knowing or a commitment or persistence in questioning that brings us to communities of faith. Thomas has become the sign to the church of the individuality of the journey of faith, even as it is rooted in tradition and occurs within a community.

The reading from 1 Peter claims that we who inherit the faith from the stories of others are also disciples. The text is highlighting the distinction in the early church between those that knew the people who knew Jesus and those who have joined the community because they have heard the stories of Jesus. It was a pertinent issue at the time, of course, when some who knew Jesus in the flesh were still living. Today all of us who know Jesus are people who have heard the stories from others, like Thomas, but we can still be tempted to prioritize those who knew Jesus first or those who had a more profound and personal experience of Jesus than others.

Whether we are lifelong Christians, new to the faith, or still exploring from the edges, Jesus invites us all to reach out and touch him, as Thomas did. There is no judgment for asking questions or for needing a little more convincing than someone else. We are all on the journey together, sharing our stories as we grow closer to one another and to Jesus.

Easter 3: Walking with Jesus
Luke 24:13–35

Then beginning with Moses and all the prophets, he interpreted to them the things about himself in all the scriptures. As they came near the village to which they were going, he walked ahead as if he were going on. But they urged him strongly, saying, "Stay with us, because it is almost evening and the day is now nearly over." So he went in to stay with them. When he was at the table with them, he took bread, blessed and broke it, and gave it to them. Then their eyes were opened, and they recognized him; and he vanished from their sight. They said to each other, "Were not our hearts burning within us while he was talking to us on the road, while he was opening the scriptures to us?" (Luke 24:27–32)

Today we read of what must have been the most beautiful seven-mile walk of all time. Even with eyes prevented from seeing him, we have the tenderness of storytelling that must have been like Philip and the eunuch, close and specific, filled with questions and wonder at a beautiful new way to understand themselves, their heritage, and recent events. Storytelling combined with a long walk might remind us of hikes or similar journeys we have taken with friends. Stories told with ease outside the confines of our day-to-day life.

What if we assume that our eyes too are prevented from seeing much of the time? We seek out these special places, like a church service, to listen differently. If we are lucky, we feel safe enough to be open to hearing something new.

Our worship is often structured like the story we have today. We gather and sing, in essence talking among ourselves. There is reading and preaching, maybe not as intimate (or long) as a seven-mile walk, but similarly, when it is done well, we are stirred up and brought to a new place in which we literally move to a table and offer and receive hospitality, for some of us liturgically at a holy table, for others of us in refreshment and fellowship. For Christians, it is in these acts of fellowship that we believe Christ is made known in community. This Gospel reading outlines the ritual acts of Christian people through the millennia.

Researchers are learning that as we walk our brains integrate information in ways specific to the act of walking. Our brains connect information we already have in ways that we might not otherwise. Some of us prepare sermons walking or work out difficult problems by walking. Can you imagine this walk? These two on the road are reviewing the harrowing events of the past few days and are walking in the night under the spell of terror. Jesus appears as a stranger and proclaims to them the stories of the liberation of their people.

In what circumstances do we share our stories today? Over coffee with a close friend? While working side by side on a project with a colleague or fellow volunteer? In the more formal setting of a Bible study or support group? It is by sharing these parts of ourselves that we grow closer in relationship; and every so often there is a moment of revelation, of true connection, where we suddenly see more deeply into ourselves and one another.

Easter 4: Someone to Watch over You
John 10:1–10

The one who enters by the gate is the shepherd of the sheep. The gatekeeper opens the gate for him, and the sheep hear his voice. He calls his own sheep by name and leads them out. When he has brought out all his own, he goes ahead of them, and the sheep follow him because they know his voice. (John 10:2–4)

What a beautiful idea: that there will be those that lead whose very voices might tell us they are for us. We are safe. We will be cared for, and we will know them because they enter through Jesus himself and the sound of their voices will draw us. This is the Davidic vision of the kingdom. David the shepherd boy knows of comfort and safety. He plays his lyre and keeps watch over the vulnerable from his childhood. Jesus says there will be people like that for us.

A friend from India once commented to me, "The tree does not stand far from the apple." I think it is an inversion of "the apple does not fall far from the tree" that may have been more about something being lost in translation than a different philosophy. In his version of things, the tree has agency, not the falling apple. It's not even clear that the apple has fallen or will fall. Almost as if, no matter how hard we apples try to be ready for the fall and work with its momentum to get somewhere free of the shadow of the tree and thrive, we will remain in the shadow of the tree. From the perspective of the tree, we can keep close and safe all who are ours.

Would that life were so clear. Most of us have as much reason to want to be free of that sheep gate as we would to want to be safe within it. We are an individualistic culture, within which each of us strives fully to express or attain our uniqueness, whether in success or in creativity. We might not do so well as Americans with the idea that we are waiting to be led and hoping not to be deceived, but the readings imply that this is a piece of the spiritual journey. Depending on anyone else means risking your emotions and sense of self-sufficiency, but that risk is necessary for being in relationship with anyone, including God.

Into these shepherding images, Jesus introduces the idea of a kind of enclosure within which the sheep are safe. We, these sheep, then await the right voice and will fulfill our calling under its guidance; and the gate itself will protect us, because not all who desire to enter through the gate will be able to do so. It would be a mistake to view our individual congregations as a gated and guarded haven, but together with all God's people (including those sheep Jesus says a few verses later were his but "do not belong to this fold") we gather as a flock to learn and know what it means to know, trust, and follow the Good Shepherd.

Easter 5: Living Stones
1 Peter 2:2–10

Come to him, a living stone, though rejected by mortals yet chosen and precious in God's sight, and like living stones, let yourselves be built into a spiritual house, to be a holy priesthood, to offer spiritual sacrifices acceptable to God through Jesus Christ. For it stands in scripture: "See, I am laying in Zion a stone, a cornerstone chosen and precious; and whoever believes in him will not be put to shame." To you then who believe, he is precious; but for those who do not believe, "The stone that the builders rejected has become the very head of the corner." (1 Peter 2:4–7)

Among the recurring images in Scripture are stones. From the very beginning there are stone pillars to mark the acts of God: stone for building homes and fortresses; stones as the site of wells; stones for altars; water-bearing stones; tomb-sealing stones; and stones thrown to mark the judgment of a community. One of Jesus' most devoted disciples, Peter, is called the rock, on whom Jesus will build his church (Matt. 16:18).

In the first epistle of Peter, Jesus is presented as a rejected stone, implying a flaw or lack in some way that would have made him not good enough to occupy the most important, foundational role—and yet he does. Like him, Peter says, we are living stones.

St. Mark's in the Bowery is the oldest site of continuous worship in New York City. It is a pile of stones, beautiful multihued New York stone, stacked and solid. When the wood, slate, and steel of the roof burned in the 1970s, the stone walls stood firm, ready to frame a new day in the life of St. Mark's. Those old stones were piled on each other between 1795 and 1799, a time when the Episcopal Church in the United States of America was a new and unlikely idea, and this community's attempt to be an independent parish was a bold and adventurous new choice. Most of the buildings from that time in Lower Manhattan have been razed, and the religious communities that were founded there have all moved uptown. Because St. Mark's is the grave site of Peter Stuyvesant, the last Dutch governor general of New Amsterdam, this site is dedicated as his memorial. Essentially these stones and the graves they watch cannot be moved.

Even in places less historic than St. Mark's, every church with a building regularly has to discern whether these stones (or bricks or boards) will be an idol or a tribute to the work of God through the ages. For as Peter reminded us, we the people of the church are "living stones," building a "spiritual house." As stones working together, we must discern how we can frame a well of living water and not become a wall keeping people out.

Jesus, the unlikely stone, is our chief cornerstone. So, unlikely as we may feel being dubbed "living stones" for Jesus, we are simply following in his footsteps. If we are in Jesus and Jesus is in us, new life can indeed spring forth from these old stones.

Easter 6: The Air We Breathe
Acts 17:22–28; John 14:15–21

"And I will ask the Father, and he will give you another Advocate, to be with you forever. This is the Spirit of truth, whom the world cannot receive, because it neither sees him nor knows him. You know him, because he abides with you, and he will be in you. I will not leave you orphaned; I am coming to you. In a little while the world will no longer see me, but you will see me; because I live, you also will live. On that day you will know that I am in my Father, and you in me, and I in you." (John 14:16–20)

The night before Jesus was crucified, when tensions were running high in Jerusalem and Jesus himself warned that he would soon be leaving them, his disciples were understandably anxious about how they would survive without him. Jesus responded that they would never really be without him, because God would send an Advocate, the Holy Spirit, to live in them. Through this Spirit, Jesus said, he would live on, in and through his followers.

In today's reading from Acts, Paul is speaking to people unfamiliar with the stories of Jesus, his miraculous works of healing and power, and his resurrection; but he speaks of a similar indwelling. Paul connects with the Athenians by referring to the common human feeling that there is a force at work in the world that is so far beyond us that our role is to search for this force and hope that its truth will be revealed to us. Paul describes this cosmic force, this Spirit, as one "in whom we live and move and have our being." God is like the air to us, sky to the bird, or water to a fish. God is like the environment so essential to our living that we cannot imagine it, because we cannot imagine being without it. We would not be alive without it.

For us who know Jesus, this understanding of God's Spirit living within us goes even further. If God, made human in Jesus, who conquered death at the hands of the state, is as present with and essential to us as the very air we breathe, then our liberation from earthly powers is also essential to our being. We are free from all that holds back the human condition: hunger, fear, racism, isolation, poverty, wealth. Whether we like it or not, in claiming Jesus' resurrected life, we claim liberation from the limits of the human experience. We "live and move and have our being" in this freedom.

As Christians there can be a purely spiritual component to this claim that shapes our orientation to suffering and rejection. We have hope in the face of inevitable suffering because of Christ's conquest over death. But this freedom also shapes how we live together and relate to one another. This freedom empowered the disciples as they boldly went on to proclaim Jesus' love and grace in hostile places. If liberation is in the very air we breathe, our every action and interaction will exude the peace and hope we know in Jesus. We will work to free others from any earthly powers that inhibit their flourishing. We will promote compassion and justice to overcome discrimination, poverty, and suffering of all kinds.

What would our community and our world look like if we saw every breath we took as immersing ourselves in God, and every exhaling as an opportunity to breathe God's liberating love back out into the world?

Easter 7: Bearing Witness
Acts 1:6–14

So when they had come together, they asked him, "Lord, is this the time when you will restore the kingdom to Israel?" He replied, "It is not for you to know the times or periods that the Father has set by his own authority. But you will receive power when the Holy Spirit has come upon you; and you will be my witnesses in Jerusalem, in all Judea and Samaria, and to the ends of the earth." When he had said this, as they were watching, he was lifted up, and a cloud took him out of their sight. (Acts 1:6–9)

We've spent this Easter season exploring the closeness we can experience with Jesus Christ and with one another. The examples and stories shared by Jesus and his earliest followers show us what it means to live and relate to one another as attentive, bold, sometimes vulnerable, always free disciples of Christ.

The first disciples were also learning those lessons, as they traveled with Jesus for three years and then tried to soak up every bit of wisdom they could in their time with Jesus after his resurrection. No wonder they thought the big moment had come, the finale of Jesus' life and work—that Jesus would now restore the kingdom of Israel, as he had long talked about. "Is this it?" they asked. "Will you bring the kingdom now?"

Imagine their shock when Jesus replied, in essence, "No, but *you* will."

He reminded them of his promise to send the Spirit to be with them, adding that this gift then comes with an assignment: to tell the story of Jesus throughout the world. "Be my witnesses," he said.

To be a witness means both to see and to share. Like one who observes a crime or a marriage, a witness affirms publicly what he or she has seen. Those first disciples had seen a lot in their time with Jesus—miraculous healings and feedings, storms calmed and hearts transformed. Jesus' last command to them was to share what they had seen so that others, both near and far, would know who Jesus was and what God did through him.

That command is one passed down through the generations, well beyond those who knew and touched Jesus in the flesh. The second and third generations of Christ's followers, on down to us today, haven't known the closeness of Jesus' physical touch—his healing hand or warm embrace—but we can be close to him in spirit as we seek to know and follow his teachings and as we build deep and real relationships with one another. Seeing Jesus at work in those ways, we can share what we have seen. Sharing our stories with one another, we can offer encouragement to the hopeless, the promise of justice to the mistreated, and healing to the broken. In these ways, our stories bear witness to the powerful, loving, liberating work of Jesus Christ and continue to build God's kingdom here on earth.

Summer Series 1: God's Creative Connection

Six Parts: Pentecost through Proper 9

The creative work of the Spirit on Pentecost began way back in Genesis.

JACQUELINE J. LEWIS

Series Overview

This six-week series begins with the creative agency of God's Spirit at Pentecost, when God uses the power of language to create and connect a new people. Even as God is doing a new thing, we know this same creative Spirit has been at work since the very beginning, from the creation of the world to the creative ways God works to connect with humanity. Spending the first five weeks after Pentecost in the book of Genesis, we learn more about how God works creatively to redeem humanity, restoring the created order to its original, "very good" status and reconnecting what we have divided. God's vision of a world of persons connected to one another and to God will be realized, even if God has to use some very creative methods to do so.

	Sermon Title	Focus Scripture	Theme
Pentecost Sunday	The Power of Communication	Acts 2:1–12	God speaks in whatever language we need to hear.
Proper 5	Spoken into Creation	Gen. 1:1–2:4a	God's voice creates and invites us to create as well.
Proper 6	Creative Hospitality	Gen. 18:1–15; (21:1–7)	When we welcome guests, we welcome God.
Proper 7	Creating Promise Out of Pain	Gen. 21:8–21	God works to redeem what humans mess up.
Proper 8	God Will Provide?	Gen. 22:1–14	We trust God when we don't understand.
Proper 9	Designing Love	Gen. 24:34–38, 42–49, 58–67	God brings people together for lifelong relationships.

Tips and Ideas for This Series	Make this summer series colorful and creative with an engaging variety of sounds, visuals, and interactive experiences. Using several voices in worship each week—varied by age, gender, and race—is a great liturgical tool for this series. Consider amplifying the diversity of music in worship. Find popular music that supports the theme, for example, Luther Vandross's "Love Power" on Pentecost or Bette Midler's "From a Distance" on Proper 5. Use different media and art forms to enhance the message each week. Offer a way for the congregation to get creative, perhaps working together on a mixed-media collage built over the course of the series or participating in an open-mic night where people can share their creative talents.

Pentecost Sunday: The Power of Communication
Acts 2:1–12

All of them were filled with the Holy Spirit and began to speak in other languages, as the Spirit gave them ability. . . . Amazed and astonished, they asked, "Are not all these who are speaking Galileans? And how is it that we hear, each of us, in our own native language? Parthians, Medes, Elamites, and residents of Mesopotamia, Judea and Cappadocia, Pontus and Asia, Phrygia and Pamphylia, Egypt and the parts of Libya belonging to Cyrene, and visitors from Rome, both Jews and proselytes, Cretans and Arabs—in our own languages we hear them speaking about God's deeds of power." (Acts 2:4, 7–11)

I love reading the names of all these peoples present at Pentecost. I love the way they feel on my tongue.

I love the specificity, the particularity. All those Jews from all over the known world gathered in one place, hearing the good news in their own language. This is what is miraculous to me, powerful to me.

To be sure, this story is amazing! Stunning! Spectacular. The rush of a violent wind. Tongues like fire, landing on each person. The cacophonous sound of many Galilean voices speaking many languages. Perplexing, awe inspiring, a shocking sight at 9:00 in the morning. Of course this provoked speculations of drunkenness. Unlike anything they'd seen before, this was certainly a creative way for God to invite the diverse people of the world into the fledgling community of Christ.

As Peter explains, prophecy is being fulfilled. God's Spirit has been poured down on the people of God—this Spirit that would provoke us all to dream God's dream. This Spirit would lead to the salvation of humanity, to the righting of wrongdoing, to reconciliation among people and with our God.

This is not just good news. It is the best news.

The coming of the Spirit is a miracle.

And the way people hear of this coming is miraculous as well. The Pentecost moment is a multivocal one. God deems it that all of God's people will hear the good news of God's amazing grace and power in the language they understand—a creative way to speak to diverse peoples simultaneously, and an example to us in communicating the gospel creatively to others.

The church is called to tell of God's stunning mercy in a multivocal way so that people can hear, can be saved. This means translation—yes, to Spanish and Mandarin, but also in music and prayers and liturgy that reach across generations and cultures. It means getting conversant in the ways millennials speak. It means importing cultural idioms that make God's word plain and accessible to teenagers and children. It means taking risks to translate the gospel into "so what?" sound bites that can be tweeted and texted and posted on Facebook.

God created a new community at Pentecost through effective communication, but the creative work of the Spirit is as old as time. From the moment God spoke the world into being, God has been working in creative ways to connect all humanity to one another and to God. In the following weeks, we'll see how God's creative connection worked in the lives of Abraham and his children and continues to work in the world. We have some translating to do, people of God, so that all will know that God's love is for them and that God will do anything—anything—to connect with them. This is the best news, and God's people need to hear it, by any means necessary.

Proper 5: Spoken into Creation
Genesis 1:1–2:4a

In the beginning when God created the heavens and the earth, the earth was a formless void and darkness covered the face of the deep, while a wind from God swept over the face of the waters. Then God said, "Let there be light," and there was light. (Genesis 1:1–3)

Last week we explored how God creatively connected different people at Pentecost by empowering the apostles to speak in a variety of languages. We're backing up this week, all the way to the beginning.

The beginning of order, the beginning of ordered time. The beginning of human-divine partnership. The first of the Bible's two creation stories in Genesis highlights the creative power of our holy God, again through the power of speech.

In the beginning when God created or began to create, the Spirit of God hovered over the deep, bearing witness to the agency of God to call forth life out of a watery, not-yet-productive space, like a cosmic womb. In the Hebrew Scriptures, the word *bara* is used only to describe the creating agency of God. God's breath/spirit—*ruach*—hovers over the womb-like space, moves deliberately, blows over the watery space.

God's voice orders the heavens and the earth, orders everything, and creates everything. The Word calls the creation forth with intention and will. The very expression of the call invites participation: "Let there be," "Let us make." God is in community with what is becoming. God's Word fills the womb-like sea with light and darkness, with a separation of the waters above and on the earth, with day and night and sun and moon and stars. With plants and trees and animals that crawl, creep, fly, and walk on all fours. With an animal that walks on two legs—a human being, created in "our" image. This cosmic "we" includes Spirit and Word and God but also every being in heaven and then even the Adam. God's partnership with the creation is generative and generous. God is not the only one with creative power.

Humankind is created in God's image, in love, for love, to care for the creation. In the image of God, reflecting the divine essence, the human one extends God to the created order. Male and female represent God's care to and for the creation. We are God's agents commissioned to care for what God has made, to steward what God has created. Maleness and femaleness are particular gifts that represent God without hierarchy or preference. The very goodness of our gender is to be celebrated as a representative of the particularity of God.

The human ones are commanded to share power with God, to share creative responsibility with God. Like God, to be fruitful and multiply and fill the earth. To have dominion—*rada*—to nurture and care for the earth, to develop the earth.

Here is the spirit/breath of God, moving over the deep. Here is the Word of God, calling forth, declaring goodness. Here is the creating God sharing power with humanity, relating to all creation. Dancing a Trinitarian dance.

And then, like our creating God, we are to rest.

Proper 6: Creative Hospitality
Genesis 18:1–15; (21:1–7)

"Let a little water be brought, and wash your feet, and rest yourselves under the tree. Let me bring a little bread, that you may refresh yourselves, and after that you may pass on—since you have come to your servant." So they said, "Do as you have said." (Genesis 18:4–5)

God appears to Abraham. It is not clear that Abraham knows it is God, but there are three men standing near Abraham's tent, standing in the heat. Abraham is hospitable. He offers them water to wash their feet and in charming understatement offers to bring "a little bread" for his guests. In fact, he asks Sarah to make cakes and overzealously tells her exactly how she should make them. He kills a tender calf and asks a servant to prepare it. He takes curds and milk to the strangers, along with this impromptu feast, and watches them eat.

There is something very powerful in the way Abraham cares for the messengers, cares for God. We who are the readers already know what Abraham comes to know. The three men are God. God has taken on human form. Abraham does not know this. So his hospitality is not to impress God; it is to be hospitable, as is customary and is culturally prescribed. The men say that they will return and that Sarah, old, barren Sarah, will bear a child. This makes her laugh out loud. Sarah's laughter indicates that she also does not know who the men are. God directs the question about Sarah's laugher to Abraham. Is anything too wonderful for the Lord? In the face of the Divine, Sarah wants to deny her laughter, her lack of faith. But this God knows all about her barrenness, her desire, and her disbelief.

For many of us, hospitality is a creative act. We may enjoy cooking for family and friends, decorating the house for a party, or preparing a centerpiece to look just right. Whether fancy or informal, our creative efforts are designed for connection, to make guests feel welcome and comfortable, to facilitate conversation and the building of relationships.

Hospitality toward God is extended when we offer it to the men, women, and children in the midst of us. When we do it unto them, we do it unto God. Extending ourselves to the stranger involves risk and vulnerability. God extends hospitality to humankind by stopping by, caring about our business, understanding our desires. This is no quid pro quo, though. Sarah and Abraham are not rewarded with child because of their hospitality. It is divine favor; it is divine *choice*, divine creative agency, that brings life to barren wombs. It is divine choice to show up at our tent, at our door, in our sanctuary and bring life-giving love.

Is there anything too wonderful for God? There is mystery imbedded in this question. Do we know the limits of God's power? Does God limit God's power? This text invites a curiosity about the nature of God that cannot be fully satisfied. Our willingness to open our doors and the doors of our hearts invites a relationship that will surprise us.

Proper 7: Creating Promise Out of Pain
Genesis 21:8–21

But God said to Abraham, "Do not be distressed because of the boy and because of your slave woman; whatever Sarah says to you, do as she tells you, for it is through Isaac that offspring shall be named for you. As for the son of the slave woman, I will make a nation of him also, because he is your offspring." (Genesis 21:12–13)

Hagar is a slave woman, an Egyptian woman. A woman in a culture in which men rule, a woman used by another woman and her man to fulfill their dream of progeny. Of course Abraham and Sarah were within their rights to use her in this way. But one has to question the culture in which this was right.

The baby—Ishmael—grows, as do Hagar's status and Sarah's resentment. Sarah banishes mother and child from the family home, sending them out into the wilderness. Abraham is distressed—not enough to halt the action, it seems, but distressed nonetheless. God promises Abraham that God will make a nation of Ishmael. Bread and a skin of water are what Abraham gives to Hagar as he sends her off into the wilderness.

With food and water gone, Hagar prepares for the death of her child. And here then is the extraordinary thing. God appears to Hagar herself. God hears the cry of the child, and the God who is attuned to the sound of human suffering responds with a promise of nation building and with a well from which they can drink. The last verses of today's reading tell us that the boy grew up strong and married an Egyptian woman.

The presence of God is evident in relationship to all these characters. A promise to an aging couple, a promise to be kept despite their fear and cunning, because God is God and keeps God's word. Care for the slave woman and her child. Care for this family on the margins. Care that does not keep them in their circumstance but responds to their changing circumstance. They are cast out, and God does not stop the action. But God meets them in the wilderness and provides a future and care in the present.

We often wonder why there is suffering in the world, why God allows people to use and abuse other people (whether it is culturally acceptable at the time or not). God is ever present, however, with those who suffer, those on the margins, and creatively works to bring goodness and care even where we humans have brought distress and alienation.

Hagar will name God "The one who sees." This God who sees is still watching the sibling rivalry between the children of Ishmael and the children of Isaac. Are God's grace and care large enough to support both promises? Why have the promises of land and progeny caused such turmoil? Does God have a creative solution in store for these peoples?

I am not sure one sermon can address that sufficiently. But this creating God of Genesis 1—this God who surprises Abraham and Sarah with the promise of progeny, this God who makes the same promise to a slave girl from Egypt—this same God is a provider and a way maker for all those cast out and put down in our society. To the immigrant, to the incarcerated, to those injured by racism, who wonder if their lives matter, to the poor and destitute: God will show up as creative love and power, even and especially to the least among us.

Proper 8: God Will Provide?
Genesis 22:1–14

God said, "Take your son, your only son Isaac, whom you love, and go to the land of Moriah, and offer him there as a burnt offering on one of the mountains that I shall show you." (Genesis 22:2)

This text is a troubling one. Abraham and Sarah have been promised progeny. They tried to make it happen the way they thought they should, bearing and dispatching Ishmael along the way. Isaac is the child of promise, a testimony to God's faithfulness in the face of our laughter and doubt.

Now Abraham is told to take Isaac and make a sacrifice of him. Abraham is obedient, obedient to the point of having his hand raised ready to slay his beloved son. And God sends a ram in substitution. The child is saved, and Abraham has proven his faithfulness.

It would be easy to say this was God's creative way of testing

Abraham, affirming their connection and covenant by providing a way out in the end. But I don't like it. I really don't.

Maybe, as some scholars suggest, this story has pre-Israel roots, where child sacrifice was a norm and is now coming to an end. Maybe this story is written in the time of exile, when the theology of Israel is rooted in being tested by God. Adults die, children die, and faith in God means remembering deliverance in times past and expecting deliverance in times to come.

Maybe this is about the ups and downs of Abraham and God's intimate relationship. You know, Abraham has not always behaved well, and so testing is appropriate. One scholar, Walter Brueggemann, notes that God is being tested too, that this test raises God's awareness.

Scholars also write about Abraham's increasing vision—he sees the place where he is to make the sacrifice, he sees the ram in the bushes. Abraham trusts in the God who sees and the God who saves and the God who provides.

Scholars write about God's intent. God did not intend Abraham to sacrifice his boy. Well, why ask Abraham, why test him?

There are many theories attempting to explain this disturbing passage, like scholars of poetry or appreciators of abstract art venturing to guess the true meaning of a creative work. We will never fully understand, but there is value in the considering and questioning.

Maybe God's command for Abraham to put Isaac on the altar of sacrifice is meant to raise our hackles. It raises mine. But the story as it is told also raises my awareness that the God of Abraham has some vulnerability. This story shows God making a request that puts God's trustworthiness on the line. Can Abraham trust a god who asks such a thing of him? Can we?

I am somewhat comforted by the idea that God seems to be learning. Is this possible? As the flood causes God to grieve God's choice to destroy creation and start over, I sense that God's asking Abraham causes God to pause, causes God to provide a ram in the bush. This might be difficult to proclaim, but I think it merits a question in the sermonic moment about the nature of God. If God can be God and learn, perhaps we can be a reflection of God and learn.

I also think there is space here to ask what it means to follow God without question. Might we question God's will, interrogate God's intent with our own ethics and moral courage? Abraham obeys God because Abraham trusts God. In the trusting relationship, there is testing, perhaps mutual testing. God provides a relationship in which we can test and be tested, one in which we keep becoming, one to which we can keep returning. Perhaps it is in the testing that God creates a people, a partnership people with whom to be in the universe.

Proper 9: Designing Love
Genesis 24:34–38, 42–49, 58–67

And they called Rebekah, and said to her, "Will you go with this man?" She said, "I will." So they sent away their sister Rebekah and her nurse along with Abraham's servant and his men. . . . Isaac went out in the evening to walk in the field; and looking up, he saw camels coming. And Rebekah looked up, and when she saw Isaac, she slipped quickly from the camel, and said to the servant, "Who is the man over there, walking in the field to meet us?" The servant said, "It is my master." So she took her veil and covered herself. (Genesis 24:58–59, 63–65)

Whether we're married or single, we all love a good love story. The subject of so many movies, novels, and best-man speeches, the tale of how two people met and fell in love can touch our hearts. But despite certain claims about "biblical marriage" and "dating God's way," there isn't much in the Bible we would recognize as marriage, or even courtship, as we know it today.

This story of Rebekah making her way to Isaac is similar to other matchmaking stories in the Hebrew Bible. We are reminded of Jacob and Rachel, of Moses and Zipporah. Men and women meet at wells. Families are involved. Sometimes servants too. Relationships are inaugurated. But God's creative and creating energy is there in the background, and we catch glimmers of the faith, risk taking, and commitment we know in our own relationships.

This time it is a servant sent by Abraham to find a wife among his kinsfolk for his son. Echoes of call, journey, and faithfulness follow. Rebekah actually follows in Abraham's footsteps, leaving home and country to fulfill God's purpose.

I am inspired by the partnership between God and humanity at play in this text. These are not puppets; these are people shaping history within the context of God's ultimate will and way. These are people shaping history inside the space and grace of God's plan for humanity. Abraham trusts his servant prayerfully to discern whom God has appointed to be Isaac's wife, and offers him an "out" if the chosen woman is not willing to come. Rebekah is not forced to go, but she freely chooses to leave home for the unknown.

I am inspired by the faithfulness of this unnamed servant. Obedient to his master, conversing with God in prayer and in praise, following through with patience to fulfill a father's loving wish: a wife for his son, a wife from among their people. This servant is faithful to Abraham and faithful to God. This servant has a spontaneous and rich prayer life, offering petitions and praise to God with ease that must come from practice.

I am also inspired by the intimate relationship between Isaac and Rebekah. There is chemistry, there is tenderness, and there is love. Our creator God loves us enough to give us pleasure and joy and sexual tension and expression. Our God loves us enough to comfort us with relationships that are deep, profound, engaging, and intimate.

A father's love, a servant's faithfulness, a wife's journey to her husband's heart. This is not exactly how we connect with potential spouses today, but God is still there in the background, creating intimacy, creating a container for comfort, designing loving relationships. The same creative spirit that brought light out of darkness and promise out of pain brings love out of loneliness. From the vastness of the universe to the intricacies of the human heart, there is cooperation between us and God as we hope, discern, and step out in faith to form lifelong bonds for God's purpose and our delight.

Summer Series 2: Broken—Good News for Tough Times

Six Parts: Proper 10 through Proper 15

Hope and encouragement in difficulty with Paul's letter to the Romans.

JACQUELINE J. LEWIS

Series Overview Paul's letter to the Romans is addressed to people he had never met, in the hopes of encouraging and building up this community to which he dreamed of traveling. He knew the Christian life was a perilous one, and the world in which the church was growing and spreading was unpredictable and increasingly diverse. In this series covering some of the letter's most intriguing and inspiring passages, we learn how God sustains us in the midst of brokenness, both within and without, helping us find wholeness and unity, no matter what crises we are facing.

	Sermon Title	Focus Scripture	Theme
Proper 10	Broken Spirits, Broken Bodies	Rom. 8:1–11	Our sin and pain damage our human bodies as well.
Proper 11	Labor Pains	Rom. 8:12–25	God will bring restoration, in spite of our pain and brokenness.
Proper 12	Inseparable	Rom. 8:26–39	No amount of brokenness can separate us from the love of God in Christ.
Proper 13	All–Inclusive Grace	Rom. 9:1–5	God chooses us all, despite human differences.
Proper 14	The End of the Law	Rom. 10:5–15	Grace restores what is broken—not anything we can do.
Proper 15	God Is in Control	Rom. 11:1–2a, 29–32	Though brokenness remains, we can trust in God's mission of restoration.

Troubles are universal to the human experience, so use this series to draw in people on the periphery of the church and those who have grown distant in the busyness of the summer. A prime visual for the series might be a shattered piece of pottery, reconstructed gradually over the course of the series. As shards on the altar take shape, people will see as they hear the message of God restoring us in the midst of our brokenness.

Proper 10: Broken Spirits, Broken Bodies
Romans 8:1–11

For the law of the Spirit of life in Christ Jesus has set you free from the law of sin and of death. For God has done what the law, weakened by the flesh, cannot do; by sending his own Son in the likeness of sinful flesh, and to deal with sin, he condemned sin in the flesh, so that the just requirement of the law might be fulfilled in us, who walk not according to the flesh but according to the Spirit. (Romans 8:2)

From violence and disaster on the nightly news to the personal, physical, or relational pain of our own lives, it's plain to see that we live in a broken world. We begin this series today with the internal brokenness of our own spirits, pain that can be both the cause and the effect of human sin. Paul's arguments about sin in Romans 7 and 8 can be difficult to follow. Sin is difficult. The thing I know is wrong to do is the very thing I want to do, he says. Just knowing it is wrong, because the law tells me it is wrong, makes me want to do it. Who can deliver me from this body of sin and death? (Rom. 7:19–25).

Only Jesus is the answer to this question. God, Paul argues, sent the Son into the world to *be* sin(ful) as we are, to take sin out of the world. In love for us, and with power to heal us, God incarnates the purpose of the law in the body of Jesus and wipes condemnation out, delivering God's people in the way that law could not. Paul makes it sound so easy, as if our relationship with Christ makes choosing what is right, living "according to the Spirit" automatic. But like so many things, particularly when it comes to human fallibility, this is much more easily said than done! There remains a tension between Spirit and flesh, Spirit being the ways of God and flesh being the ways of the world.

It is a common misunderstanding that Paul is referring to our souls and our bodies here. We know that body and soul are inextricably connected, as our bodies are deeply impacted by the state of our spirit. Broken hearts can lead to broken bodies. Ulcers, cancer, sleeplessness—our *sōma* is impacted by our spiritual condition. And not only our bodies but the body of our human family. Greed, malice, unbridled hatred, and fear due to our differences—all the ways our souls are still broken by sin—these are literally killing us. Black and brown bodies are especially in danger.

To set the mind on things of the flesh means living according to the broken ways of our world, succumbing to discrimination or hatred due to gender or sexual orientation, race, ethnicity, or religion. This leads to death. Not just to bodily deaths but to soul death as well. To the death of hope. To the death of justice.

Life in the Spirit, on the other hand, liberates us from hatred and frees us to love. Focusing our minds on things of the Spirit—compassion, kindness, fairness, unity—can heal our broken spirits and empower us to help heal our broken world.

Proper 11: Labor Pains
Romans 8:12–25

For the creation waits with eager longing for the revealing of the children of God. . . . We know that the whole creation has been groaning in labor pains until now; and not only the creation, but we ourselves, who have the first fruits of the Spirit, groan inwardly while we wait for adoption, the redemption of our bodies. (Romans 8:19, 22–24)

Barack Obama's election and reelection are two of the most amazing events in my life to date. As an African American clergywoman, I am not sure I can yet articulate the sense of pride and the hope for a healed nation this represented to me. Yet, despite all the hope, all the promise of a new day, our nation is embroiled in racial tension. It is almost as though a pendulum has swung as far to the right as it can, and we are at war with one another. Uncivil discourse, black men, women, and children suffering at the hands of the state.

I am in pain; we are in pain.

Labor pains.

Paul writes his letter to the Romans with the pain of a broken world in mind. Christians in many places are suffering at the hands of the Roman government, and many wonder if the glorious reappearing of the risen Christ will soon occur. He offers a message of comfort and empowerment: "All who are led by the Spirit of God are children of God." But this status is not a mark of privilege. As "joint heirs with Christ," we suffer with Christ "so that we may also be glorified with him." Paul tells the people that the suffering of this day is nothing compared to the glory about to be revealed in us, to us, for us. All creation is waiting, like a woman in childbirth, to see the revealing of the children of God.

Labor pain is not a fruitless pain. It is pain with a purpose, with a promise of new life emerging. We are that new life, ever forming and reforming under God's skillful hands.

Like those to whom Paul was writing, the glorious birth may not be in our lifetimes. We are still not the people God created us to be. God is still working with us, pushing us, guiding us to live as the new creations we were made in Christ. We are in the birth canal; the labor pains are the stretching and pulling back of the status quo. When the pain is over, after we have been squished through the canal, after some ripping and tearing of our old vices and hateful patterns, we will be revealed as the children of God we were born to be.

This kind of creation and rebirth is often uncomfortable, but God is in charge of the pain, in control of the stretching and tearing and rupture and disruption. God is using all of it to recreate us, to change us, to transform us. There is no pain that God cannot use or redeem. There is no struggle that God can't use to strengthen us.

This is God's power to create beauty from brokenness, to bring life out of pain.

Proper 12: Inseparable
Romans 8:26–39

For I am convinced that neither death, nor life, nor angels, nor rulers, nor things present, nor things to come, nor powers, nor height, nor depth, nor anything else in all creation, will be able to separate us from the love of God in Christ Jesus our Lord. (Romans 8:38–39)

How many times have I turned to these words in Scripture? How many times have I referred others? My mother is grieving a new prognosis related to her lung cancer. The miracle drug has stopped working. She is herself a miracle, living with stage 4 non-small-cell lung cancer for over five years now. She who prays every day, on her knees, before leaving her bedroom. She of bedrock faith, who nurtured six children to believe in the power of prayers, struggles with her fate, in the hands of the God in whom she trusts. What next? What now? "Read Romans chapter 8," I say, while hugging her thin shoulders.

Nothing separates us from God; this is Paul's testimony. Not our inability to pray, for when we know not what to pray, God's Spirit prays on our behalf, in sighs too deep for words.

Not our inability to see God's plan for our lives, for while we are blinded by disease and grief, what we cannot see is still in place, calling us, knowing us, shaping destiny.

Not our circumstances, for though we feel abused or even abandoned, our God is one who uses all of life to our good. To teach us something, to strengthen a place in us, to give us compassion toward others. Our God does not bring the cancer, does not cause the disaster, but holds our broken pieces together while we lean into the everlasting arms, and creates the conditions for our love to open up spaces for transformation.

Since God loved us enough to send Jesus into the world to teach us what it means to be human with a divine spark, what would God withhold? Since God is on our side, on the side of love, who can be against us?

These words of assurance—that nothing in all of life, not even death, can separate us from the love of God—are powerful words to preach in summertime, when sunshine dares make light of our troubles, when the miracle of the resurrection might be a faint springtime memory and the miracle of the incarnation is pushed off for winter hope. The brokenness of our hearts and our world takes no vacation. With warm sun on the face, with humid summer winds at the back, God's people need to know the blessed assurance of the love of God that does not wane, not with long days or longer nights.

This text summons testimony, not about magic protection bubbles; we are not promised that. But about the very present help of God that stands with us in our trials and tribulations. The kind of presence that is sometimes best experienced in retrospect. Was not God there in that hospital room, when the chaplain prayed? Did you experience the light? Was not our God there, as we held hands in the circle and sang "Nearer My God to Thee"? Sharing stories about the way God has shown up in the real, lived lives of God's people gives weight to Paul's experience of the powerful presence of the Holy. Any distance or disconnect we feel from God is in our head, clouded by doubt or obscured by fear. In difficult times, we need the stories of those who have come through, reminding us that we are incapable of frustrating God's love and care. God is closer to us than we can ever fathom.

Proper 13: All-Inclusive Grace
Romans 9:1–5

They are Israelites, and to them belong the adoption, the glory, the covenants, the giving of the law, the worship, and the promises; to them belong the patriarchs, and from them, according to the flesh, comes the Messiah, who is over all, God blessed forever. Amen. (Romans 9:4–5)

Paul's wrestling here with the rejection of Jesus by the Jews feels almost like insider conversation. It is why context counts in our exegetical work, in our teaching and preaching. Paul has assured the Christians in Rome that there is nothing in all creation that will separate them from the love of God. This is the meaning of grace, grace with the power to transform individual lives and communities, to repair what is broken within us and between us. God has a plan for humanity that includes redemption; God has taken on flesh to make it so. Particular flesh—Jewish flesh—this is the flesh of the chosen, the people of the promise.

Yet, Paul is arguing, those very people of the promise have rejected the means of grace, the incarnate Word of God, by whom and through whom it is God's intent to redeem. Can the connection to God in Christ be forfeited by willful rejection? Paul has to address this, and address this he does. This text is not about a moment in life when doubt appears. This text is about the relationship God has to the people God chose. This text is about God's faithfulness to God's word.

The move that Paul makes is evangelistic. To be chosen by God is not an act of biology. It is an act of faith: God's faithfulness and our faith in the One who chooses us. Paul illustrates God's choice in this way: Isaac (not Ishmael, the firstborn as per tradition) is the child of promise. Similarly, in the next generation God chooses the younger Jacob rather than firstborn Esau through whom to bless the nations. God's choice/election supersedes tradition and birthright. God's choice supersedes biology. God's choice to bless God's people is not thwarted by the rejection of Christ by those who are biologically Jewish. God's choice, not Israel's biological heritage, is what enables God's plan of salvation for the people of God everywhere.

What a hopeful word for an increasingly interreligious culture, where we tend to see difference and fragmentation more than unity and wholeness. Can we imagine God's choice extending beyond our imagination? Beyond Jews to Gentiles, yes. Beyond Jews and Christians to Muslims? Beyond Muslims to those outside of the Abrahamic traditions? Is God, who is able to do more than we can ask or imagine, able to be God for the so many disenfranchised who claim "none" when asked about faith? Who are the people in your community who need to know that biology does not legislate for God's choice, that God's faithfulness and intent to redeem God's people knows no bounds?

What makes a people for God is God's desire to have a people. On any given Sunday at Middle Collegiate Church in Manhattan, a Muslim man named Mohammed will be in worship, both morning and evening. A Jewish therapist named Susan will be there too. On first Sunday, when we celebrate the Eucharist, and we say, "All is prepared, you are welcome just as you are, to fellowship with the risen Christ," Susan and Mohammed are among the hundreds who make their way down the center aisle to the table of grace, grace that would bind together all that our human distinctions would declare broken.

Proper 14: The End of the Law
Romans 10:5–15

For one believes with the heart and so is justified, and one confesses with the mouth and so is saved. (Romans 10:10)

From the beginning (or near to it) our human sin has kept us from full unity with God. God, of course, remained faithful, making and keeping promises to Abraham and rescuing the Hebrew people from slavery in Egypt, but still the people were determined to go their own way. The law was given to Moses to help the people rectify this broken relationship with God. Instead, according to Paul, the law led the people of Israel to "seek to establish their own [righteousness]" rather than God's (Rom. 10:3). In midrashic fashion, Paul wrestles with the law throughout his letter to the Romans, describing it as somewhat of a barrier to salvation by faith, being cumbersome to keep and nurturing self-reliance instead of reliance on God. The good news Paul shares with the Romans: What the law could not do, the incarnation can.

Jesus is the end of the law, the fulfillment of the law, and the telos of the law. God's intent to be at one with God's people is manifest in the Christ. Black gospel music sings, "Trouble in my way. . . . I have to cry sometimes. I lay awake at night, but that's alright. Jesus will fix it, after a while." Jesus can heal the broken relationship between creature and Creator and among the created order. Our heartfelt belief, confessed with our mouths—this is the one God sent to save the world—redeems us, reconciles us to the God who loves us.

In place of the law and its 613 commandments is the commandment of Christ to love God with all you have and to love your neighbor as yourself. This is true for Jews, and this is true for Gentiles. Paul's midrash revokes the sense that good works can save us, that any human has the capacity to save herself. Only God, only grace, can set us free, can release us from condemnation.

Deuteronomy 26:5–11 confesses the God who drew Jesus out of the womb of the chosen people and gave him back to them in a gracious act of love. God now chooses all who would believe in the One who was sent. Grace repairs the brokenness we feel. Brokenness is the gap between the people we strive to be and the fallible people we are. It is the gap between God's perfection and our own imperfection. It is the divisions we create and perpetuate between all of us in God's creation. Jesus restores what was broken, fulfilling God's promise of salvation, fulfilling the law. Jesus is the end of the law.

Proper 15: God Is in Control
Romans 11:1–2a, 29–32

For the gifts and the calling of God are irrevocable. Just as you were once disobedient to God but have now received mercy because of their disobedience, so they have now been disobedient in order that, by the mercy shown to you, they too may now receive mercy. For God has imprisoned all in disobedience so that he may be merciful to all. (Romans 11:29–32)

God is on a mission. God has a plan. We may screw it up, but God works through it all. God calls a people and chooses them. They are disobedient, and God saves them anyway. They are taken captive and once again freed.

God gives the law and knows it will not be obeyed. God sends judges and prophets.

God sends the Christ, the rock of salvation, hewn out of God's own people.

They reject Jesus; and this, even this, God uses so that Gentiles may be grafted into the plan of God for salvation.

Oh yes, God has a purpose and a plan. God is in control.

Throughout our series on Paul's letter to the Romans, we've seen how God repairs the brokenness in our own souls through grace and unwavering, inseparable love. We've seen how God overcomes the brokenness in human relations, uniting us in Christ as chosen, beloved children. God's plan is restoration and wholeness. Paul trusts in this as he sorts through the frustrating divisions between Jews and Gentiles, the law and God's grace, and waxes poetic about spirit and flesh, labor paints, height and depth, and chosenness.

To Paul's mind the rebellion of all creation is purposed by God so that God might show mercy to all. God uses the salvation of the Gentiles to inspire jealousy in the hearts of the chosen ones, Paul says. See the mercy of our God and how it extends to all people? Even this is part of the plan of God.

It can be difficult to talk about God's plan or God being in control, because we still see so much brokenness in our world. If God is in control, why do people kill one another in the streets? Why do some have more than enough, while others languish in poverty? Why do I lose the ones I love, and why does there seem to be no end to my grief?

Those are life's unanswerable questions, but in spite of all that remains broken, we can trust that God is still on a mission, working all things for good. For healing. For restoration. And this is grace. Though the ways of God are mysterious and though the arc of human history bends in ways that may seem to defy God's goodness, God's purpose is mercy and God's method is grace.

We are invited to participate in God's mission of restoration, working with God to heal the broken places. How, then, do we respond with our lives?

Fall Series 1: No Fair!

Three Parts: Proper 18 through Proper 20

God's idea of fairness is fortunately very different from ours, the Gospel of Matthew shows.

BRIAN ERICKSON

Series Overview

One of the first lessons of social interaction we learn as children is that things don't always seem fair. Sometimes our brother gets a bigger scoop of ice cream, or a friend gets a longer turn on the swing. As adults, maybe we feel the boss passed us over for a promotion or raise. The gospel of Christ is not merely personal, but social. Followers of Christ are called to model the kind of selfless love that Jesus exemplifies, even when people seem utterly undeserving of it. The amazing grace we so joyfully sing about for ourselves is not so easy to swallow when we watch someone else receive it, but this is the heart of Christian community. As we grow in Christ, we learn to love like Christ, even when it's not fair. This series focuses on three passages from Matthew's Gospel that challenge our notions about church life, forgiveness, and grace.

Tips and Ideas for This Series

This series begins around Labor Day, when school is back in session and churches are gearing up for fall activities. Emphasize how this series will discuss issues we often face in our social interactions. Graphics for bulletins and screens might depict obviously unequal portions of a treat, such as ice cream or cake, or a child's pouting

	Sermon Title	Focus Scripture	Theme
Proper 18	How to Fight like a Christian	Matt. 18:15–20	Jesus gives a plan for settling conflict in the church.
Proper 19	The Math of Forgiveness	Matt. 18:21–35	Real grace means losing count of wrongs.
Proper 20	A Fair Wage	Matt. 20:1–16	We don't get what we deserve.

expression that even adults can relate to (though they may never show it!).

Proper 18: How to Fight like a Christian
Matthew 18:15–20

If another member of the church sins against you, go and point out the fault when the two of you are alone. If the member listens to you, you have regained that one. (Matthew 18:15)

Most of the time, Jesus speaks in nebulous parables that invite reflection and prognostication. But occasionally in the Gospels, he is remarkably practical and direct. This is good news and bad news, of course, as Jesus' practical instructions may be easier to understand but leave much less wiggle room in terms of interpretation. Jesus takes it for granted that there will be "in-sinning" against one another in the church, but something as important as relational hurt within the body of Christ cannot be left to chance. When it comes to forgiveness within the Christian community, Jesus says, "Do it like this."

The irony, of course, is that churches are often the most indirect, passive places in the world. One church I know was so intimidated by their elderly longtime organist that they couldn't fire her, so they just threw her a retirement party. When that didn't work (and I'm not making this up), they just gave away the organ. In the very places where the gospel should be manifest in our interactions with others, we may be even more likely to gossip, whisper behind closed doors, and nurture old grudges in the dark, while vehemently denying them in the light.

If we are to forgive as God forgives, we have to pay close attention to the way God forgives us. In God's economy, forgiveness is not a feeling; it is a choice made in faith. We, the stiff-necked, need to hear that a lot, because many of us assume that being able to forgive is a matter of feeling like it—that we will know it's the right time to forgive because we will want to—but Jesus implies that moment is not coming.

So Jesus spells out conflict resolution in three easy steps. First, go directly to the person who has wronged you, and speak alone. This simple directive alone would change the course of Christian history. Before we discuss it with others, before we harbor it so long that it slowly poisons us against the possibility of reconciliation or wait until they catch on to our signals and come to apologize, go and find the one who has sinned against you. Is this fair? Absolutely not. Does it sound like Jesus? Unfortunately yes.

Step two of the Jesus plan for reconciliation is to involve others. But again, Jesus is not saying, "Go and talk about this person behind their backs." Jesus is saying, "Bring in others whom he or she might listen to." The proper role of having others be part of a conflict, according to Christ, is to give some perspective to the issue.

If that step does not work, then Christ calls on us to involve the church. This invites imagining how much work we would need to do in our own faith communities to make them places of healing and reconciliation for our members, much less the outsiders. The point is clear: the church is meant to be mediator in a world of misunderstanding, peacemaker in a world of passive-aggressiveness.

We often forget that Jesus' wonderful declaration that he will be with two or three gathered in his name comes in the middle of a discourse about hard conversations and reconciliation. According to Jesus, the church ought to be reducing conflict through direct discussion, accountability, and transparency. When the church fails to live this out, when the church fails to invite Christ into our conflicts, we shouldn't be surprised when it's hard to see Jesus in our midst, no matter how many are gathered.

Proper 19: The Math of Forgiveness
Matthew 18:21–35

Then Peter came and said to him, "Lord, if another member of the church sins against me, how often should I forgive? As many as seven times?" Jesus said to him, "Not seven times, but, I tell you, seventy-seven times." (Matthew 18:21–22)

Peter is always direct with his words, the patron saint of those of us born without a filter between their brain and their mouth. Having heard the instructions on how Christians are to deal with conflict, he now wants a number. He's caught Jesus in a rare moment of straightforward speech, and this seems like a good time to draw a line in the sand as to exactly how forgiving the forgiven need to be.

And give Peter credit; he's learned from his previous mistakes. He knows that Jesus will set the number high, probably ridiculously high; so Peter shoots even higher. Not once, not twice, not thrice, but seven times. When can I write this person off? When we step away from Scripture and imagine someone wronging us seven times, Peter's formula sounds pretty radical.

The problem with counting how many times we forgive is that we're not really practicing grace; we're just extending our patience. Keeping count of wrongs is a means of unforgiveness, for the past is never really washed away; it's just relegated to the archives. When we choose to forgive, we have to be ready intentionally to stop rehearsing and rehashing that moment of pain. A lot of times folks will speak forgiveness, but whenever anything else happens in the relationship, those old wounds get opened up all over again.

When we choose to forgive others, we have to take the risk of restoring the relationship back to where it was before we were hurt. It may not ever grow beyond that, but we have to be willing to get back to where we started. That means taking the risk of being hurt all over again. You have no guarantees this will not happen again. We have to risk that, just as God has taken that risk with us.

In the seventeenth chapter of Luke, Jesus tells the disciples, "If a fellow believer sins against you, and then comes and repents, you have to forgive them. If they do it seven times in one day, and seven times they come back and repent, you have to forgive them seven times." By the way, it's right after Jesus says this that the disciples respond, "We need more faith!"

Being people of forgiveness means we are not waiting until someone earns our forgiveness. That is as impossible as our trying to earn the love of God, and it is just as unfaithful. But the tension here is that the forgiveness Jesus calls for is a reckless and seemingly irresponsible practice that could easily lead to the kinds of abusive, imbalanced relationships that plague our world. Surely Jesus isn't calling for his followers to be doormats, right?

There will sometimes be consequences. We should not forgive serious wrongs when we don't yet believe there has been true repentance, but once we know there has been repentance, we have to let go of those obstacles that keep us distant from the person who has hurt us. Perhaps the measure of assurance for our own salvation is not some ecstatic religious experience, but whether or not we too will live out the kind of unfair grace that has been shown to us by our Redeemer.

Proper 20: A Fair Wage
Matthew 20:1–16

Now when the first came, they thought they would receive more; but each of them also received the usual daily wage. And when they received it, they grumbled against the landowner, saying, "These last worked only one hour, and you have made them equal to us who have borne the burden of the day and the scorching heat." But he replied to one of them, "Friend, I am doing you no wrong; did you not agree with me for the usual daily wage?

Take what belongs to you and go; I choose to give to this last the same as I give to you. Am I not allowed to do what I choose with what belongs to me? Or are you envious because I am generous?" (Matthew 20:10–15)

Someone asks Jesus what the kingdom of God is like. What they are asking Jesus, what we are asking Jesus, is, how do we tell the difference between the way the world works and the way God works?

His answer comes in the form of a story. There was a gentleman who owned a vineyard, Jesus says, and it came time for the harvest. Most of the time a farm can be run by a few hardworking folks, but when harvesttime comes around, you need extra hands. So the gentleman who owns the vineyard heads out to the street corner and hires a group of day laborers. They agree on a wage—not an exorbitant amount, but a fair amount. They jump in the back of his pickup and head off to the vineyard for a long day.

As the day goes on, the overseer keeps coming in and saying, "We need more workers." At 9:00 a.m. At noon. At 3:00 p.m. And even at 5:00 p.m., though closing time is at 6:00. Each time, the owner heads back to the corner, where there is still a long line of hopeful day laborers, and takes as many as he can fit in the back of the truck. The last crop of workers barely has time to get their hands dirty before the bell rings and it's time to quit.

The owner, unusually, has the last workers hired stand at the front of the line and, even more unusually, when he hands them their pay, he gives them the full day's wage for their one hour of work.

As the word spreads down the line, to the 3:00 workers, the noon workers, the 9:00 workers, and finally those who have labored since the crack of dawn, the excitement builds. "If he gave them that much, imagine what he'll pay us." But as the line moves up, the pay scale does not. Every worker, down to the first one hired that morning, receives the same thing.

When those early risers had agreed on the wage that morning, it sounded fine. Generous, even. But now that they've seen someone else get it for much less work, they are furious. The coins in their pocket, that they hoped for all afternoon when the sun was bearing down on them, now feel downright insulting. This isn't fair; they deserve more than the others.

They demand an explanation, and all they get is, "It's my money, and my business. I'll do with it what I want."

Jesus finishes his story with another one of those nonsensical gut punches he likes to leave us with: "So the last will be first, and the first will be last." And that, friends, is what the kingdom of heaven is like. That is the last word.

Like the first who find themselves suddenly last, sometimes I want to yell, "They don't deserve God's grace! They didn't earn it! They didn't even try! It isn't fair!"

But then I realize where I am. Standing on a lonely street corner, desperate and hopeless with no place to go. When he comes along. And says he has a place, even for undeserving me. And so I hop in the truck.

Fall Series 2: The Enemies of Gratitude

Five Parts: Proper 21 through Proper 25

A stewardship series exploring the things that keep us from being content and grateful.

BRIAN ERICKSON

Series Overview The fall is typically the season in which most churches make their case for financially supporting their ministry while also teaching the biblical principles of giving. This series offers an opportunity to teach gratitude by calling out the things that keep us from being truly grateful. In each sermon, we see how a misplaced focus—on how things could be or used to be better, how we're not getting what we think we deserve, or simply how life's struggles are keeping us down—prevents us from seeing all the blessings that are right in front of us. While the Scripture selections move back and forth from the Old Testament to the New, the need for "an attitude of gratitude" is made clear in each week's lection.

	Sermon Title	Focus Scripture	Theme
Proper 21	Nostalgia	Exod. 17:1–17	Glorifying the past blinds us to present blessings.
Proper 22	Worry	Phil. 4:1–9	It's not about less stress, but more trust.
Proper 23	Entitlement	Matt. 22:1–14	None of us "deserves" the invitation, but we share it anyway.
Proper 24	Greed	Matt. 22:15–22	Give to God what is God's (i.e., everything).
Proper 25	Disappointment	Deut. 34:1–12	Don't let loss keep you from appreciating the good.

Tips and Ideas for This Series	Stewardship series can be challenging, especially when interpreted as begging and guilt-tripping congregants into giving more. With a focus on gratitude, discussion of giving becomes more about giving back to God in response to all God has given us. Consider including testimonies in the service from people whose stories of gratitude in the face of each Sunday's "enemy" have led them to give back to the church and community, whether financially or in other ways.

Proper 21: Nostalgia
Exodus 17:1–17

But the people thirsted there for water; and the people complained against Moses and said, "Why did you bring us out of Egypt, to kill us and our children and livestock with thirst?" (Exodus 17:3)

An entire nation, thousands of people, are delivered from certain death when God makes a way for them through the Red Sea. God hears their prayers and makes it happen.

But then, the story says, they forget. In Exodus 14, we read the story of God doing the incredible, answering the Israelites' prayer and pushing aside the water to give them a path to freedom. And sure enough, Exodus 15 begins with them dancing. For three days they dance with excitement and gratitude before God. Every child of Israel sings a song of praise before God.

But within just a few verses, the miracle has worn off. The Israelites are parched; they go looking for a water fountain, only to discover that the facilities out here in the desert are sorely lacking. They get hungry, and they reminisce about the buffet line back in Egypt. Their empty bellies cause them to have nostalgia about their slavery.

This is one of the signs you have really lost it: when you start to idealize your past, and your past involved being a slave to the Egyptian Pharaoh: "Back in the good ol' days, when we spent all day making bricks and building pyramids, when we had no rights, and the Pharaoh occasionally killed all our male children, *those were the days.*"

In slavery, every day is the same. There is something comfortable about suffering, because it is predictable. Freedom can be much more trying. Out here in the wilderness, when they have to depend on God, when they are in uncharted territory, there is no predictability. They wake up every day having to trust that God is going to lead them somewhere. They are suffering from postmiraculous stress disorder.

The Israelites, trapped in rosy revisions of their past, are blinded to the almost constant provision of God. They are numbed to the now, trapped in the spiritual lands of Massah ("test") and Meribah ("find fault"). They wander in their grumbling, and it should be no surprise that they go in circles for forty years.

Nostalgia never leads you forward, because nostalgia casts an impossible standard—a candy-coated, much-improved rendering of what once was. Nostalgia is Egypt 2.0, with the warts and the thorns removed. The present can never match an idealized past, leaving us stuck in the quicksand of our edited memories, perpetually ungrateful for the place we now find ourselves.

This postmiraculous stress disorder still strikes God's people (we may be the most prone to it), leading some faithful Christians to remember earlier days through a Norman Rockwell revisionist lens. Whether it is holding on to the church of our youth (which ceased to exist many years ago) or clinging to a season of our own lives in which things were better than they are now, nostalgia quietly steals our joy and makes us indifferent to the flowing streams of living water God has provided here in the wilderness.

It is telling that this generation of exodus wanderers never makes it to the promised land, perhaps because their nostalgia won't let them get there. Liberation and hope lie in wait for those who can stop pretending that the past was perfect and who can walk in faith toward God's future. How would the church be different if we could move forward together?

Proper 22: Worry
Philippians 4:1–9

Rejoice in the Lord always; again I will say, Rejoice. Let your gentleness be known to everyone. The Lord is near. Do not worry about anything, but in everything by prayer and supplication with thanksgiving let your requests be made known to God. And the peace of God, which surpasses all understanding, will guard your hearts and your minds in Christ Jesus. (Philippians 4:4–7)

"Don't worry about anything." It sounds simple enough, but this may be the most difficult of all biblical instructions to keep.

It ought to be especially difficult for Paul, who has plenty to worry about. He is writing this letter in chains, as he sits on death row. He is scheduled to be executed for preaching the gospel. His body has been beaten, he has been stoned almost to death, he has endured shipwrecks and angry mobs, and now he will die for preaching the gospel of Jesus Christ.

But his command is simple: "Rejoice." And in case the first time did not take: "Again, I say, rejoice." Celebrate your way through the chaos.

Earlier in the letter, writing from prison, Paul says it clearly, "I will continue to rejoice, for I know that through your prayers and the help of the Spirit of Jesus Christ this will result in my deliverance. . . . Christ will be exalted now as always in my body, whether by life or by death. For to me, living is Christ and dying is gain."

All around him, the church is being assaulted, the apostles are being persecuted, families are being torn apart, and fear is reigning in the hearts of the believers; and Paul's word to them, facing his own death, is simple: Don't worry about it.

The powerful thing about Paul's instruction here is how incongruent it is with his own context and the circumstances surrounding his readers. Pop culture teaches a peace that ignores, a peace that detaches, a peace that hides from the news in order to lower your blood pressure and give you some perspective. Paul doesn't just say, "Be joyful, because things are going well"; for Paul, nothing is going well. He doesn't say, rejoice in your family, or in your job, or in your well-being, or in the fact that you live free from all dangers. He says, "Rejoice in the Lord."

We invest our trust in a lot of places where it is not safe. We try to be happy in all sorts of ways; we try and make ourselves feel right in all sorts of things that cannot last. A confidence in temporal things will always be temporary. All of it can be taken. When we build our joy on the sand of this world, we should not be surprised when the storm comes along and takes it away.

"So don't worry about anything," Paul says. The reality is that some of us hear that word from Paul, and it just makes us worry more, because we worry too much, and now we're worried that we're too worried. But this isn't a psychological trick. Paul isn't telling us to think happy thoughts. He has seen up close and personal the pain of this world, the darkness of this world. He is just as overwhelmed by the evil that grips God's creation, but he believes in another story.

Paul says that God's peace passes all understanding. He says that it makes no sense. It's not something you think your way into; it's not something you arrive at logically; it is something you trust in. And when we have that peace, God will guard our hearts. The word he uses is a military word, for a sentry watchman. Paul says that the God of the universe will stand watch over your heart and protect it from whatever the world can throw at you.

Letting go of our worry is not a matter of ignoring what's wrong; it's a confidence in what is right. It's dropping anchor in the good news of Christ Jesus rather than waiting for the news of the world to calm us down. It's sobering to imagine how little a worried Paul would have accomplished.

Ridding your life of worry is not a matter of reducing stress but of increasing trust. "Rejoice," Paul says. And if the first time doesn't take: "Again I say, rejoice."

Proper 23: Entitlement
Matthew 22:1–14

Then he said to his slaves, "The wedding is ready, but those invited were not worthy. Go therefore into the main streets, and invite everyone you find to the wedding banquet." Those slaves went out into the streets and gathered all whom they found, both good and bad; so the wedding hall was filled with guests. (Matthew 22:8–10)

The wedding banquet is a common theme for Jesus' teaching, particularly when he wants to envision the coming kingdom of God. For his contemporary listeners, there may have been no more significant social event than a wedding, where a family's honor was put on display for days of feasting and friends. One can only imagine the extravagance of a king's wedding banquet for his son, when the normal constraints of a checking account are removed. Before Jesus even unfolds his story, his listeners are imagining what it would be like to have a place at such a feast.

But, as is the case with most of Jesus' stories, there is a twist, to say the least. At the wedding of the century, the guests fail to show. Not only do they fail to make an appearance, but they brutally beat and kill the messengers sent to call them to the feast. Matthew, of course, is drawing our attention to the fate of the prophets, but the violence shown to the king's servants is no less disturbing. What should be a cause for joy turns to death and destruction as the king returns the violence shown to his messengers.

It makes sense that this detail is omitted in the other Gospel telling of this story (Luke 14:16–24), as it is hard to imagine any sort of positive resolution after such a massacre. The preacher does well to remember that the Gospels are forged in a time of animosity between the early Christians and certain Jewish leaders, and it is easy to imagine that Matthew reframes Jesus' original parable to suit the venomous nature of his own context.

But the overall message is certainly meant to mirror the version told in Luke, which is that those original invitees turned their back on the invitation, and the king's response is to welcome the un-welcomeable. Carefully separated from the anti-Semitic simplicity that we often apply to this parable, it teaches us something about all those who are too comfortable in their standing with the king. The good news is meant for the hungry, for those who would drop everything for an invitation to the banquet. When we lose sight of the radical grace of the invitation, we have forgotten who we are.

The ballroom is crowded with the good and the bad. Our birthright as the followers of Christ is to remember none of us deserve to be here, and so we should never impose our quality-control standards on anyone else the king wants to invite to the banquet. Our job is to go and tell, to invite all, and to leave to the host any thinning of the crowd.

Whenever we allow ourselves to believe that we deserve what we have, or that we are somehow more worthy than another, we will find ourselves incapable of gratitude. The proper response to the king's invitation, Jesus declares, is to run breathless to the banquet, dressed for the marriage of heaven and earth, wondering how we ever got put on such a guest list.

Proper 24: Greed
Matthew 22:15–22

Then he said to them, "Give therefore to the emperor the things that are the emperor's, and to God the things that are God's." (Matthew 22:21)

There's something deep inside most of us that cringes at the suggestion that what we have doesn't belong to us. If we work for it, we want control of it, and we don't trust other folks to know how best to spend it. One of the foundational irritants leading to America's Revolutionary War was "taxation without representation." Being taxed without getting a say-so.

And if you think *we* don't like paying taxes, meet the residents of Jerusalem during Jesus' time. Israel is an occupied territory, a Roman province. The Romans let the Jews have their temple worship, but they are taxed unfairly to support the Roman capital, and they enjoy very few rights, because they are not truly Roman citizens.

There is a group of Jewish religious leaders on one side of the aisle determined to overthrow the pagan Roman government, to kick them out of Jerusalem. On the other side of the debate are the Herodians, the Jews who have benefited rather nicely from the Roman occupation. As you might imagine, the Pharisees and the Herodians did not get along very well. The only platform they share is that Jesus needs to go. This unusual partnership is something like Hillary Clinton and the Tea Party teaming up.

They plant a question in the crowd, a question about paying taxes to the Romans. If Jesus says it's unlawful to pay taxes (as the Pharisees think but are too afraid to teach publicly), then the Romans will snatch him up for being an instigator. If he says that it's fine to pay taxes to the Romans, then the religious zealots in the crowd will stone him for going against God's Word. It's a no-win situation for Jesus.

"Is it lawful to pay taxes to the Roman emperor?" Jesus answers their question with another question, as he is prone to do: "Anybody got a coin?" He's not about to do a magic trick; he just doesn't even have a coin on him. The King of Kings, Lord of Lords, has nothing in his wallet.

You've got to imagine this is an embarrassing moment for the Herodians and the Pharisees as they dig into their pockets and produce a coin, because the Pharisees shouldn't even have one. They publicly teach that Roman currency is appalling to God, and here they are in the courts of the temple; so if they have one, they have exposed their hypocrisy in front of the crowd.

They nervously hand Jesus the coin, and he looks at it as if he's never seen one before.

"Who is this on the coin? There seems to be someone's picture on this coin." The word in Greek is "icon." "Whose icon, image, is on this coin?" Jesus asks them.

Well, duh. It's the image of the emperor. Maybe he's not as smart as he looks.

Without going any further, Jesus says, "Render unto Caesar that which is Caesar's, and give to God what is God's." The literal translation would be: "Pay back Caesar what belongs to him, and pay back God what belongs to God." Give to them what they deserve.

He's not talking about taxes at all. Give to God what has God's image on it. This is bigger than a tax, bigger than a picture on a coin. This is a question of what belongs to God.

It is still a no-win situation for preachers to talk about money. Even two thousand years later, we walk on eggshells when it comes to dealing with our stuff. Stewardship campaigns crash attendance; it feels more like going to the dentist than cheerful giving. But perhaps our problem is not so much with the giving, but with remembering who this stuff really belongs to.

Jesus says, let Caesar have his little coins. But let the people of God decide today whom they serve. Let the followers of God decide today that what they have, what they are, what they do, what they think—it all belongs to the One who knew you before he knit you together in your mother's womb.

Ask yourself, "What belongs to God?" Then find a way to put it back in God's hands.

Proper 25: Disappointment
Deuteronomy 34:1–12

The LORD said to him, "This is the land of which I swore to Abraham, to Isaac, and to Jacob, saying, 'I will give it to your descendants'; I have let you see it with your eyes, but you shall not cross over there." Then Moses, the servant of the LORD, died there in the land of Moab, at the LORD's command. (Deuteronomy 34:4–5)

This is one of the most interesting plot twists in all of Scripture. More than any other Israelite in the desert, Moses has earned the right to cross that river and enter the promised land. From the fiery shrubbery that first called him out of shepherding, through the Red Sea and the tempests of whining and complaint he has endured, Moses should be a shoo-in for a passport.

What's striking here is that, while later interpreters will spend countless pages trying to make sense of this turn of events, Deuteronomy simply states it is a result of the misdemeanor at Meribah (Num. 20:1–13). Moses didn't follow the letter of the law, and as a result God will keep both him and his brother from setting foot in the promised land.

It's easy to read a passage like this and become distracted by the seemingly graceless way in which God treats Moses. And it is easy to spend an entire sermon trying to justify God's actions or explain how the ancients would have interpreted events like death to have divine meaning and purpose to them.

But perhaps the deeper truth here is the nature of disappointment, that sometimes life, even the life of faith, does not make much sense. Wonderful would-be parents are unable to conceive a child. Fervent prayers in the oncology ward seem to fall on deaf ears. The one who is right and true and colors within the lines finds herself standing atop Pisgah, so close to what she desires but unable to touch it.

The word "disappointment" means what it sounds like, to miss an appointment. To have a scheduled expectation broken, a previously calendared promise erased. The greater the promise, the more devastating its disappearance.

Like Job, most people who have been through the wringer of life have a long list of complaints against their Maker. God has quite the rap sheet, and it's no wonder that so many well-intentioned followers of Christ find their faith dashed against the rocks of disappointment. It's hard to be grateful when the thing you most want and need and desire and pray for is taken away.

But there is also great power in those who see their own stories as a part of something greater. Scripture records that Moses knows in advance that his ministry will end just short of his intended destination, yet he spends his last breaths in blessing and praise. Maybe he wasn't taking this journey just for himself.

None of us can assign meaning to someone else's suffering, but when the sufferer can see purpose even on Pisgah, healing can occur. Folks like Viktor Frankl have been telling us this for a while, but in our day of instant gratification and convenience, many of us have forgotten the discipline of disappointment.

It's never our work to assign meaning to others' dashed hopes and dreams or to command joy in the face of disappointment. But what we can do is look to the faith of Moses, perhaps best displayed not in front of the Pharaoh but sitting alone with his God watching the horizon of his life's work, feeling not resentment but gratitude. What we all need is some perspective on Pisgah, to cling to the central claim of our faith: that a grander story is being told. We can rejoice and give thanks for our place in that story, in spite of disappointments we've faced along the way.

Fall Series 3:
The Good News about Death

Four Parts: All Saints', Proper 27
through Proper 29 (Reign of Christ)

Facing a difficult topic as people with resurrection hope.

BRIAN ERICKSON

Series Overview

While we speak of death often at funerals, we rarely tackle the subject head on in our Sunday routine. Yet at the core of the Christian faith is a word about death and life beyond death. If the book sales of *Heaven Is for Real* and others in the genre are any indication, people are hungry for a word of life in the midst of death. The lections for this period, stretching from All Saints' to Christ the King, offer the preacher a wonderful opportunity to model for the congregation what it means to speak openly about death and the Christian hope of resurrection and perhaps clear up some of society's misguided notions at the same time.

Tips and Ideas for This Series

Talking about death can be difficult, and this series may spark many emotions in those who have suffered a recent loss. Consider offering

	Sermon Title	Focus Scripture	Theme
All Saints' *(observed in place of Proper 26)*	The Other Side of the Curtain	Rev. 7:9–17	We remember those who came before us, and we worship knowing death is not the end.
Proper 27	Grieving with Hope	1 Thess. 4:13–18	We grieve in the paradox between human loss and eternal life.
Proper 28	How Many Shopping Days Left?	Ps. 90:1–12	Life is a gift; use it wisely.
Proper 29 (Reign of Christ)	The Last Word	Eph. 1:15–23	No matter what life (and death) bring, Christ has the last word.

special times for grieving persons to gather and share their stories, in a certain room before or after the service, or at support groups throughout the week.

All Saints' Sunday: The Other Side of the Curtain[1]
Revelation 7:9–17

Then one of the elders addressed me, saying, "Who are these, robed in white, and where have they come from?" I said to him, "Sir, you are the one that knows." Then he said to me, "These are they who have come out of the great ordeal; they have washed their robes and made them white in the blood of the Lamb. For this reason they are before the throne of God, and worship him day and night within his temple, and the one who is seated on the throne will shelter them. They will hunger no more, and thirst no more; the sun will not strike them, nor any scorching heat; for the Lamb at the center of the throne will be their shepherd, and he will guide them to springs of the water of life, and God will wipe away every tear from their eyes." (Revelation 7:13–17)

We like our Scriptures comforting, and it's hard to find Revelation comforting at first glance. It is hard to get a nice coffee-mug verse out of the Revelation of John, and I have a hard time imagining a Precious Moments Bible with the cover depicting the four horsemen of the Apocalypse.

But Revelation's primary intent is to comfort the saints on this side of God's "big reveal." It is to give a word of hope to those whose worlds have come apart. Revelation is not a map to the end; it's a promise to those who feel as if they are already at the end, that a new beginning awaits.

In the passage assigned for today, John describes a glorious moment where a countless number of faithful people—those who have lived through the "great ordeal" and have died and are now with Christ—are seen robed in white and singing praises to God. Imagine the endless sea of white robes, Christians who were bruised and beaten by life, who spent their days in fear of persecution, now singing at the top of their lungs.

Their robes have been cleansed with the blood of the Lamb. Blood seems like an unusual choice for detergent. But what a powerful image! The suffering, the stains of our brokenness and fear and worry, are washed clean, not by our own doing, but by the faithfulness of Jesus Christ. Jesus' suffering redeems our suffering.

1. Most churches will mark All Saints' on this Sunday rather than use the Proper 26 lections, so the readings and sermon have been altered to reflect that.

If we're honest, we don't know what to do with death in our culture. When someone we know loses a loved one, we don't know what to say. When we lose someone precious to us, we don't know how to ask the living for what we need. Revelation is a reminder that for the early Christians (and for many of our sisters and brothers around the world today), death was a constant reality. Not just death, but martyrdom, as they were persecuted for their belief in Jesus Christ.

Whenever a faithful member of the church died, the living would gather in the place they had died, or in the catacombs near where they lay buried, to remember their faith. The early Christians knew that their faith didn't come out of nowhere; it was their inheritance, passed on to them by those who had come before. Perhaps the reason we have such a hard time with death in our culture is that we are so quick to forget those who came before us.

So, on today of all days, may we give thanks for those who have stepped into that unseen horizon of grace—who have shaped us into the people we are, who have loved us and failed us and everything in between, and who call us now to a life of hope, to a life of daring to believe death and pain do not have the final word. This means worshiping, even in the wreckage of this war-torn world. It means seeing what the world cannot see, that God has revealed a truth too precious to tell, that we are a family, all God's children, and that one day we will sit together at a great feast, robed together in a white not made by bleach but by blood.

Proper 27: Grieving with Hope
1 Thessalonians 4:13–18

But we do not want you to be uninformed, brothers and sisters, about those who have died, so that you may not grieve as others do who have no hope. For since we believe that Jesus died and rose again, even so, through Jesus, God will bring with him those who have died. . . . Therefore comfort one another with these words. (1 Thessalonians 4:13–14, 18)

As one pastor is fond of saying, the mortality rate for human beings is hovering at around 100 percent. Death is the great equalizer, irrespective of vocation, wealth, social status, class, and creed. It comes for all of us.

As a result, it makes sense that the Thessalonians (and we, their theological descendants) have some serious concerns about death. What about those who have died before Jesus comes back? Why does death seem still to have such a sting, if Christ has won the victory?

Paul spends a lot of time in his Thessalonian correspondence calling the believers to test what they hear, before they receive it as truth. Paul is clear that there is much in the world and in the church that is good to the ear, but not necessarily good news.

This may be particularly true when it comes to death. At the core of our Christian faith is a word about death, broken wide open on Easter Sunday, but there is likewise no other Christian doctrine that has been so revised by the surrounding culture. The Greeks and Egyptians believed that the soul went on to some sort of afterlife, and some of the Jews even believed in a resurrection at the end of time. So simply to say that Christians believe that there is something on the other side of death is not really to express the Christian hope. There is more to it.

The Christian approach to death must somehow paradoxically embrace the reality of human loss and the hope of eternal life. Many of our funeral liturgies begin with the announcement that we have come to praise God and acknowledge our human loss, all at the same time. Perhaps this is exactly what Paul means about "grieving with hope." Paul never suggests that faith exempts us from the need to grieve. Christians know full well the pain of death, even death on a cross. Grieving with hope will always mean acknowledging our loss (and taking seriously the sadness of others around us), while trusting that a larger epic is unfolding.

Nancy's son Tripp suffered from cystic fibrosis. As Tripp lay in the hospital in his final days, Nancy asked him if she could read Scripture to him to comfort him. She wasn't sure what to read him, and he could sense that, so he told her to turn to page 1649. The numbers 16 and 49 were two of his favorites, since Joe Montana was number 16 and he played for the 49ers.

She flipped open her Bible, but it ended on page 1334. There was no page 1649, because the New Testament started over with page 1. She was about to tell Tripp to try again, when she did the math in her head and realized that page 315 of the New Testament would have been page 1649, so she turned there.

There she found these words, from the apostle Paul to the Thessalonian church: "But we do not want you to be uninformed, brothers and sisters, about those who have died, so that you may not grieve as others do who have no hope."

Tripp turned to his mother, his CO_2 level rising and his lungs failing, and he said, "Mommy, those are the sweetest verses."

We live in the shadow of death, but we wait for the dawn. We grieve, but not as others do, for we are the people of hope.

Proper 28: How Many Shopping Days Left?
Psalm 90:1–12

For all our days pass away under your wrath;
our years come to an end like a sigh.
The days of our life are seventy years,
or perhaps eighty, if we are strong;
even then their span is only toil and trouble;
they are soon gone, and we fly away. (Psalm 90:9–10)

As we approach the holidays, it is inevitable that the shopping calendar takes over. There is something ominous about the countdown to Christmas, where we are constantly reminded of how little time we have left to complete our necessary purchases. Knowing that we only have a certain amount of time brings a sense of urgency to what otherwise would be ordinary days.

The shopping days countdown inspired me to wonder what it would be like to know how many days each of us had left to walk the earth. The most recent data suggests that the average life span for an American citizen is a little over seventy-eight years, 78.56 years, to be exact. Women still live longer than men, and obviously that is an average, but for our purposes, let's say most of us get seventy-eight years and some change to walk this earth. That's around 28,647 days we have to spend being alive, to spend however we wish. Shopping, standing in line, waiting in traffic, wondering why this line is called the express line—whatever it is that brings you a sense of fulfillment and joy.

There is even a website (convertunits.com/dates) that will let you put in two dates and it will give you the range between them so that you can see how much of your allotment you've already spent. It's rather sobering. What if we all woke up every morning and we could see how many days we had left? What if, above the mirror in your bathroom, there was a big digital countdown, letting you know how many days you had to work with?

Our psalm for the day agrees with the current national average, that we have somewhere between seventy and eighty years to be alive. The psalmist's mood reflects a significant portion of the Old Testament witness, presumably composed prior to any Jewish theology of bodily resurrection. It seems rather depressing at first glance, declaring human life an insignificant blip on the cosmic radar.

The deeper truth here, however, is that we who are like dust in the wind are precious to God. Elsewhere the psalms will ask, "What are people that you are mindful of them?" Or put another way, "Don't you have better things to do than love us?"

Ironically, it is our fragility, so easily forgotten, that makes our living so precious. It is the urgency of our mortality, the ticking countdown clock, that makes each moment matter. Death makes earthly life precious, because it reminds us that we can take no day for granted. When we live as if we will never die, we tend to waste the life we have. We worry about things that don't really matter, we fret over things that are not in our control, and we become consumed by stuff that is not eternal.

But when we remember that our place in this universe is not a status we've earned, but a gift graciously given, we will better recognize the sacred weight of every second.

Proper 29 (Reign of Christ): The Last Word
Ephesians 1:15–23

God put this power to work in Christ when he raised him from the dead and seated him at his right hand in the heavenly places, far above all rule and authority and power and dominion, and above every name that is named, not only in this age but also in the age to come. And he has put all things under his feet and has made him the head over all things for the church, which is his body, the fullness of him who fills all in all. (Ephesians 1:20–23)

I am fascinated by people's last words, the thing they choose to leave us with. In some ways, our first words as a child and our last words at death are some of our most important. John Wesley, the founder of Methodism, spent his dying breath saying, "Best of all, God is with us." Henry Ward Beecher, the great evangelist, used his last breath to say, "Now comes the mystery." And Jesus, according to Luke's Gospel, said from the cross, "Father, into your hands I commend my spirit."

We have a lifetime of words that we don't pay much attention to. We send e-mails, we text message, we exchange casual small talk, but we have only one chance to say our last word. Our conclusion. Our final reflection on this life and what it was all about. What we remember, and the way we want to be remembered.

Christ the King Sunday is the last word of the Christian year. This Sunday was first celebrated in 1925, when the world was still reeling from World War I and dictators were laying the foundations for World War II. In Europe and in Mexico, there were great forces of secularization in the government, doing all they could to weaken the influence of religion, particularly Christianity. So the church sent a bold statement on the last Sunday of the Christian year, saying, "Do what you will, but Jesus Christ will have the final word."

In the opening verses of Ephesians, we hear that refrain loud and clear. In the midst of chaos, fear, illness, and even death, Christians hold fast to the image of Christ enthroned above all—above every name, above every earthly power, above every authority. Christ gets the final word.

These are spiritual words, but they are also deeply practical ones. Paul does not intend for us to relegate Jesus to a heavenly throne that has no weight on earth. Jesus' kingship transforms every allegiance, every relationship, even our understanding of life and death. Christ's place in eternity demands our attention in the here and now. The work of faith is to live in the confidence of God's final word in Christ.

Today we proclaim to the world that Christ is the firstborn of all creation, the one for whom angels sang, the one through whom all that came to be. But in giving Christ the last word, we declare that in the here and now, he is our king.

He is our king as we sit in the waiting room, as the test results come back, as we weep over the grave, as we watch the wars escalate and the darkness deepen. He is our king when hope seems lost, that voice we will listen to when promises seem shattered, when our lives have no direction, and when we can't imagine anything tomorrow could bring that might fill this hole within us.

This is the great now-and-not-yet of Christian life, that we celebrate a victory the world cannot see, a hope that defies every instinct, a king enthroned on a cross. Therefore we need not be afraid of any power this world can wrangle, for Christ gets the last word.

Year B

Advent/Christmas Series: Coming Soon

Six Parts: First Sunday of Advent through First Sunday of Christmas, including Christmas Eve

The expectation and arrival of the Messiah is a grand, movie-like epic.

THERESA CHO

Series Overview The flow of the Advent season plays out like a movie. We get a hint of the highlights of the Christmas story in Advent 1, where we are invited to stay tuned to what is to come. Through the life and actions of John the Baptist, the scene and life of Jesus Christ is set up, as we are drawn in to remember the meaning of baptism and our own wilderness experience. The suspense heightens in the middle of the Advent season as we witness through the lives of Elizabeth and Mary that nothing is impossible for God. All this builds up to the climax of

	Sermon Title	Focus Scripture	Theme
Advent 1	Stay Tuned!	Mark 13:24–37	Something big is coming—watch and wait!
Advent 2	Baptismal Limitations	Mark 1:1–8	John the Baptist's limitations set him up to play an important role in Jesus' story.
Advent 3	John, the Doppelgänger	John 1:6–8, 19–28	The juxtaposition of John and Jesus shows us who our main character really is.
Advent 4	The Subjunctive Space	Luke 1:26–38	Plot twist! Elizabeth and Mary see the possibilities of what God can do.
Christmas Eve[1]	The Foggy Fringe	Luke 2:1–14, (15–20)	A different perspective helps us see the main event in all its glory.
Christmas 1	The Cliffhanger	Luke 2:22–40	The credits roll—what do we do now?

1. If Christmas Eve falls on a Sunday, Advent 4 can be used in the morning and this sermon used for evening candlelight services or a Christmas Day service.

the Christmas story, where the Christ child is born, but not in a way that we expect. The plot twists and ends in a cliffhanger that invites us to wonder how we are called to participate in the story.

Tips and Ideas for This Series

Movies are the way in which most people see epic stories unfold these days. Play up the epic quality of the Christmas story with movie-themed graphics on your bulletin and/or screen. Include references to your favorite films that complement the part of the story you are discussing each week. Small group gatherings to watch favorite Christmas movies and discuss their connection to the biblical Christmas story would be a fun way to incorporate fellowship and Bible study to a busy season.

Advent 1: Stay Tuned!
Mark 13:24–37

"Therefore, keep awake—for you don't know when the master of the house will come, in the evening or at midnight, or at cockcrow, or at dawn, or else he may find you asleep when he comes suddenly. And what I say to you, I say to all: Keep awake." (Mark 13:35–37)

Today is the First Sunday of Advent. We enter a season that journeys through a story that is familiar to so many. It is like a favorite movie that we have seen over and over again. We can recite our favorite lines, chuckle in anticipation of an upcoming funny scene, cringe in knowledge of what is going to happen next, or begin to tear up at those moments that always seem to tug at our heartstrings.

If the story of the birth of Christ is our favorite movie, then today's Scripture reads like the movie trailer. Imagine the voice-over setting the scene: "In those days, after the suffering of that time, the sun will become dark, and the moon won't give its light . . ." The camera pans over to a fig tree that is beginning to sprout new branches, shoots, and leaves. The voice-over continues: ". . . but nobody knows when that day or hour will come, not the angels in heaven and not the Son. Only the Father knows." The trailer ends, "Watch out! Stay Alert!" This trailer shades this familiar birth story of cute sheep, wise men with gifts, holy angels, and curious shepherds into a suspenseful, action-filled, ominous plot titled "Advent Apocalypse."

The Christmas story read in this way is a far cry from the G-rated version we may tell our children. If read in this way, how does it affect the way we enter into this Advent season—a season known for expectation, preparation, and waiting? Are we merely waiting for baby Jesus to be born, or are we waiting for something more?

This parable of the Fig Tree is not concerned about revealing what we are waiting for as much as it is illuminating how we should wait. Nowhere does this trailer reveal the release date of this movie. It can arrive at any time; so constantly check your listings. Stay tuned!

There is a sense of urgency because what this parable describes is not an event that will occur in the far-off future. It is here and now. Therefore, there is no time for patience or complacency. On the contrary, we are to wait impatiently.

What would it look like if we lived our life alert, not missing out on the beauty and miracles before us, not denying the ways that Jesus speaks to us and calls us? How can we be constantly on the lookout for places that desperately call us to make known God's forgiveness, generosity, justice, abundance, and love? What if we entered into this Advent season already out in the fields like the shepherds, ready to receive the angel's message that the time has come, or like the astronomers, constantly searching until they spot the star that will guide them to what they have been looking for?

Stay tuned. Stay alert. The story we think we know so well may just have a twist we didn't quite expect.

Advent 2: Baptismal Limitations
Mark 1:1–8

John the baptizer appeared in the wilderness, proclaiming a baptism of repentance for the forgiveness of sins. And people from the whole Judean countryside and all the people of Jerusalem were going out to him and were baptized by him in the river Jordan, confessing their sins. (Mark 1:4–5)

If the First Sunday of Advent was the trailer, today is the setup. The scene is set, and we are meeting the first of our characters. We find John the Baptist in the wilderness. Before Jesus even arrives on the scene, the work is already in progress. John is baptizing, receiving confession, and preaching of "one stronger than I." While it may seem that John is doing much of the work that Jesus is coming to do, John is clear that his work is limited. His work is merely in preparation of the One who will baptize with the Holy Spirit.

What John models here is the kind of waiting that requires not only action but the kind of action that prepares people to receive the good news of Jesus Christ. John is changing hearts.

Often during a baptism we are reminded to remember our own baptism—not the event itself, which may be impossible for some, but the meaning of baptism. We are reminded that we are truly loved, forgiven, and accepted without any reason of deserving or earning it. We are reminded that we are created as God's children in God's image. We are reminded that God calls us to serve just as we are—no more, no less.

Here John gives us one more thing to remember about our baptism. Baptism is an active preparation for receiving the good news of Jesus Christ. Our hearts are changed. Therefore, baptism is an active part of preparing in Advent. As we remember our baptism, we are reminded that we join John the Baptist in preparing the way by engaging the world in a heart-changing manner. We are reminded that we are capable and worthy, just as we are. John the Baptist merely wore clothes of camel hair with a leather belt. The limitations of being out in the wilderness did not restrict John's ability to do good work. Instead, they set him up to play a major role in the Jesus story.

A young woman, Sheena Matheiken, started the Uniform Project when she found herself consumed and drained from the lack of creative inspiration while working in an advertising agency. She came up with an unusual creative challenge: she limited herself to the same black dress for an entire year, yet she had to create a unique look every single day. She paired this creative challenge with an ethical cause: to raise money to send less fortunate kids in India to school.

Her project quickly gained notice, and she found others wanting to join her along the journey. Not only did people want to donate to her cause, but they also wanted to participate in her black-dress experiment. Sheena received many donations of accessories to wear with her black dress from people's wardrobes, vintage stores, and designers. Soon people were coming up with their own black-dress projects and sharing photos on social media.

By setting limits for herself, Sheena unleashed a spark of creativity that was contagious and life changing for herself, the people involved, and the children who could now go to school. Limitations have a way of freeing us to discover that it does not take much to be an active participant in this Christmas story.

Sheena's limitations prepared the way for others to find their own creative solutions to color the world. John the Baptist's limitations prepared the way for hearts to be changed in anticipation of the One. What will our limitations prepare the way for?

Advent 3: John, the Doppelgänger
John 1:6–8, 19–28

There was a man sent from God, whose name was John. He came as a witness to testify to the light, so that all might believe through him. He himself was not the light, but he came to testify to the light. (John 1:6–8)

We are now in the middle of Advent season, but ironically we are not as close to the heart of the Christmas story. In fact, it may seem that we are nowhere approaching it, since there has been no mention of Jesus thus far. Jesus does not enter into today's Scripture either, at least not overtly.

Instead, the exposition phase of the story continues with John the Baptist. The identity of John the Baptist is still confusing to many. All we know is that "he came as a witness to testify to the light." Then we get a litany of all the things that John is not.

We know he is not the light to which he testifies.

Is he the Christ? He is not.

Is he Elijah? He is not.

Is he a prophet? No.

Is he a doppelgänger of some sort? Certainly John the Baptist's actions and demeanor are confusing him with the One that is to come. "Doppelgänger" is a German word that literally means "double-goer." There are quite a few stories of people meeting their doppelgänger, their look-alike.

Neil Richardson met not only his look-alike but someone who shared many habits, hobbies, a lifestyle, and mannerisms. In a small town northeast of London, Richardson met John Jemison. Richardson moved to this town after he retired and was frequently mistaken for John. Apparently they had a lot in common: a love for British constitutional history, a profession as a religious education teacher, and even a son who played the didgeridoo. Although they are quite certain they are not related, it is a mystery how much their lives parallel each other, beyond just looking alike.

In many ways, John the Baptist is Jesus' doppelgänger. The very actions of John the Baptist confuse those around him to the point that they believe he is the One. If he is not the One, he is questioned, "Why do you baptize if you aren't the Christ, or Elijah, or the prophet?" John the Baptist responds that his actions are merely testifying to the One who is to come. As disciples, we also testify to the coming of Christ, so how might we act as Jesus' doppelgänger as well?

John the Baptist's actions not only foreshadow the actions of Jesus. His insistence on what he is not foreshadows Jesus' own journey in the wilderness, where Jesus testifies to what he is not. John's wilderness experience is his preparation for Jesus. Jesus' wilderness experience is his preparation for his ministry. What is our wilderness experience preparing us for?

Advent 4: The Subjunctive Space
Luke 1:26–38

"And now, your relative Elizabeth in her old age has conceived a son; and this is the sixth month for her who was said to be barren. For nothing is impossible for God." (Luke 1:36–37)

On this Fourth Sunday of Advent, we inch closer to the heart of the Christmas story as Jesus' birth is foretold through the relationship of Elizabeth and Mary. If John the Baptist prepares the way for Jesus, then John's mother, Elizabeth, sets the stage for Jesus' mother, Mary. While there are differences between Elizabeth and Mary regarding marital status, age, and circumstances, the plot twist revealed through them is the miraculous nature of God's work.

Elizabeth is six months pregnant. Prior to this, Elizabeth's husband, Zechariah, received a message from an angel, Gabriel, who foretold that Elizabeth would be pregnant, despite her previous inability to become pregnant and her old age. Through the story of Elizabeth, we see that truly nothing is impossible for God.

It is this same angel who appears to Mary and announces a similar incredible happening. She too is to become pregnant—and with God's Son, no less. Her disbelief is understandable.

In the space between Elizabeth's story and Mary's story exist the impossible possibilities of God's abundance. In the space between barren and elderly Elizabeth and the teenage Mary blooms a miracle so great that it testifies, "Nothing is impossible for God."

The question is, why is Elizabeth's story necessary? Why is it just as important for Elizabeth's story as for Mary's story to be rooted in impossibilities? Is it so that Mary would believe? Could it be that seeing the extremes of what is possible for God reveals to us that there are no bounds to what God can do? No despair too deep. No pain too unbearable. No situation too hopeless. No sin unforgivable.

Often times, we believe our faith must be grounded in credulity and certainty. However, being certain of what we know is true and possible has a way of suffocating opportunities for God to surprise us. What if faith is rooted in the space we create between the extremes of what we understand to be impossible so that the Holy Spirit has room to move, breathe, and expand? How would that change how we interact with the world, engage in the Christmas story, relate to our brothers and sisters in Christ?

Phuc Tran, an instructor of Latin, German, Greek, and Sanskrit, has a deep passion for grammar, particularly the use of the subjunctive and indicative. Indicative case captures the factual statements made about what is actually happening or has happened. The subjunctive holds all the nuances of possibilities and potentialities. Indicative says, "I go there." Subjunctive says, "I could go there," "I would go there," "I might go there."

When he was growing up, the use of the subjunctive was incredibly helpful to Tran, whose family barely escaped to the United States from Vietnam. His ability to ponder the "what ifs" gave him strength to survive the harsh indicative reality of leaving his homeland during a war-stricken time.

The power of the indicative is that it roots us in reality and the truth of who we are. But it also prevents us from grasping alternate possibilities and can make us feel stuck and trapped, accepting a reality that doesn't have to be. The power of the subjunctive is that we can imagine not only the possible but also the impossible.

Like Mary and Elizabeth, we must hold on to the indicative nature of who God is so that we can fully embrace who we are. Like Mary and Elizabeth, we must also embrace the subjunctive of what God can do. Like Mary and Elizabeth, we are called to connect the dots between the God whom we know, and have always known, and the God who is guiding our future.

Christmas Eve: The Foggy Fringe
Luke 2:1–14, (15–20)

And when the angels returned had left them and gone into heaven, the shepherds said to one another, "Let us go now to Bethlehem and see this thing that has taken place, which the Lord has made known to us." So they went with haste and found Mary and Joseph, and the child lying in the manger. When they saw this, they made known what had been told them about this child. (Luke 2:15–17)

Today we come to the climax of this Christmas story, where Christ the child is born. All the familiar characters converge on this one scene to pay honor to the Christ child. It all begins with Mary and Joseph, who are required to take a long trip back to their city of origin so that they can participate in a census and be properly counted.

Usually at the ninth month of pregnancy, doctors advise their pregnant patients not to fly or travel, let alone travel by donkey over rocky terrain to a far-off city.

This event of the Christ child being born requires not only Mary and Joseph but all the characters in this story to travel. The angel comes down from above to send a message below. The shepherds who receive the message move away from their flock and fields to a humble stable in town. Later in the story, we will hear how the astronomers traveled across country, guided by the navigation of the stars. Even Herod moved—not physically but certainly emotionally from confidence in power to fear of losing that power.

God is subtly pulling and tugging Mary and Joseph, spectators, and those in power to the fringes, to places out of their comfort zone. Therefore, this story of Christ being born is not a sweet tale that fills our hearts with warmth and comfort. On the contrary it pulls us, tugs us, and yanks us out of our comfort zone.

This story does not take place in the center of the action, power, and everyday happenings; instead the story lures us on a journey farther and farther away from what is familiar and logical. Why is this so important?

San Francisco is subjected to two natural phenomena: fog and earthquakes. Mark Twain once said, "The coldest winter I ever spent was a summer in San Francisco." It is true that summers in San Francisco are considered the coldest season, mainly due to a dense fog that invades the city and hangs around for a couple of months. The fog can be quite thick, immersing itself through every cavity it can find.

If you simply remain in San Francisco, you will eventually believe that the sun no longer exists. Not until you venture out of the city, do you begin to see blue sky and feel the warm air. It is quite a sight to see how the fog sits on the city like a puff pastry on a hot bowl of French onion soup. You cannot get this perspective unless you move to the fringes. If you remained in the city, you would assume that the whole world was covered in fog. On the fringes, you capture a whole new view.

Maybe that is why the Christmas story moves us out to the fringes, so we can gain a whole new perspective on the birth of Jesus Christ. Being born on the outskirts gives us a glimpse into the who, what, where, and how of Jesus' life and ministry. We are invited then to be active participants in the life and ministry of Jesus in a way that may be uncomfortable but where justice will be realized.

Christmas 1: The Cliffhanger
Luke 2:22–40

When they had finished everything required by the law of the Lord, they returned to Galilee, to their own town of Nazareth. The child grew and became strong, filled with wisdom; and the favor of God was upon him. (Luke 2:39–40)

The holiday frenzy is over and we come to the end of the Christmas story. Today we get a glimpse into the life of Jesus as a child. We are in that in-between time of Christmas and New Year's. Christ is born, and we enter into the new year with a change of perspective and focus. The world will never be the same, because a miracle has happened. We spend much of December preparing and waiting for Christmas, reminding ourselves that Christmas is about more than just giving and receiving presents but about how the birth of Christ changes our world forever. We move from this miracle to focusing on the new year with reflection and resolution. We reflect on what has happened in the past year and try to resolve our regrets for the new year. But what do we do about this in-between time, when Christmas is over and the new year has yet to come? The truth is, Christmas isn't over.

The story does not finish where the ending feels complete and no loose ends are hanging. Instead, we are left with a cliffhanger, a hint that the story has just begun and an itch yearning for a sequel.

We get a clue about what we are to do in the in-between time. Here we see that Mary and Joseph observe longtime traditions and rituals by having Jesus circumcised, named, and presented. In the midst of these ritual acts, Jesus is blessed by Simeon, who claims that Jesus' life is set to walk down a prophetic path, mixed with God's steady protection and the fulfillment of ancient prophecies and the faithfulness of God's people. The whole Christmas story, therefore, names and claims the process in which we are to live out our faith.

As the credits roll, we sit with something stirring inside us. The Christmas story is not over. It has just begun. As you walk the prophetic walk surrounded by God's guidance and the support of God's people, as you live into the season of Christmas, as you are grounded in a real faith, an active faith, how is God calling you to obey, to serve, to pick up your own role in Jesus' story?

Epiphany Series: Jesus, Man of Mystery

Six Parts: First Sunday after Epiphany through Transfiguration

Who is this Jesus, who tries to keep his identity a secret?

THERESA CHO

Series Overview As Jesus' public ministry begins, he remains a somewhat mysterious figure. Like a good spy, magician, or stealthy detective, Jesus plays things close to the vest and reveals things only when he is ready.

	Sermon Title	Focus Scripture	Theme
First Sunday after Epiphany (Baptism of the Lord)	The Reveal	Mark 1:4–11	Baptism is the beginning of Jesus' revealing his identity.
Second Sunday after Epiphany	Now You See It, Now You Don't	John 1:43–51	Jesus invites us to come and see, but it is not always obvious what we are looking at.
Third Sunday after Epiphany	An Urgent Mission	Mark 1:14–20	Immediately the disciples followed Jesus, not even knowing why.
Fourth Sunday after Epiphany	Extra! Extra! Read All about It!	Mark 1:21–28	Jesus insists his identity be a secret, yet his actions stir the people to spread the news.
Fifth Sunday after Epiphany	Secrets, Secrets, Secrets	Mark 1:29–39	Jesus continues to keep his identity a secret, but his actions often free others who have been living in secret.
Transfiguration Sunday[1]	Exposed	Mark 9:2–9	Christ's transfiguration circles back to an earlier revelation about his identity.

1. Transfiguration Sunday is observed on the last Sunday before Lent begins. Depending on the date of Ash Wednesday, the season after Epiphany can range from four to nine Sundays. This series can be shortened or lengthened as needed.

Through six weeks of Gospel readings, we see Jesus begin to reveal himself more and more, while at the same time insisting on keeping his identity a secret. As we explore Jesus' mysterious identity, we may discover more about ourselves and a purpose that causes us to live with a sense of urgency.

Tips and Ideas for This Series

Invite Christmas visitors to return in the new year for a compelling look at a most basic question of Christianity: who is Jesus? The "Man of Mystery" theme can be enhanced with imagery and examples from a variety of secret-keepers and secret-revealers: spies like James Bond, illusionists like David Copperfield, detectives like Sherlock Holmes.

Baptism of the Lord: The Reveal
Mark 1:4–11

And just as he was coming up out of the water, he saw the heavens torn apart and the Spirit descending like a dove on him. And a voice came from heaven, "You are my Son, the Beloved; with you I am well pleased." (Mark 1:10–11)

Today's Scripture from the Gospel of Mark clearly marks the beginning, the jumping-off point of the good news of Jesus' ministry. This is also the only clarity that we will readily receive, because Mark is known for his secrets.

Yet Mark begins with a teaser of sorts for all we will discover about Jesus later on. After Jesus is baptized, the heaven splits open, and the Spirit in the form of a dove swoops down while a voice from heaven declares, as the Common English Bible puts it, "You are my Son, whom I dearly love; in you I find happiness." This beginning seems contrary to the secrecy motif that is often associated with Mark. Or is it?

Often in a good story, the reveal is essential in moving a plot along. The reveal may give new information that a character is not who we thought all along or another sort of twist in the plot. We are invited in the beginning to witness Jesus' baptism only to discover, through a dramatic but mysterious voice, that Jesus is the Son of God. What isn't so clear is what Jesus' being the Son of God means for us. We've received just enough information to pique our curiosity and decide to follow along as Jesus' story unfolds.

In many churches, this Sunday exploring Jesus' baptism involves a remembrance of our own baptism. What does Jesus' baptism tell us about our own? Is it the beginning? If so, the beginning of what? Maybe, like Jesus, the big reveal is yet to come, and we are invited to journey with Jesus and our fellow disciples to discover secrets along the way. And maybe, just maybe, when we encounter these secrets, we will receive epiphanies both small and large, not only about ourselves, but about God as well. As important as baptism is, it is the journey ahead that is essential. It is a journey that is not meant to be traveled alone but together in community. Only in community can we compare notes and share clues and encourage each other along the way.

The Appalachian Trail is a brutal two-thousand-mile hiking path stretching from Georgia to Maine. Many hikers descend on the mountains with backpacks full of gear and supplies to sustain them along the journey. The hike tests one's physical, emotional, and spiritual strength. While many may trek the path alone, they really are not alone, because there have been many testimonies of encounters with "trail angels." These good Samaritans have a mysterious knack for showing up with food, water, or transportation right when hikers are approaching desperation. Such encounters provide strength and encouragement to continue on the journey.

Baptism is not the final reveal, but simply a stop on this human-transformation trail we are on. For Jesus, it was one significant moment that revealed just enough of his identity to compel others to start the journey to know him more. Baptism is a reminder that where we are going is more important than where we have been.

Second Sunday after Epiphany: Now You See It, Now You Don't
John 1:43–51

Philip found Nathanael and said to him, "We have found him about whom Moses in the law and also the prophets wrote, Jesus, son of Joseph from Nazareth." Nathanael said to him, "Can anything good come out of Nazareth?" Philip said to him, "Come and see." (John 1:45–46)

The mystery continues with today's Scripture. Jesus has encountered Philip and Nathanael. We are given no clue to whether there was a prior relationship between Philip, Nathanael, and Jesus. We also don't know if word had spread about Jesus and therefore they at least recognized his name. All we know is that Jesus told them to follow and they did.

We may be able to assume that since Philip came from the same hometown as Andrew and Peter, who were already following Jesus, that mere association was good enough for them. But that still does not explain their absolute willingness to drop everything for someone they knew so little about.

What was it about Jesus that caused people to follow him with little to no evidence? The only scrutinizing question was when Nathanael asked if anything good could come from Nazareth. Nathanael finally succumbed to belief when Jesus said he knew his character when he saw him under the fig tree. Nathanael was amazed as if he had seen a magic trick.

There is a lot of psychology behind the art of magic, using the techniques of misdirection and cognitive illusion. Illusionists convince observers that they have discovered the solution to the trick. Once observers are convinced, they are less likely to pay attention to clues that pop up as to how the trick is really done, because they are distracted by finding confirmation that their own theory is correct. By creating cognitive illusions and directing our attention elsewhere, we are too distracted to notice obvious changes happening in front of us. For example, when a magician makes a coin disappear from passing it from one hand to another, we assume it is in the other hand. When the other hand is revealed to be empty, it is as if the coin had disappeared, when in fact it had been palmed and never left the hand in the first place. Once we have one solution in mind, it is hard to consider—or even notice—alternatives.

Because John the Baptist was preparing the way by preaching and baptizing, people were convinced that all signs pointed to him being the One. They were so convinced that they didn't even recognize that the One was in their midst. Even after John corrected them that he was not the Christ, Elijah, or a prophet (John 1:20–21), there was still doubt that anything good could come out of Nazareth. It was not until John told his two disciples that Jesus was the One they were looking for that they went and followed.

It seems natural that people were disillusioned with who Jesus is. Jesus was unlike anything they had encountered before. Yet, like a good illusionist, Jesus is not forthcoming with evidence or clues that give away all of who he is. All he does is invite us to come and see. These magician-like techniques are not meant to be deceptive. I wonder if it is Jesus' way of shaking us up so that we are open to the possibilities instead of distracted by our own conclusions and assumptions. As Jesus said to Nathanael, "Do you believe because I told you that I saw you under the fig tree? You will see greater things than these!"

So let us come and see.

Third Sunday after Epiphany: An Urgent Mission
Mark 1:14–20

And immediately, they left their nets and followed him. (Mark 1:18)

Today's Scripture continues the story of Jesus collecting disciples and followers. Unlike John, Mark gives us a little more back story into the lives of Simon, Andrew, James, and John. They are fishermen. However, besides their occupation, we receive no further clues that explain their eagerness immediately to quit their jobs and leave their family to follow Jesus. Likewise, it is also unclear why Jesus chose these particular twelve. Were they exceptional? Did their fishing abilities reveal a particular skill that would be useful in Jesus' ministry? In spite of all these questions, there is an undeniable sense of urgency to Jesus' call on these men's lives and their response.

It is almost a cliché among action adventure stories. The almost-retired secret agent is compelled to go out on "one last mission," and of course that mission ends up being the most challenging and death defying of his or her career. It is in our time of complacency, when we are content with ordinary life, that we are often most rudely shaken into action.

For Candy Chang, creator of the "Before I Die" campaign, it was the sudden death of a dear friend that woke her up from living a life of complacency, to a life with a sense of urgency. Thoughts of death and grief brought clarity to what was meaningful in her life. With an abandoned house across the street from her New Orleans home, Chang wondered how she could use this abandoned property as a public space that would connect people, making neglected space into constructive space, a place of loneliness into a reminder that we are not alone.

Chang turned the house into a chalkboard and wrote the sentence, "Before I die, I want to . . ." The blank spaces were invitations for passersby to complete the sentence with their own words. The words ranged from silly to profound, from sadness and regret to hope and joy. Words such as, "Before I die, I want to sing for millions . . . plant a tree . . . live off the grid . . . hold her one more time . . . follow my childhood dream."

From their ordinary work on the seashore, Jesus awakened the disciples to a new sense of meaning and life-changing purpose that compelled them to drop what they were doing right away and follow him. This deep sense of urgency overrode any need for full understanding of what was at stake or even a complete grasp of whom they were following. It was enough to take a step of faith.

Jesus can be secretive, but he's not often subtle. As he says in Mark

1:15 (CEB), "Now is the time! Here comes God's kingdom! Change your hearts and lives, and trust this good news!" Jesus clearly has something to accomplish, though the goal may not be immediately revealed to us. His call is bold and clear, shaking would-be followers out of their complacency. What urgent mission might God be calling you to?

Fourth Sunday after Epiphany: Extra! Extra! Read All about It!
Mark 1:21–28

They were all amazed, and they kept on asking one another, "What is this? A new teaching—with authority! He commands even the unclean spirits, and they obey him." At once his fame began to spread throughout the surrounding region of Galilee. (Mark 1:27–28)

Earlier in this chapter, God already let the secret out that Jesus is God's own Son, but we get the sense from today's Scripture reading that there is a lot more to discover about Jesus. The first miracle recorded in the Gospel of Mark is not a run-of-the-mill miracle like turning water into wine or multiplying food; in dramatic fashion, Jesus casts a demon out of a person he finds in the synagogue.

You would think that if Jesus wants his identity to be kept a secret, he would do this quietly. However, he does it with such authority that people around him, who are already impressed with his teaching abilities, spread the news all over Galilee. The person with an evil spirit professes that Jesus is the holy one from God, and Jesus speaks harshly, telling the demon to come out of the person. His teaching and healing both cause the people around him to react in astonishment and respond with the same type of urgency and authority to share the news of who Jesus is.

His actions reveal a key element of Jesus' identity: he is one with authority. Yet Jesus insists on keeping his identity a secret. So why does Jesus insist on the secrecy of his identity and yet continue to act in a way that undermines keeping his secret? The more that Jesus teaches and performs miracles, the more people are amazed and drawn to him. It's as if the mystery is part of Jesus' message itself.

In superhero stories like Superman and Spiderman, the chief newspaper editor is often determined to reveal the hero's identity, not for any humanitarian reason but out of sheer sensationalism. Headlines shouting "Secrets Revealed!" compel us to buy magazines, but such cheap bids for readership rarely leave us satisfied. *Breaking the Magician's Code* was a television show that revealed secrets of many standard magic tricks. I remember watching a show, eager to know how a certain trick was done, only to be left with a feeling of disappointment that the mystery was gone. The mystery created space within me to wonder at all the possibilities; compelled me to watch more, to see if I could figure it out for myself; and opened my sensibilities to believe in the impossible.

Jesus spends much of his ministry teaching, healing, loving, and speaking truth in a way that creates space for people to wonder alternative possibilities for their life than what is dictated to them with rules, laws, and commandments. People are compelled to follow to see if they can figure out for themselves who Jesus is. People are open to believing the impossible because they see the impossible happen before their eyes.

How do our actions reveal who Christ is to the world, not by shouting explanations of Christ's identity, but instead by acting in a way that creates space, compels, and opens others to believe the impossible?

Fifth Sunday after Epiphany: Secrets, Secrets, Secrets
Mark 1:29–39

And he cured many who were sick with various diseases, and cast out many demons; and he would not permit the demons to speak, because they knew him. (Mark 1:34)

Jesus continues to heal, exorcise, and teach, all the while not letting the demons speak in order to keep his identity a secret. News of Jesus' ministry is spreading, and people in need of his healing touch are flocking to Jesus.

As much as Jesus insists that his identity is kept a secret, I cannot help but notice that the people who need healing are people who have to live their life in secret. Oftentimes, demon-possessed and ill people were ostracized from community. Jesus' healing them not only makes them whole and accepted back into community but also releases them from a life of living in secret. With their new lease on life and freedom from their deepest secrets, they can fully discover ways they are called to follow Jesus.

Frank Warren collects secrets. He got a crazy idea to hand out three hundred self–addressed postcards on the streets of Washington, DC, asking people to share a secret they had never told anyone. Frank collected many secrets and created the PostSecret Project, where online he shared many of these secrets written on postcards.

The secrets were silly: "I give decaf to customers who are rude to me at Starbucks"; shocking: "Everyone who knew me before 9/11 believes I'm dead"; soulful: "Dear birthmother, I have great parents. I found love. I'm happy"; fearful: "When people I love leave voicemails on my phone I always save them in case they die tomorrow and I have no other way of hearing their voice ever again"; and kind: "I like to make mix CDs and leave them in random mailboxes."

Secrets revealed have a way of freeing us to live into our identity, accept ourselves for who we are, and connect us to our deepest humanity and others we have yet to meet. Frank Warren says, "The secrets I receive reflect the full spectrum of complicated issues that many of us struggle with every day: intimacy, trust, meaning, humor, and desire." The PostSecret Project gave a venue where unheard voices could be heard and untold stories could be shared.

Just as quickly as Jesus healed Simon's mother-in-law, she was quickly restored to her family and community. While we do not know how serious her ailment was, I wonder what possibilities lay ahead of her once she was healed. For the many who were healed and freed, I wonder what joy they found in living freely and openly rather than in secretive shadows on the fringes of society.

What secrets are keeping you from living fully? Is shame keeping you in the shadows? Jesus understands and can bring healing. Freed from all that holds us back, we can connect to one another and live fully in community and openness.

Transfiguration Sunday: Exposed
Mark 9:2–9

Six days later, Jesus took with him Peter and James and John, and led them up a high mountain apart, by themselves. And he was transfigured before them, and his clothes became dazzling white, such as no one on earth could bleach them. (Mark 9:2–3)

In today's Scripture, we see Jesus transformed, his holiness exposed through light and likeness to revered prophets of old. He stands on a mountaintop, where so many monumental events of Scripture occur. His clothes become a blinding, otherworldly white. Moses and Elijah, the ultimate character references for a Jewish leader, appear beside him. While this revelation of his identity is still limited to a few (on the way back down the mountain, he again tells them not to tell anyone!) and will not be fully revealed to all until his death and resurrection, this amazing moment on the mountaintop sends a big message about Jesus' identity.

God's words at the transfiguration, "This is my Son, the Beloved," add to the power of the moment but also remind us of a simple truth.

These are the same words spoken at Jesus' baptism, where we began just a few Sundays ago. The mystery has come full circle. In spite of all that we've learned about Jesus—his urgency, his authority, his power to heal, and now his place among the greatest prophets—the secret to his identity still lies in his status as God's Son, in that baptismal revelation of the One to whom he belongs. Sometimes the solution to a mystery has been present from the beginning, right in front of our noses.

Likewise, our baptismal identity is important to our walk as we follow Christ. When we circle back to this core truth, we are reminded that we are beloved children of God and gain layered epiphanies of how abundant God's love truly is. Love is what connects us in creation and call. We are reminded of that love in our baptism. We are reminded of that love when we follow Jesus. We act on that love when we share the good news with others. God is revealed to us through the abundant love of Jesus Christ.

At Jesus' transfiguration, he is surrounded by those past and present: Peter, James, John, as well as Moses and Elijah. We too are surrounded and do not journey alone. We carry with us the cloud of witnesses who have lived before us. We carry with us our family, friends, colleagues, and strangers in our midst. Together we are transformed. Together we are a beacon of light to others, inviting them to join on the walk as we circle back to the One who created us, loves us, and calls us to follow him.

We can never fully understand this mysterious Messiah we follow, but by walking in his ways of love and daily answering his invitation to "come and see," we can grow closer to Christ and participate in his revelation to the world.

Lenten Series: Covenant

Six Parts: First Sunday in Lent through
Palm Sunday

Trusting in God's everlasting covenant with us.

PAUL ROCK

Series Overview Most adults have had the experience of signing a contract or other legal document. To borrow money, rent an apartment, or buy a car, we are asked to sign on the dotted line. Contracts are built on distrust, protecting ourselves from liability if the other person doesn't hold up his or her end of the bargain. Yet healthy human development and relationships are built on trust. Trust becomes possible

	Sermon Title	Focus Scripture	Theme
Lent 1	A Global Guarantee	Gen. 9:8–17	God's covenant with Noah and what it means for how we view creation today.
Lent 2	Promises We Can't Keep	Gen. 17:1–7, 15–16	God's covenant with Abram and Sarai is based not on faithfulness but need.
Lent 3	Contracts and Covenants	Exod. 20:1–17	A contract provides coverage as we meet each other half way. Covenants are all in, and God's love covers all.
Lent 4	Unbreakable	Eph. 2:1–10	There's nothing we can do to make or break God's covenant with us—it's all God.
Lent 5	Marriage Vows	Jer. 31:31–34	God's commitment to us is deeply personal and intimate, like a covenant of marriage.
Lent 6 (Palm Sunday)	What Happens When You Assume?	Mark 11:1–11	God's covenant through Christ defies all our assumptions and expectations.

only when we willfully and lovingly yield all authority and power and make ourselves vulnerable. The deepest and most eternal trust that undergirds our souls comes from a relationship with God, who has given all to be with us and keeps not only God's promises but ours as well, in an unbreakable love known as covenant.

Tips and Ideas for This Series

Covenants are easily contrasted with contracts, to great effect, but the distinction can be missed by some. Be cautious if using imagery of a traditional, "sign-on-the-dotted-line" contract on your bulletin or screen. A large rock and strong, all-caps typography can effectively express the concept of God's immovable, unbreakable covenant with us. Video clips or images from movies, including *Noah* and *The Mission*, or films depicting the giving of the Ten Commandments can be effective illustrations in worship.

Lent 1: A Global Guarantee
Genesis 9:8–17

God said, "This is the sign of the covenant that I make between me and you and every living creature that is with you, for all future generations: I have set my bow in the clouds, and it shall be a sign of the covenant between me and the earth. When I bring clouds over the earth and the bow is seen in the clouds, I will remember my covenant that is between me and you and every living creature of all flesh; and the waters shall never again become a flood to destroy all flesh." (Genesis 9:12–15)

In 2002 something horribly frightening happened to our world. In February that year, a chunk of arctic ice the size of Connecticut broke free from the eastern tip of the Antarctic Peninsula and floated into the sea, exposing a massive swath of ocean that had been ice-bound for more than twelve thousand years. As this floating glacier (and others that will follow) melts, climatologists predict that places like the Maldives, Solomon Islands, Fiji, parts of Bangladesh, and eventually coastal cities in our nation will slowly but steadily be submerged. An incremental, methodical flood is taking place in the world.

Today's Scripture tells the story of another flood, not a steady rise in sea water, but a sudden deluge from heaven that covered even the tops of the mountains with water. Apparently, just six chapters into the book of Genesis, God's good creation had become polluted beyond repair, as we read in Genesis 6:11–14: "The earth was filled with violence. And God saw that the earth was corrupt; for all flesh had corrupted its ways upon the earth. And God said to Noah, 'I have determined to make an end of all flesh, for the earth is filled with violence because of them; now I am going to destroy them along with the earth. Make yourself an ark of cypress wood.'" Noah heeded God's instruction, and he and his family and two of every creature entered the ark and were spared.

After 150 days, we are told, the waters receded, and eventually Noah and his cargo descended from the ark. Imagine for a moment what that landscape looked like. Have you visited a town devastated by a hurricane or wiped out by tornado-force winds and rain? Everything stripped and lifeless, the ground soggy and gray, as far as the eye can see. That's what Noah, the ark's inhabitants, and God looked upon postflood: global destruction, a holocaust cloaked in a natural disaster.

God had been sad enough with the actions of humanity to destroy them, but God was also saddened by the destruction the flood had caused. And we hear a distinct tone of regret as God made a promise to Noah, his family, the birds, the animals, and the earth never, ever again to destroy the earth. To mark this promise he placed a bow in the sky and established his covenant, not just with Noah or humanity, but with "every living creature . . . all flesh . . . the whole earth."

When we think about God's biggest agreements with humanity, God's most sweeping promises, our minds typically go to Moses and the Ten Commandments or perhaps Abram and Sarai. But before those covenants with specific men and women, God made the biggest promise of all—to humanity, to the creatures we share this earth with, and to the earth itself: "I will never destroy you again."

Can we make the same promise to God? The corruption and violence God saw before Noah are still an ever-present part of life on earth. We still treat one another poorly, putting ourselves ahead of others and allowing the fulfillment of our own desires to trample whole societies and even the earth itself. As costewards of God's creation, how then shall we live our lives to ensure that every living creature can live fully into and under this promise?

Lent 2: Promises We Can't Keep
Genesis 17:1–7, 15–16

"As for me, this is my covenant with you: You shall be the ancestor of a multitude of nations. No longer shall your name be Abram, but your name shall be Abraham; for I have made you the ancestor of a multitude of nations. I will make you exceedingly fruitful; and I will make nations of you, and kings shall come from you." (Genesis 17:4–6)

Do you remember the story of "Stone Soup"? It's been told in many languages and cultures throughout the ages. In the Portuguese tradition, a wandering monk with an empty pot and a ladle in his knapsack makes his way through a village, asking townspeople for something to eat: a crust of bread or scraps from their tables. Time after time he is ignored or sent away empty-handed.

In response, the monk announces to the townspeople that that evening he will host a feast and serve the most amazing of meals, stone soup. Curious, the townspeople slowly gather at dusk as the monk starts a fire, places his pot on it, and fills it with water. Then, from his bag he takes a stone and carefully drops it into the simmering kettle. After stirring for a time he takes a sip and declares it quite good—but not quite ready. "Why not?" the curious villagers ask. "Because it needs a pinch of salt and pepper and I seem to have none left in my bag." One of the townspeople runs to his home and returns with salt and pepper, which is tossed into the boiling pot with its solitary stone. After tasting again, the monk tilts his head in contemplation. "You know what would make this stone soup even more delicious? Sliced onions!" Another townsperson runs off and returns with sliced onions, excitedly splashed into the pot. The routine repeats itself again and again, with people adding carrots, slices of beef, garlic, potatoes, and so on, until the pot is filled to the brim with a feast and the people are licking their lips with anticipation. A large table is set in the town square and spoons and bowls laid out. One by one the townspeople's bowls are filled by the monk, and together they sit and enjoy an evening of warm laughter and camaraderie over a meal of amazing stone soup.

In Genesis 17, God makes an amazing claim. A promise to Abraham and Sarah. God promises to make them the parents, grandparents, and great-grandparents of a multitude of nations; as many descendants as the sands of the seashore! But there are serious problems with God's amazing claim. Besides the fact that Abraham is ninety-nine and Sarah not far behind, Sarah is also barren. For decades they have tried to have children, but Sarah's barrenness is a constant source of pain and inadequacy. As God speaks to them of a feast of nations, Sarah and Abraham know very well that their pots are empty.

But they have faith. And their faith, we have been told, is the reason God chooses them as the father and mother of many nations. But when we look more closely at these two, it doesn't take long to see that they also do some awful things to their own family and tell big lies when it suits them. They are, indeed, faithful, but they are also selfish and at times despair, just like you and me. But when God is looking to do something new, to birth a people who will bear his mark and through whom all nations will be blessed, more than any of Abraham or Sarah's characteristics, perhaps God is drawn to their barrenness. An empty pot is an opportunity for God to fill us up, perhaps with the help of others in our community.

Do you ever feel as if you have nothing to offer? That your pot is bare and dry? Such pain can be deeply humbling and leave us empty. But maybe that's not the worst place to be. Because God is known to speak to and use barren vessels and out of them to serve a feast of grace.

Lent 3: Contracts and Covenants
Exodus 20:1–17

Then God spoke all these words: I am the LORD your God, who brought you out of the land of Egypt, out of the house of slavery; you shall have no other gods before me. You shall not make for yourself an idol, whether in the form of anything that is in heaven above, or that is on the earth beneath, or that is in the water under the earth. You shall not bow down to them or worship them; for I the LORD your God am a jealous God, punishing children for the iniquity of parents, to the third and the fourth generation of those who reject me, but showing steadfast love to the thousandth generation of those who love me and keep my commandments. (Exodus 20:1–6)

Let's start off with a bit of a pop quiz or, really, more of a morality check. Reading today's Scripture, a list of moral decrees, think back over the past week, over the past year, or over your entire life and see if you have failed at maintaining any of these commands.

How did you do? Most likely we all did well when it came to things like not coveting our neighbor's ox or murdering, but if we've ever missed a putt or been stuck in traffic, we've probably used God's name in vain at least once. Working on the Sabbath and coveting our neighbor's car or high-tech gadget are practically a way of life these days. Overall, if we're human, we've failed. We all fail, perhaps daily, to keep these moral directives we call the Ten Commandments.

In truth, we are destined to fail. It's inevitable. It's part of our human fabric. God promises to deliver us, to provide for us, to be our Lord and Savior. In return, God asks for us to follow ten rules. Actually, our Jewish brothers and sisters recognize an additional 603 *mitzvoth*, or commandments, in the books of Moses, things God asks us to either do or not do. And we fail at them. Although God is always faithful, we are serial defaulters.

So what does God do about our inability to keep up our end of the contract? God makes a covenant. And covenants are fundamentally different from contracts.

Contracts are formalized agreements based on mutual assent. They work quite well for employment situations or business transactions. Each partner gives as much as is necessary, and in the end a mutual goal is achieved. But the primary beneficiary is me. It's about getting out of it what I put in—or, hopefully, more. So, once my counterpart falters or defaults, the contractual agreement can be broken.

If this was the case with God, the lawyers would have come calling centuries ago, and God would have moved on to the next partner planet, and we would be left figuring out a bankruptcy plan to make amends for our failed obligations.

But from the beginning, God's agreement, God's business plan with us, has been rooted not in contract, but in covenant. Yes, God expects us to love and obey, to advance God's will, and to care for each other, but our failure to do so, our mistakes and inabilities, does not affect God's commitment to us. While biblical writers employ economic, judicial, or contractual language to explain our relationship with God, those are partial metaphors attempting to explain the illogical nature of covenant. Contracts are governed by the rules of bargaining. Covenants are governed by the irrational but eternal rules of love.

Remember the Noetic covenant we explored at the beginning of this series? After the flood, God, with no prompting from humankind, declared, "As for me, I am establishing my covenant with you and your descendants after you." God has chosen to covenant with us, with the earth. No response, no bargaining on our part was required. A covenant is a deep, soul-level connection that binds one to the other. And God has chosen to be bound together with us.

To be clear, God made these covenants with full understanding and appreciation of our strengths and talents and faith and with full understanding and appreciation of our imperfections, failings, and inabilities. God knew what God was getting into with us, the same way a wise parent knows what's in store when they raise a child. No matter how many times a rule or command is given or explained, failure is inevitable. Imperfection is understood. But love and grace endure. There is an old Jewish proverb that says when God decided to create the world, he foresaw all the sin humans would commit against God and each other. The only way God could continue was to decide to forgive the world before he created it.

But God, who is rich in mercy, out of the great love with which he loved us even when we were dead through our trespasses, made us alive together with Christ—by grace you have been saved—and raised us up with him and seated us with him in the heavenly places in Christ Jesus, so that in the ages to come he might show the immeasurable riches of his grace in kindness toward us in Christ Jesus. For by grace you have been saved through faith, and this is not your own doing; it is the gift of God—not the result of works, so that no one may boast. (Ephesians 2:4–9)

If there was a fundamental belief in Protestantism that could serve as our mission statement, the cornerstone of our belief, it might be summed up by Ephesians 2:8: we are saved through no work of our own but only through the grace of God.

One of my favorite movies is *The Mission*. It is centered on the work of Jesuit priests in eighteenth-century South America. Robert De Niro plays a former soldier named Rodrigo, who would ride into the highlands, capture natives, and sell them into slavery. In a fit of rage over a woman, Rodrigo ends up killing his own brother, which causes him to seek refuge and retribution for his sins at the Jesuit monastery in the city. Disgusted with what he has become, Rodrigo asks for a cell where he can be left to die for his sins. The Jesuits are there as missionaries, called to carry Christ's love to the highlands, so the lead priest works out a deal with Rodrigo. Because he won't accept God's forgiveness, Rodrigo will do penance. The penance will be to join the Jesuits as they make the arduous climb up a mountain to live with and share the good news of Christ's love with the natives he had once enslaved. Rodrigo agrees, but only if he is allowed to drag his weapons and armor, the metal vestiges of his former life, behind him in a massive rope net, in order to make the journey even more painful and difficult.

After a long and grueling trek, the priests arrive in a jungle village, with Rodrigo slowly bringing up the rear, exhausted, knowing he will most likely be killed by the natives once they recognize him. Indeed, this looks to be the case as a villager runs to the muddy and depleted slave trader, grabs a fistful of his hair, and forcefully puts a knife to his neck. Taking notice, the chief calls out to the villager, who then removes the knife from De Niro's neck and, instead, methodically cuts the ropes binding Rodrigo to his net of weapons and armor. The tangle of rope and metal is shoved from a cliff into the river. Disbelieving and free, Rodrigo breaks down sobbing. Villagers and Jesuit brothers surround him with hugs, tears, and laughter and lead him into a life of living out his forgiveness in freedom.

No matter how hard we try, my friends, we will never be free until we trust in the comprehensive and unbreakable promise of God's love for us. A love that comes to us, scoops up our imperfect lives, becomes one with us, and even lives the life that we cannot. A life that responds to God's enduring love with enduring love. That responds to God's commitment to us with perfect obedience. Here's the overwhelming truth: only God can keep God's covenant, and so, in Christ, God became us. Through faith in Christ we are saved, not by works. And that faith is unbreakable because it begins and ends, is initiated and answered, by the perfect love of God.

What is the heavy weight of past regret or shame tied around your neck? What is that insult, that failure, that pain you can't let go of? We all carry burdens that feel impossible to lay aside. God's covenantal love promises to ease your burden. Christ carried that cross for you, and you are free. God wants you to know it is time to cut the cords and be free to do the good works of an unbreakably forgiven life.

Lent 5: Marriage Vows
Jeremiah 31:31–34

The days are surely coming, says the LORD, when I will make a new covenant with the house of Israel and the house of Judah. It will not be like the covenant that I made with their ancestors when I took them by the hand to bring them out of the land of Egypt—a covenant that they broke, though I was their husband, says the LORD. But this is the covenant that I will make with the house of Israel after those days, says the LORD: I will put my law within them, and I will write it on their hearts; and I will be their God, and they shall be my people. (Jeremiah 31:31–33)

We've been talking about promises, contracts, and covenants during this Lenten series and also about the differences between them and what distinguishes a covenant. But "covenant" is not a term we often use today, and so the concept is still murky. When a typical person hears "covenant," their mind goes to land use or building restrictions. So today the prophet Jeremiah is going to help us grasp and envision what this covenant thing looks like, and he paints a vivid and very personal picture.

Jeremiah writes his letter to the Hebrew people as they are being disciplined in exile, far away from their home—in a type of "time-out" in Babylon. As a prophet of YHWH, Jeremiah assumes the voice of God and tells Israel that God wants to have a serious, relationship-defining conversation. "Let me tell you how I'm feeling about us," God says. "Let me tell you where I think this relationship is going. My desire is not just to be friends, but to deepen things. The covenant I am making with you will be a covenant whose codes are not written in stone, but on your hearts." God is taking things to a whole new level, more personal, more intimate. As Jeremiah explains the intensity of this commitment, we come to see that God is hopelessly in love: "I will put my law in their inward parts, and write it in their hearts; and will be their God, and they shall be my people."

Here's something interesting. The word "religion" comes from the Latin verb *religare*, which means "to connect, to bind together." My faith, your faith, our relationship with God are not about getting ourselves or others to fall in line with a proper way of thinking. It's not about getting ourselves to fall in line with a proper way of doing things. What this faith, what this community, what our covenant with God is about is to get us, not to fall in line, but to fall in love.

A friend who raised his children in Southern California told me that he loved to come home at the end of a summer day. His kids would run to give him a hug, and he would hold them tight and kiss them. He could taste from their cheeks and smell in their hair that they had spent the day at the beach; they were sandy, salty, and warmed with goodness. That taste and smell and feeling doesn't happen if you just drive by the beach or sit up in a restaurant that overlooks the sea. You need to be down by the water, playing in the waves, digging in the sand.

What God wants, more than our hard work or our disciplined obedience, is that, when someone draws close to us, they can tell, they can see, they can smell and taste that we have been with God, that God's ways are written in the depths of our heart, that we intimately know the Lord, that we are indeed his people. That's covenant.

Lent 6 (Palm Sunday): What Happens When You Assume?
Mark 11:1–11

Many people spread their cloaks on the road, and others spread leafy branches that they had cut in the fields. Then those who went ahead and those who followed were shouting, "Hosanna! Blessed is the one who comes in the name of the Lord! Blessed is the coming kingdom of our ancestor David! Hosanna in the highest heaven!" (Mark 11:8–10)

In a world with its surplus of violence, how do we wage peace? How do we address and push back against the systemic violence in our nation and our cities? How do we address the pain and frustration caused by the larger forces that employ the violence of oppression, unjust laws, or racism?

This is what the people on the streets of Jerusalem were crying out for two thousand years ago as Christ came riding into town on that most intimidating of beasts, the foal of a donkey. You may have heard the quip about what happens when you assume: you make a . . . donkey . . . out of *u* and me. Both the Romans and the Jews in Jerusalem that day were doing a lot of assuming. Everyone assumed they knew exactly what Christ's promise to bring the kingdom of heaven meant. Jewish zealots, with daggers at the ready, were eager to spill Roman blood and take their roles in a new Davidic monarchy. Pharisees and Sadducees were concerned about their religious leadership. Centurions were ready to ensure that *Pax Romana* was maintained, no matter the cost.

Jesus came proclaiming, promising that the kingdom of God was near, and everyone assumed they knew what that meant. All were eager to make sure their expectations about this new covenant were met, beginning with the crowds.

Jerusalemites young and old poured out into the streets and waved branches shouting Hosanna! "Hosanna" is not an easy word to translate, but most biblical and linguistic scholars believe it is a transliteration of two Hebrew terms smashed into a compound word that is most easily rendered, "Save us!" "Save us, king of Israel!"

Interestingly, the same phrase was shouted from those very same streets in Jerusalem 150 years prior to Palm Sunday. That was when a Hebrew family called the Maccabees helped stir up a revolution that somehow drove the mighty Roman occupiers out of the city. The Maccabees governed Jerusalem for a time until, inevitably, Rome regained control of the city and established puppet Hebrew kings, like Herod, to enforce Roman rule. "Hosanna!" the people called out to the Maccabees. "Hosanna!" the people called that Palm Sunday morning, "Save us! Blessed is the one who comes in the name of the Lord—the King of Israel!"

Well . . . when you put it that way, it sounds kind of seditious. Because it was. Palm Sunday was a street demonstration. It was a rally that could have easily become a riot. The air was buzzing with tension and energy. So Jesus on his donkey rode into the occupying kingdom of Rome, with its wealth and military power; and into the kingdom of simmering violent revolution, with daggers and pitchforks at the ready. He rode right into the middle of it all and . . . did not join ranks with the zealots and their daggers, and he certainly didn't side with religious leaders or the powers of Rome. Jesus confronted the assumptions inherent in our expectations and presented a different kind of kingdom, a different definition of power.

While the Romans assumed Christ might stir up another revolution, and the people on the streets assumed he would affirm God's covenant with Israel by ushering in a new earthly Davidic kingdom, Jesus introduced another way, another kingdom, a deeper covenant that found its strength in simplicity, its wealth through generosity, its leadership through service, its power through sacrifice. No one's blood runs in the streets except his own, and radicals and Roman republicans alike are challenged and transformed. Jesus begins a revolution of grace, justice, forgiveness, and hope.

Easter Series:
Belong, Behave, Believe

Six Parts: Easter Sunday through the
Sixth Sunday of Easter

Reversing the typical order of entry into faith—you belong even before you believe.

PAUL ROCK

Series Overview   When thinking about what makes a person a Christian, we often start with belief. Someone confesses faith in Jesus, then learns what is expected of his or her behavior as a Christian, and finally the person

	Sermon Title	Focus Scripture	Theme
Easter Sunday	Insider Knowledge	John 20:1–18	Mary didn't recognize the risen Christ until she heard her name and she knew she was known.
Easter 2	In Defense of Doubt	John 20:19–31	The strength of our faith does not come from certainty; it is forged in the furnace of doubt.
Easter 3	Eating with Ghosts	Luke 24:36b–48	Jesus meets his scared disciples with an invitation to fellowship.
Easter 4	When You Say Nothing at All	Psalm 23	Sometimes the most powerful way to communicate belonging is to say nothing and simply be present.
Easter 5	Follow the Verbs	Acts 8:26–40	Philip and the Ethiopian eunuch show us how to walk with "the other" on the road to belonging.
Easter 6	When Jesus Interrupts	Acts 10:44–48	Jesus continues to interrupt and rearrange our understanding and ordering of salvation.

finds belonging in a community with other Christians. But Jesus didn't work that way, nor does that pattern work for many on the outskirts of the church today. In this Easter series we explore the ways in which Christ lived out a gospel of homecoming and modeled the primary need for and power of belonging, even before we know what exactly we believe or how we are to behave.

Tips and Ideas for This Series

Easter visitors may not feel as if they belong in a congregation they visit only a few times a year. They may not be sure what they believe, or even how a Christian is supposed to behave. This series serves to remind visitors and longtime members alike that in Christ, we all belong, regardless of belief or behavior. This may comfort some and unsettle others, but it will go a long way toward making visitors feel welcome and starting to incorporate them further into the life of the church. Be sensitive especially during this series (and, ideally, always) about using insider lingo that may make new people feel as if they don't really belong.

Easter Sunday: Insider Knowledge
John 20:1–18

Jesus said to her, "Woman, why are you weeping? For whom are you looking?" Supposing him to be the gardener, she said to him, "Sir, if you have carried him away, tell me where you have laid him, and I will take him away." Jesus said to her, "Mary!" She turned and said to him in Hebrew, "Rabbouni!" (which means Teacher). (John 20:15–16)

In the 1950s and 1960s, the heyday of organized religion in the United States, there was a pattern almost everyone followed, or at least we appeared to. We woke on Sunday, got into dress clothes, went to Sunday school and worship, and topped it off with a hearty lunch. If you were new to a town, you quickly found a respectable church, and sometime in the first few months you went to a new members' class. There you made sure you understood what these Methodists or Catholics or Presbyterians believed. At the end of the class, you confessed that you believed it too. In the meantime you tacitly or intentionally learned how to behave. People here wear this; we don't wear that. We stand at this time, appreciate this sort of music, conduct ourselves in this manner, and so forth. And then, finally, you joined. You became a member, and at that point, you officially belonged.

Believe, behave, belong. That was the pattern. It was a wonderfully effective method for accepting and integrating people into a believing community. But the curious thing is, when you pay attention to how Jesus worked, how he transformed confused or dubious individuals into disciples, you see that Jesus didn't follow this well-worn methodology.

Just look at how the disciples and Mary responded to idea of Jesus' resurrection that first Easter. These were people who had spent years with Christ. Jesus had spoken to them numerous times about his death and resurrection. He'd made analogies, he'd looked them in the eye, he'd warned them of what was to come. They'd even seen, first-hand, Jesus raise people from the dead and yet . . . as the disciples ran away from the tomb, it says they didn't understand. And Mary? She talked to two angels who confirmed Jesus' resurrection, and still she wept and was confused. If you're sitting here this Easter morning and you're not exactly sure you know how you're supposed to behave, and if you're not exactly sure you believe, then listen closely: You're in the right place.

The people who were the most in the know didn't know what was going on. They weren't even close to having it all figured out. Those who should have had their doctrine nailed down and who should have been displaying behavior that confirmed their steadfast faith undoubtedly were not at all sure this was real, and they were behaving strangely. And then the gardener walks up to Mary and says her name, and it all begins to fall into place—and the order has been reversed.

First, before you behave or you believe, you belong. First, God says, know that I know who you are. I know your name. "Mary, it's me," Jesus says.

You see, Mary had experienced Jesus as a young woman. In both Luke and Mark's accounts she met Jesus early on in his ministry, and she was a mess. The story goes that Jesus cast seven demons from her. You don't forget that anytime soon. But the Jesus who stands before her now, she doesn't recognize. Jesus says, "Whom are you looking for?" Maybe she doesn't recognize this Jesus because there's been some time between her dramatic experience of knowing Jesus as one who needed desperately to be known and forgiven. Maybe she's grown so used to listening to the teacher, trying so hard to believe, working so hard to behave like the respectable woman that she so badly wants to be. And then Jesus, the gardener, says her name.

Friends, here's my Easter confession: I don't fully understand the resurrection. Never will. You'll never fully understand it either. And none of us will ever behave the way we think we're supposed to, but know this: You belong. You have a place here. You are known and you belong. That's a good place to start.

Easter 2: In Defense of Doubt
John 20:19–31

But Thomas (who was called the Twin), one of the twelve, was not with them when Jesus came. So the other disciples told him, "We have seen the Lord." But he said to them, "Unless I see the mark of the nails in his hands, and put my finger in the mark of the nails and my hand in his side, I will not believe." (John 20:24–25)

I like this Thomas guy. Think about it: anyone whose common nicknames include both "Saint Thomas" and "Doubting Thomas" has to be interesting, someone difficult to nail down, someone we all can relate to. But what do we really know about Thomas?

Church tradition tells us that after Thomas had become convinced of Christ's resurrection, he headed east, farther than any other apostle, to share the good news in India. To this day, Thomasite churches exist in India, tracing their heritage back to the proclamation of the gospel by Thomas. Earlier in John's Gospel, there's a scene where Jesus is talking to his disciples about returning to Judea, the very place where the crowds had almost stoned him on their last visit. While some of the disciples advise caution, Thomas is quoted as saying, "Let us all go, that we might die with him!" This guy has spunk.

I think Thomas would have a lot in common with many of us today. He was passionate, he wasn't afraid to travel, he was opinionated, he was a skeptic, and he was alone.

Our text says that the disciples were together in the house where they met when Jesus came to them; yet later it clarifies that Thomas was not with them. I wonder where exactly he was. Maybe he was out trying to land a job, now that the Jesus movement had come to a dramatic and horrific end. Maybe he was at the tavern trying to forget the pain and disappointment he was wallowing in. And maybe he was just out, alone.

At any rate, at some point these convinced disciples run into Thomas. "You're never going to guess what happened!" they tell him. And he doesn't. You see, Thomas was in the Garden of Gethsemane that night when the soldiers dragged Jesus away. He'd seen Christ's body nailed to the cross and seen him die. His calling as a disciple, so full of promise just a week ago, is over. Now, for some reason he has been left out of a miraculous incident. Thomas hasn't seen or experienced anything. He is still on the outside, and mere testimony about a supposed resurrection is not going to be enough.

There's a continuum for belief. The more we've lived, the more pain we've endured, the more advertisements we've heard, the more times we've been deceived, the less likely we are to be taken in or titillated by testimony. We are not born doubters; those who are wise learn to doubt, as a matter of discernment.

As you know, the traditional structure of church in Europe has been dying for the last sixty years. But an exception has been the organic growth of ecumenical gatherings called the "Thomas Mass." Starting in Helsinki in 1988, ministers, artists, musicians, and civic leaders worked together to create a prayerful service that would again fill their cathedral, not with departed churchgoers, but with doubters, seekers, searchers, and believers alike.

Recognizing that Europe had become a continent of skeptics, they named the service after Thomas "the Doubter." It immediately began to spread across Europe, and services are prayerful and participatory rather than passive. People engage with God at prayer stations, painting walls, and creative expressions of the sacraments.

Thomas cannot believe based on others' testimony. It isn't going to happen, and this doesn't seem to bother Jesus, who doesn't scold but comes alongside Thomas and invites him to place his hand in Jesus' side. And Thomas believes, saying, "My Lord and my God!"

Cynics, take heart, and rejoice this Easter season. God forms community, God forms honest faith from the clay of our doubt. In the words of Fyodor Dostoyevsky, one of the more eloquent doubters of the modern era, "It is not as a child that I believe and confess Jesus Christ. My hosanna is born of a furnace of doubt."

Easter 3: Eating with Ghosts
Luke 24:36b–48

While in their joy they were disbelieving and still wondering, he said to them, "Have you anything here to eat?" They gave him a piece of broiled fish, and he took it and ate in their presence. Then he said to them, "These are my words that I spoke to you while I was still with you—that everything written about me in the law of Moses, the prophets, and the psalms must be fulfilled." Then he opened their minds to understand the scriptures. (Luke 24:41–45)

Here are the disciples, gathered together in a home in Jerusalem, trying to make sense of their world, which has been turned upside down. Jesus, their dear friend, Lord, and leader has been tried, publicly mocked, and brutally crucified. Because of their cowardice, they have watched him die from a distance and now find themselves huddled in grief, despair, and fear. And as they attempt to hatch a go-forward plan in someone's living room, Jesus himself, unexpected and unannounced, appears among them. As we picture this event, I want us to wipe from our minds any image of a clean and polished Jesus. This Jesus has been crucified, dead, and buried. Remember, when Mary first saw him, she thought he was a gardener. Who knows, he may have been limping, and there are definitely large, fresh scars on his hands and his feet that tell the story of where he has been.

And the disciples? They're freaking out. The Scripture says they are startled and terrified, because they think they are seeing a ghost. Jesus quickly reads the situation; knowing he has only precious hours left with these friends who will advance his kingdom, he has them come close, really close—close enough so that they can take his hands in theirs and rub his feet with their fingers. As they come in close, touching Jesus' hands and feet, feeling his clothing, stroking his face to ensure he is no phantom, Luke says this: "While in their joy they were disbelieving and still wondering, he said to them, 'Have you anything here to eat?'"

While the disciples are disbelieving and still wondering, Jesus asks for some food. Quite forward of him actually. In this culture, having someone into your home for a meal signified deep intimacy, friendship, and unity. You've touched my feet, held my hands, rubbed my back; now let's eat.

So here is Jesus, having just returned from the brutal, lonely, and eternally victorious journey from life to death and back. But his executive team, his closest partners in ministry, the future of the church, are freaking out and filled with disbelief. But Jesus doesn't seem concerned with their beliefs. He invites them in to touch and then invites himself to a meal in their home. When they know that they belong, that this is Jesus, that he is really with them, then he begins to open their minds to understand the Scriptures. Again we see the pattern: first belong; then you can begin the process of behaving and figuring out what you believe.

While the opening of the Scripture and the teaching are vitally important, they come after the fear has been dispelled and belonging has been established and a meal is shared. Recall what Christ instructs us to share until he comes again; it is not a lecture or an anthem or confession, but a meal. To repeat, regularly, the act of invitation, of drawing together, of sharing food, of pausing long enough to lean in and touch and taste and be fed and filled together. Eating together is an essential part of Christian behavior, right up there with caring for the poor and gathering for worship.

Our strength does not come from our certainty. Our faith is not about etiquette. It's about community. It's about identity. It's about grace. And when we've touched grace and tasted community, we can be witnesses, even while we continue to wonder, in Jerusalem and to the ends of the earth.

Easter 4: When You Say Nothing at All
Psalm 23

Even though I walk through the darkest valley, I fear no evil; for you are with me; your rod and your staff—they comfort me. You prepare a table before me in the presence of my enemies; you anoint my head with oil; my cup overflows. Surely goodness and mercy shall follow me all the days of my life, and I shall dwell in the house of the LORD my whole life long. (Psalm 23:4–6)

Medical diagnoses and prescriptions tell us that on any given day, about 25 percent of us are struggling with situational, seasonal, or chronic depression. Twenty-five percent. And then there are all those who struggle undiagnosed. That's a lot of people. Mental-health experts are calling it an epidemic. People born in the last five decades are up to ten times more likely to deal with depression than those born in the 1930s, 1940s, or 1950s.

Suicide used to be a middle-aged man's desperate attempt to end the pain. But in last few decades suicide rates among the young have quadrupled, while rates of suicide among strict Amish communities have remained stable. This seems to indicate that the ever-increasing pace of life and mounting stresses and responsibilities in this mobile, global economy, where we are inundated with massive doses of advertisements and bad news and increased costs and fragmented communities, have placed an increasingly unbearable burden on our human souls, emotions, and relationships.

Today there are a lot of anxious and painfully sad people in our society and in our church, daily walking through what seems to be a long valley of shadows. Friends, you are not alone, and we're in this together. You belong.

Feeling blue is the common cold of our human existence, a fever that comes and goes and stays above or just below the surface of our humanity, an angst made even more stark when compared with the episodes of love and peace and joy that we have known in life—those seasons when our life was nothing but green pastures and our cup and table were overflowing. As the author of Ecclesiastes himself notes, God has woven eternity into our souls, and yet those souls live in an imperfect and painful world.

So, in this in broken and beautiful in-between place, Scriptures like the Twenty-third Psalm help us. I memorized these lines years ago, and when I wake with an anxious thought in the night, David's words about the Good Shepherd often begin rolling through my mind. "The LORD is my Shepherd, I shall not want. . . . He restores my soul." And when I visit someone in the hospital or pray and talk with someone over coffee or over the phone about a particular hardship, sometimes I'll share a Scripture like this or remind them of promises or truths that we can claim and lean on as followers of Christ.

Then there are times when teachings, truths, words, even Scriptures lose their influence. Sometimes the pain and weariness are such that the most powerful thing we can provide is our presence. Sometimes telling people what to believe or how to behave, although well intentioned, is misplaced, and the best teaching, the most important words, are those we leave unspoken. We've all been there.

It's interesting to note in this most famous of psalms the Good Shepherd brings such poetic, profound, and enfolding comfort *with no words spoken*. The Lord says nothing, but he makes me lie down, he leads, he is with, he comforts, he prepares, he anoints, and he dwells with me.

If you are one of the fortunate ones this morning who are not wrestling with or feeling wrestled down by depression or anxiety, there is a good chance there is someone in your family or a dear friend who is. It's important for us to know that God is aware and that the Good Shepherd is there and is with those sheep who feel lost—with those who are having a hard time keeping up, with the ones who are walking through the deep valleys. Beliefs and behaviors rarely heal hearts. Belonging does.

Easter 5: Follow the Verbs
Acts 8:26–40

Then an angel of the Lord said to Philip, "Get up and go toward the south to the road that goes down from Jerusalem to Gaza." (This is a wilderness road.) So he got up and went. Now there was an Ethiopian eunuch, a court official of the Candace, queen of the Ethiopians, in charge of her entire treasury. He had come to Jerusalem to worship. . . . So Philip ran up to it and heard him reading the prophet Isaiah. He asked, "'Do you understand what you are reading?" He replied, "How can I, unless someone guides me?" And he invited Philip to get in and sit beside him. (Acts 8:26–28, 30–31)

In today's reading, we meet a couple of great characters, Philip and the Ethiopian eunuch. This is the third time Philip has made an appearance in the book of Acts. He was one of the Hellenist followers of Jesus in Acts 6, chosen to take over the distribution of food from the Hebrew disciples as they went forth to proclaim the gospel. Now Philip, the Greek food distributor, is headed away from church headquarters in Jerusalem and finds himself in an absorbing interaction with our second main character, a eunuch, an official of the queen of the Ethiopians, a man who had come to Jerusalem to worship and was returning home.

When Acts was written, "Ethiopian" was a generic term for dark-skinned people who lived south of Egypt. We also know this official was not a practicing convert to Judaism; in order to perform his duty in the queen's court, he had been castrated, and Deuteronomy 23:1 makes it clear that anyone in his situation was to be excluded from the worshiping assembly. So when we read that an Ethiopian eunuch was in Jerusalem to worship, understand that this would have leapt out as a provocative juxtaposition to a first-century reader of Acts: eunuch and worship, they don't go together. So here we have Philip and a God-seeking eunuch unable to become part of the covenant community because of church law.

Fast forward to today. Our society is filled with people who are curious about God and interested in exploring theirs and others' beliefs, but most, like this Ethiopian eunuch, due to experience or hearsay, cannot make their way through all the requirements or traditions or perceptions that characterize a worshiping community. A recent survey revealed what young, nonchurchgoing Americans think of when they think of Christians. Here are the top three: (1) antigay, (2) judgmental, and (3) hypocritical. True or not, those are the barriers that we face.

In light of those barriers, I believe this exchange between Philip and the Ethiopian is an archetype for healthy, respectful, effective faith sharing and learning. Just follow the verbs.

Go—not *to* church, but *away from* church. Rather than inviting people to dine in, we need to get on our Christian bikes and practice spiritual takeout and share the good news wherever we are.

Join. Once Philip has left Jerusalem and noticed the eunuch's chariot, God simply tells him to go over and join it. Before we say anything, we go and we join. We can't expect people to join our church if we have not taken the time to join in the lives and traditions and experiences of others. And joining can take a while.

Listen and Ask. Philip heard the Ethiopian reading Isaiah. Philip had gone, he had joined, and then he listened and asked a question. Most of us excuse ourselves from sharing our faith before we even try, because we think we have to do it all. The fact is, faith sharing is already happening, and God is doing all the real work. We just need to go and join and listen and ask good questions. God leads, and we follow.

Philip sits with and gently guides the eunuch to faith in Christ. We often hear it said that we need to "lead people to Christ." This might be the case sometimes, but usually, especially in today's world, a better metaphor is to midwife. We simply assist the natural process, starting with belonging and moving toward belief as the Spirit leads.

Easter 6: When Jesus Interrupts
Acts 10:44–48

While Peter was still speaking, the Holy Spirit fell upon all who heard the word. The circumcised believers who had come with Peter were astounded that the gift of the Holy Spirit had been poured out even on the Gentiles, for they heard them speaking in tongues and extolling God. Then Peter said, "Can anyone withhold the water for baptizing these people who have received the Holy Spirit just as we have?" So he ordered them to be baptized in the name of Jesus Christ. Then they invited him to stay for several days. (Acts 10:44–48)

This is the last Sunday in our series "Belong, Behave, Believe"—which is the opposite order in which outsiders have been traditionally incorporated into the community of faith. Typically we require people to believe and behave, and then they can belong; they become members and join in the service of leading the church forward as we follow Christ.

But, as we've noted these past five weeks, Jesus modeled a backward pattern of inviting people into leadership, including people with no prior training, proclaiming belonging and homecoming to the outsider, before beliefs or behavior were taught or tailored. With our passage this morning we are again confronted with the Spirit of Christ, who even after his death and resurrection continues as an iconoclast, tipping over and reversing the understood sequence and muddying the waters of purity and polity.

Poor Peter. Can you imagine? As a disciple and leader of the Jerusalem headquarters of the new Jewish sect known as Christians, he hears the voice of God calling him to go to the home of a Roman centurion in the city of Capernaum. Not only is it improper to enter the home of a Gentile; this particular Gentile is a commander in the occupying army. Peter doesn't know what to think, but he obeys the voice and enters Cornelius's home and begins to teach the gathered outsiders about Jesus. Then all heaven breaks loose.

You see, what is supposed to happen is this: the Gentiles who are interested in joining the family of God first become "proselytes"; then they commit to a season of learning the behaviors of the faith—modifying their diets to keep kosher, learning purification rites and all the other laws of the Torah—and professing their belief in God or, in the case of these new Christians, faith in Jesus as Lord. Finally, they are baptized in water as a sign and seal of their new identity. Ever since Pentecost, Peter and the other disciples have come to understand that there is another layer in this conversion experience: baptism in the Holy Spirit, being filled with the very presence of Christ. That's how it is supposed to happen.

But just as Peter is starting the process, introducing these Roman Gentiles to the truths of the faith, the Spirit of Christ rudely interrupts and, willy-nilly, just starts baptizing all these Gentiles with the Holy Spirit! The final step! They're speaking in tongues and prophesying and clearly have been adopted and filled and blessed by God. So, like a pilot learning to fly a plane already in the air, Peter asks, "Can anyone withhold the water for baptizing these people who have received the Holy Spirit?" I guess not!

Imagine a room full of immigrants, just starting the process of gaining U.S. citizenship, suddenly being visited by the highest judge in the land who begins shaking their hands and conferring upon them all rights and privileges as U.S. nationals, before they've studied, taken their citizenship test, and said their oath of allegiance. Everyone is celebrating and congratulating each other while the authorities and bureaucrats try to figure out how to get these people stamped paperwork and passports. What is going on?

Jesus is turning things upside down again. Telling people they belong, long before they behave and believe.

If we in the church are Peter in this story, who are the Gentiles of today? And how is our ordered way of faith perhaps hindering their belonging in the body of Christ?

Summer Series 1: God at Work

Six Parts: Proper 4 through Proper 9

God's gracious actions as seen through the lives of Samuel and David.

MIHEE KIM-KORT

Series Overview This six-week walk through 1 and 2 Samuel invites us to see God's radical grace at work in unexpected ways. The stories of Samuel's call, David's unlikely anointing as king and victory over Goliath, and the lesser-known elegy where David mourns Saul and Jonathan and his official kingship over all of Israel highlight the unexpected ways God is actively working among God's people. It is a challenge to our present-day lives as we perceive God working among us—calling us, responding to us, seeing us, leading us, saving us, and uniting us, even today.

	Sermon Title	Focus Scripture	Theme
Proper 4	God Calls	1 Sam. 3:1–10	Samuel is caught off guard by the voice of God, but Eli helps him understand.
Proper 5	God Responds	1 Sam. 8:4–11, (12–15), 16–20; (11:14–15)	The people ask Samuel for a king; God disagrees but gives the people what they ask.
Proper 6	God Sees	1 Sam. 15:34–16:13	God tells Samuel to anoint little David king, for God sees his heart.
Proper 7	God Leads	1 Sam. 17:(1a, 4–11, 19–23), 32–49	David defeats Goliath because God is with the underdog.
Proper 8	God Saves	2 Sam. 1:1, 17–27	Even in times of grief, God brings light out of darkness.
Proper 9	God Unites	2 Sam. 5:1–5, 9–10	David leads his army to occupy Jerusalem, but it is God that brings victory.

Tips and Ideas for This Series

Construction signs are an obvious choice for visuals to accompany this series, but don't let static building imagery limit the active, verb-centered approach of the sermons. Three of the six focus texts feature young children as main characters, so take the opportunity to really engage children in worship, the Sundays leading up to or following vacation Bible school, for example. Father's Day will fall on Proper 6 or 7, and themes of parenthood can be woven in as appropriate.

Proper 4: God Calls
1 Samuel 3:1–10

Then Eli perceived that the LORD was calling the boy. Therefore Eli said to Samuel, "Go, lie down; and if he calls you, you shall say, 'Speak, LORD, for your servant is listening.'" So Samuel went and lay down in his place. Now the LORD came and stood there, calling as before, "Samuel! Samuel!" And Samuel said, "Speak, for your servant is listening." (1 Samuel 3:8a–10)

I was in my junior year during my undergraduate study and trying to figure "it" all out. What was I supposed to do with my life? How would I deal with my parents' disappointment? Could I really pursue ministry full-time as an actual job?

Your call story may sound a bit similar. I'd chosen the stereotypical path in college. I would go premed and double major in some type of science and English literature (for fun). And then I found myself utterly failing those science classes. Just doing horribly. And loving English. Religion. Philosophy. History. I kept thinking to myself, Who am I? I had always thrived in math and sciences, and I was supposed to become a pediatrician. The days got darker as I vacillated back and forth between what I thought I should do and what I thought I wanted to do with my life. Something else was drawing me in a different direction.

I would never have considered seriously pursuing full-time ministry in a million years until one conversation with my father in the middle of my undergraduate studies. He was attending Princeton Seminary at the time and enjoying the classes and community with numerous women who were studying to also become . . . pastors. "Pastors? But the Bible says that women are supposed to submit to men . . . and church leaders are just supposed to be only men; I can't imagine a woman being able to do it!" I argued with him over the phone, and we went back and forth.

My father—ironically the symbol of Asian patriarchy—was trying to persuade me, a woman, that women could and should do much more in the church. My father argued for an egalitarian view on the role of men and women in the church, even in the Korean church. "And you can be a leader too: an elder, a pastor, anything you believe God is calling you to be in your own life," he said to me.

Sometimes it takes someone else—a parent, a friend, a mentor—to help us hear God's calling in our lives. It was certainly that way for Samuel. God was audibly calling out to the boy, and he didn't recognize who was speaking to him until the old priest Eli caught on and told Samuel it was the voice of God.

"Speak, Lord, your servant is listening," Eli told Samuel to respond. Something I notice, though, is that Samuel was already listening and responding—to Eli. Samuel was attentive to those around him, eagerly responding to what he thought was Eli's call. Had he not been, both he and Eli would have missed what God was doing in their lives.

God is calling each of us to something, whether it is our life's vocation or a new thing God has for us to do. God's voice can be hard to discern, but there are Elis to each of our Samuels, out there listening with us and helping us to hear. By listening for God in community, we can discern together the ways God is moving in our midst.

Proper 5: God Responds
1 Samuel 8:4–11, (12–15), 16–20; (11:14–15)

But the thing displeased Samuel when they said, "Give us a king to govern us." Samuel prayed to the LORD, and the LORD said to Samuel, "Listen to the voice of the people in all that they say to you; for they have not rejected you, but they have rejected me from being king over them. Just as they have done to me, from the day I brought them up out of Egypt to this day, forsaking me and serving other gods, so also they are doing to you. Now then, listen to their voice." (1 Samuel 8:6–9a)

Mediation.

All day long it feels as if this is the main task of a parent with more than one child, although I can imagine the kind of negotiations that happen on a regular basis between parents and one child. But everything from fighting over one soccer ball or Frisbee (even though there are multiple outdoor toys of all sizes and shapes) to fighting over a particular seat at the dining room table to fighting over a specific cup—these moments make me wonder if I should have done some training on conflict resolution.

What must it have been like to be a prophet, constantly mediating between God and people? To be a representative of the people for

God and intervene on their behalf? To be the mouthpiece of God and remind the people who saved them from bondage? I can only wonder—exhausting.

While I often am surprised by how immovable a small child can be, it is easy to see God this way. After all, so many of our theological beliefs rely on an immovable God—a God who is unchanging, basically static and rigid. Yet the Scriptures suggest that actually even God can be affected by us. For years God had promised the people that God would be the people's God, the center of their universe, their protector, their king. Now the people had seen other communities who had kings, and they felt they were missing out. The grass was greener. So they complained, they pleaded, they whined, and they argued with Samuel that a king was necessary to govern them.

And God responded to them.

This always confounds me. As a parent, I try never to seem as though I'm giving in to my children's unreasonable demands. However, somehow God's gracious response—this willingness by God to bend toward God's children—communicates a marvelous grace, one that keeps us off balance, as we realize that God cannot be contained by theological statements or systems but is boundless in love and faithfulness. All this because God is in relationship with us and longs to respond to us.

Proper 6: God Sees
1 Samuel 15:34–16:13

But the LORD said to Samuel, "Do not look on his appearance or on the height of his stature, because I have rejected him; for the LORD does not see as mortals see; they look on the outward appearance, but the LORD looks on the heart." (1 Samuel 16:7)

One word of advice on parenthood continues to stay with me. It was Toni Morrison on the *Oprah Winfrey* show. "When my children used to walk in the room, when they were little, I looked at them to see if they had buckled their trousers or if their hair was combed or if their socks were up," she told Oprah in 2000. "You think your affection and your deep love is on display because you're caring for them. It's not. When they see you, they see the critical face. But if you let your face speak what's in your heart . . . because when they walked in the room, I was glad to see them. It's just as small as that, you see."

Day and night I hear my children say, "Watch this!" and "Look at me!" Though it may feel overwhelming to try to respond to three children who say this every ten seconds, it is a profound act. It roots them. It connects them. And yes, it changes their world. It says to them, "I see you." It says, "You matter."

In a world that says looks matter, brains and smarts matter, money and portfolios matter, résumés matter, muscles and sports matter, this is a strange notion: that a person, a human being—just as he or she is—matters.

When the Lord led even the wise and discerning prophet Samuel to Jesse's house to anoint the next king of Israel, Samuel couldn't help but be dazzled by the physical stature of the eldest son. "Surely the LORD's anointed is now before the LORD," he excitedly whispered to himself. Of course, we know God's response: "But the LORD said to Samuel, 'Do not look on his appearance or on the height of his stature, because I have rejected him; for the LORD does not see as mortals see; they look on the outward appearance, but the LORD looks on the heart.'"

Samuel was surprised to go down the entire line of Jesse's sons, only to find that none of them was God's chosen. Doesn't age matter? Doesn't brawn matter? Doesn't intelligence matter? But God knows what really matters. When David was finally brought in from the lowliest job, keeping the sheep in pasture, I imagine the flabbergasted look on each son's face as they watched Samuel take the horn of oil and cover David's head with the precious and sacred liquid.

What God sees is what ultimately matters. When we make the effort to see what God sees, we will encounter the anointed in the most remarkable places and, most definitely, in the most astonishing people: "the least of these," whether children, homeless, foreigner or immigrant, the stranger. And that is world changing.

Proper 7: God Leads
1 Samuel 17:(1a, 4–11, 19–23), 32–49

David said to Saul, "Let no one's heart fail because of him; your servant will go and fight with this Philistine." Saul said to David, "You are not able to go against this Philistine to fight with him; for you are just a boy, and he has been a warrior from his youth." But David said to Saul, "Your servant used to keep sheep for his father; and whenever a lion or a bear came, and took a lamb from the flock, I went after it and struck it down, rescuing the lamb from its mouth; and if it turned against me, I would catch it by the jaw, strike it down, and kill it. Your servant has killed both lions and bears; and this uncircumcised Philistine shall be like one of them, since he has defied the armies of the living God." David said, "The LORD, who saved me from the paw of the lion and from the paw of the bear, will save me from the hand of this Philistine." So Saul said to David, "Go, and may the LORD be with you!" (1 Samuel 17:32–37)

Few stories capture the imagination like the story of David and Goliath.

We have two armies facing off. They put forth their most fearsome warriors for a battle that will decide which side will serve the other. The bad guys have a giant. The good guys have . . . a shepherd boy? But we know how it ends, as David the unlikely hero, armed merely with a slingshot and river stones, brings about the demise of the terrible Philistine.

But the theme of the encounter between David and Goliath continues in the same vein as last week: what really matters. In our world, age matters. Strength matters. Physical ability matters. When it comes to war, weapons matter. Military expertise matters. But not to God.

So this story of David as the underdog is familiar because we have countless modern-day versions of it. *Rudy. Hoosiers. The Karate Kid. Cinderella Man. Million Dollar Baby.* Google "underdog movies." You will find hundreds of examples. The NCAA Men's Basketball Tournament, aka March Madness, is one long drama of the underdog. One of my favorite March Madness stories happened in 2013, when the Florida Gulf Coast Eagles, led by second-year head coach Andy Enfield, in only their second year of full NCAA eligibility, won the Atlantic Sun Tournament, beating top-seeded Mercer in the championship game, to earn their first-ever bid to the NCAA Tournament as a no. 15 seed in the south region.

In their NCAA Tournament debut, the Eagles upset no. 2 seed Georgetown 78–68. It was the third time in two years, but only the seventh time overall that a 15 seed had upset a 2 seed. With a third round 81–71 win over San Diego State, they became the first 15 seed to advance to the Sweet Sixteen. They lost in the Sweet Sixteen to Florida 62–50, to finish the season 26–11. They won the 2013 ESPY for Best Upset.

Why do we love the underdog so much?

Theories about it abound: We root for it because of schadenfreude (the bizarre enjoyment of others' misfortunes). We want the world to be just. We don't want to get our hopes up. But this story about David and Goliath is more than simply another underdog victory. We have here a fresh picture of bold and courageous faithfulness . . . of God as reflected in David's character. When someone's life is so integrated with God's life than the leading is the living out.

But this is what happens when God leads us. It is often astonishing and remarkable. Sometimes it is in the form of the least expected. More often than not, it is through a child, whether a shepherd boy or a baby in a manger. But whatever it is, we are able to accomplish more than what the world might say to us, because the one who ultimately matters is with us and guiding us.

Proper 8: God Saves
2 Samuel 1:1, 17–27

Saul and Jonathan, beloved and lovely!
*   In life and in death they were not divided;*
they were swifter than eagles,
*   they were stronger than lions.*
O daughters of Israel, weep over Saul,
*   who clothed you with crimson, in luxury,*
*   who put ornaments of gold on your apparel.*
How the mighty have fallen
*   in the midst of the battle!*
Jonathan lies slain upon your high places. (2 Samuel 1:23–25)

Grief is a thin place to me.

It has a similar tone to Holy Week. As communities all around the world pour their energy into this yearly tradition, I can feel it. I feel the collective bending toward the narrative events of the week—the Last Supper, the Gethsemane garden, Jerusalem, and Calvary. I feel the way it clashes a bit with spring awakening around me, in the trees budding pink and white, tulips and crocuses stretching to the sky, birds chasing each other in their mating rituals. It's this collision of time and happenings all around me that provides a doorway to this thin place—a realization that something is brewing beneath the surface. Some of it pours out of the cracks and crevices from the way everything brushes up against each other. The darkness of lament and grief overwhelms everything.

This is the darkness in which David finds himself today. King Saul and his son Jonathan, whom David loved dearly, have died, and David cries a mournful lament. His grief is palpable, as he tells the very land and all its people to mourn with him. With grief this profound, it is hard to see how light and life can ever emerge again.

Barbara Brown Taylor writes, in her book *Learning to Walk in the Darkness*, "If it happened in a cave, it happened in complete silence, in absolute darkness, with the smell of damp stone and dug earth in the air. Sitting deep in the heart of Organ Cave, I let this sink in: new life starts in the dark. Whether it is a seed in the ground, a baby in the womb, or Jesus in the tomb, it starts in the dark."

When we are grieving, the laughter of strangers and even the bright colors of flitting birds and summer flowers feel like a bit of an affront. A little too pretty and too happy, and too awake. Perhaps we're not ready to move on from the darkness quite yet. As Taylor says, "I have learned things in the dark that I could never have learned in the light, things that have saved my life over and over again, so that there is really only one logical conclusion. I need darkness as much as I need light."

This is the life God has for us. This is what matters. Not victory. Not conquest. Not a triumphalism. This is what matters—that God holds us in our grief and saves us even here. In the face of all the horrific injustices and inequities, and the seemingly constant stream of devastation of humanity, not only in faraway places, but right here in our own backyard, the darkness of our sufferings and need to lament remain present. I need only to invoke the names of those lives lost to police brutality in these last years—Trayvon Martin, Michael Brown, Eric Garner, Akai Gurley, Tamir Rice, Jessie Hernández, Renisha McBride, Freddie Gray, and so many more. It may be hard to see, but God is at work, redeeming human suffering and saving us from this grief by being with us right there in the darkness.

Proper 9: God Unites
2 Samuel 5:1–5, 9–10

David occupied the stronghold, and named it the city of David. David built the city all around from the Millo inward. And David became greater and greater, for the LORD, the God of hosts, was with him. (Samuel 5:9–10)

Do you remember the Occupy Wall Street movement of late 2011? That's what comes to mind when I read about David occupying the fortress of Jerusalem. I remember photos of people holding up those signs on Wall Street, and then all around the country, clogging up my newsfeed. Protesters were angered by social and economic inequality, greed, corruption, and the power big business seemed to have over the government. Signs and slogans emphasized the plight of the 99 percent versus the 1 percent that seemed to control all of America's money and power.

It made me remember the last time this kind of demonstration happened nearby. I was in seminary when the United States invaded Iraq in 2003. There were constant posters and e-mails about the location and details of the next protest—in Philadelphia, in New York City, right near me in downtown Princeton. Something about these movements spoke to me. I wanted to be there with people who were protesting, angry and passionate, united around a certain cause. I longed to feel the energy of such a gathering. I imagined that few things would be more inspiring.

Today's Scripture—the last in our series about the amazing ways God moved in the lives of Samuel and David and still moves today—describes a similarly energetic occupation. After all his years as unlikely royal anointee and warrior, David finally, officially becomes king. And his first task as leader is to capture a great city, the city of Jerusalem, and make it capital of a united Israel. The text describes the army's strategy, sneaking into the city through a water shaft until they "occupied the stronghold." Their physical presence signaled the victory for David's army and David himself.

I never went to one of the Occupy protests or the Iraq War protests in 2003, but I should have. I wanted to be a part of it. I wanted to show my support for each cause, but the thought of being present in that space was overwhelming. So I stayed back. I tried to show support through social media as much as possible—tweeting and retweeting or liking various posts on Facebook—but of course, it didn't feel quite the same as it probably would have if I had bodily been there.

Because bodies matter. Being somewhere in the flesh and blood matters. To occupy a space means to be committed to the risk of bodily harm. To occupy any space means being rooted, committed, and absolutely present. People's physical presence, gathering together to fight for a cause, is a powerful, unifying force.

So it was for David's army. Israel had been a mess of rivaling tribes and even civil war during Saul's reign. But under David, the people came together. Was it because he was the strongest, biggest, bravest leader the world had ever seen? No, we've seen how God surprised everyone with this unlikely choice for Israel's king. It is only by God's power that David succeeded as he did. The last verse of our reading praises David but credits God for the victory: "David became greater and greater, for the LORD, the God of hosts, was with him." We know from later stories about David that he was by no means a perfect king, but he sought God in all he did. His reign is considered a golden age for ancient Israel, a united kingdom, brought together by the passion of a people, united under a great king, united under God.

Summer Series 2: No Longer Strangers

Six Parts: Proper 10 through Proper 15

The keys to living as a community of faith, shown by the letter to the Ephesians.

MIHEE KIM-KORT

Series Overview This walk through the letter to the Ephesians teaches the church how to be a community worthy of the gospel. In the midst of familiar interpersonal conflicts, the writer of Ephesians reminds them that they are "now in Christ Jesus," no longer strangers to God and, importantly, no longer alienated from each other. Because of this new life in Christ they are experiencing a radical transformation of their identity—as individuals and as a community. These six weeks explore, What does it look like to live rooted in reconciliation—vertical and

	Sermon Title	Focus Scripture	Theme
Proper 10	The Family	Eph. 1:3–14	God chose us to be adopted together as a family in Christ.
Proper 11	Aliens Brought Near	Eph. 2:11–22	God reconciles divided peoples in a politically subversive act.
Proper 12	God's Powerful Love	Eph. 3:14–21	God can do things through us we cannot imagine.
Proper 13	Bound Together	Eph. 4:1–16	God calls us to unity, requiring humility and acceptance of one another.
Proper 14	Making Peace	Eph. 4:25–5:2	God calls us to make peace, dealing with anger in a righteous, loving way.
Proper 15	Overflow	Eph. 5:15–20	God fills us with the Spirit, bringing joy and thankfulness to ordinary days.

horizontal—with God and with neighbor? How do we practice it in radical ways?

<table>
<tr><td>Tips and Ideas for This Series</td><td>Though worship attendance may be lower in the summer, it can still be a good time to cultivate and reflect on community, with camps, festivals, and picnics bringing people together for fun and fellowship. Consider offering opportunities for people to gather and improve their skills in the interpersonal areas discussed in the series: a conflict-resolution workshop, diversity seminar, or training for small-group leaders in anticipation of new groups forming in the fall.</td></tr>
</table>

Proper 10: The Family
Ephesians 1:3–14

He destined us for adoption as his children through Jesus Christ, according to the good pleasure of his will, to the praise of his glorious grace that he freely bestowed on us in the Beloved. In him we have redemption through his blood, the forgiveness of our trespasses, according to the riches of his grace that he lavished on us. (Ephesians 1:2–8a)

The *Family Stone* is a heartfelt comedy that came out during Christmas 2005 with an ensemble cast including Diane Keaton, Craig T. Nelson, Sarah Jessica Parker, and Rachel McAdams. The plot follows the holiday misadventures of the Stone family in a small New England town when the eldest son, Everett, brings home his uptight girlfriend, Meredith, with the intention of proposing to her with a cherished heirloom ring. But the family is unwelcoming. Overwhelmed by the hostile reception of this family, Meredith begs her sister to join her for emotional support, triggering further complications. But one looming thread throughout the movie later reveals (spoiler alert!) that the mother has terminal cancer.

I'd expected a feel-good holiday flick. To say my countenance fell like a stone would be an understatement. Yet, even though it wasn't a lighthearted Christmas movie, I was moved by all the unexpected interactions, and later the new connections and relationships, that in turn brought healing to the family despite the mother's death. I ended up bawling my eyes out. It is always this image of family—with all its complications—that compels me to ponder the radical and beautiful possibilities of church.

We begin this series delving into the letter to the Ephesians for six weeks to explore these wonderful images of the church. It is a letter that was widely circulated and thus clearly an important document that reveals some of the struggles of a burgeoning community that might be familiar even to us today—distrust, prejudice, judgment. The writer to the Ephesian church understood the need for the community to focus on developing authentic relationships rooted in love. Being the body of Christ—united—was important for the ministry, but it was also an imperative. It was God's purpose for the church in spreading the gospel. They needed to come together, not for the sake of being some kind of social club, but to fulfil God's will. But what would heal the divisions among the people?

Some of the letter may feel superficially moralistic and prescriptive, with its instructions on putting away falsehood, giving up stealing, and forgoing "obscene, silly, and vulgar talk." But most of it is meant to be descriptive and to illuminate the possibilities of the fullness of life in Christ, specifically, in community. The letter bursts at the seams with praise, like waves crashing over each other, eager to get to the shore. It is poetry. It is art. It is music.

The letter begins with the simple promise that God chose us, adopted us to be brothers and sisters together. This is the basis for the writer's praise, and he deftly integrates this throughout the letter, whether he talks about reconciliation, blessing, or the Holy Spirit. We will continue to explore all these themes in the context of this worshipful perspective on God's choosing and adopting us in Christ and what that means for all our relationships.

Proper 11: Aliens Brought Near
Ephesians 2:11–22

So then, remember that at one time you Gentiles by birth, called "the uncircumcision" by those who are called "the circumcision"—a physical circumcision made in the flesh by human hands—remember that you were at that time without Christ, being aliens from the commonwealth of Israel, and strangers to the covenants of promise, having no hope and without God in the world. But now in Christ Jesus you who once were far off have been brought near by the blood of Christ. For he is our peace; in his flesh he has made both groups into one and has broken down the dividing wall, that is, the hostility between us. (Ephesians 2:11–14)

Looking around the table full of empty glasses, wine bottles, and little plates of half-eaten food, surrounded by people who are now close friends, I remember when they were once strangers.

We might look around our neighborhood and feel the same way

about the people who live next door to us. Once strangers, they are now people who have lent us their tools, played with our kids, and shoveled the snow on our driveways and sidewalks.

We might look around the church and feel the same way about the people who are in our pews. Once strangers, they are now people who have prayed with us, struggled with us, worked with us on mission projects locally and abroad, and fought with us when it came to deciding the color of the carpet or purchasing new furniture for the parlor.

Once strangers, says the writer to the Ephesians, "we are now brought near by the blood of Christ. He is our peace." This is no easy reconciliation, no easy peace. These are heady words, not because they have to do with ancient and eternal realities, but because these are the words of revolution. "He is our peace." These are words of treason. These are words opposed to the state. These are words meant for demonstrations and protests against empires.

"It is crucial to recognize that any talk of peace within the context of Asia Minor in the late first century under Roman rule would be politically charged talk," says Sally Brown in her online commentary. Roman emperors were perceived as vessels of the Divine and thus the originators of peace. To say that "Christ is our peace" was akin to denying the political power and authority, specifically, the divinity of the emperor and the legitimacy of the empire. Ephesians declares peace on new terms, a peace forged not by the "lords" of empire in its manifold forms, but in the blood and bone of the crucified. The cross undermines the wall dividing Jew and non-Jew, but that is only the beginning. This is only the beginning of a revolution of love that radicalizes all notions of peace, community, and church.

Sally Brown offers again: "The new household of God is not a purely spiritual reality that we visit briefly on Sundays—a weekly time-out in which we pretend peace is possible by sitting next to people we scrupulously avoid the rest of the time. The church is the daring practice of a new politics—a different kind of power, the self-outpoured, boundary-crossing power of Christ's cross." God bringing diverse and disparate people together is an affront to the divisive powers of this world. Imagine how subversive the church today would seem if "aliens" and "strangers" were all gathered together in our pews? God reconciles us to God's self, but we live out this reconciliation in courageous and creative ways through our boundary-breaking relationships with each other.

Proper 12: God's Powerful Love
Ephesians 3:14–21

I pray that you may have the power to comprehend, with all the saints, what is the breadth and length and height and depth, and to know the love of Christ that surpasses knowledge, so that you may be filled with all the fullness of God. Now to him who by the power at work within us is able to accomplish abundantly far more than all we can ask or imagine, to him be glory in the church and in Christ Jesus to all generations, forever and ever. Amen. (Ephesians 3:18–21)

My husband and I often joke there should be some kind of crisis training for parents of young children. Hostage negotiation might be helpful. Or maybe peacekeeping courses? Because right now, more often than not, I'm in survival mode.

I find myself saying things like: "You need to hold still so I can put some socks and shoes on you so that you don't get frostbite and have to have your toes amputated! Here, have some gummy bears."

"For the love of God, please stop staring off into space and get into your car seats so that we can get you to school on time! Here, have some more gummy bears."

"Please, please, please stop screaming at each other! You want some more gummy bears?"

I know it's an easy way out. Bribery is the mark of a desperate parent. But those gummy bears help us to maintain a fragile peace in our house.

At the same time I know that this is a temporary season, and we hope we aren't doing any permanent damage. We love those kids more than anything else in the world, no doubt about it. But there is so much we as parents cannot accomplish. Our parental love cannot magically make toddlers and preschoolers cooperate and care for themselves like responsible adults. It cannot guarantee that our kids and teenagers will always make good decisions.

Today's reading from Ephesians is a prayer in which the writer raves profusely about God's extravagant love for us and, immediately thereafter, God's power to accomplish more in and through us than we could ever ask or imagine. God is surely teaching us something about humility, as we try in vain to accomplish all the things we strive to do, knowing we must depend on God to fill us with this indescribable, unimaginable love that can accomplish what we alone cannot. It's hard to believe such a thing, in our moments of weakness and desperation, whether in parenting or work or any other endeavor. But believing—even more, understanding—such a thing is exactly what the writer is praying we will do.

It's a tall order, to attempt to comprehend the incomprehensible, and the writer gives us a hint as to how this might be possible: "I pray that you may have the power to comprehend, with all the saints . . ." God's indescribably powerful love is something we can try to grasp together, in community with our brothers and sisters.

This prayer at the end of Ephesians 3 is a sort of hinge point in the letter. Many readers have noticed throughout the centuries that the first three chapters of Ephesians are primarily about what God has lovingly done for us, and the last three chapters are about how we should live in response to that love. Immediately following this prayer (and beginning with next week's sermon) we read some very challenging calls to discipleship. The only way we can hope to live up to such a call is through the power of God, explored and embraced in community with our fellow disciples.

Proper 13: Bound Together
Ephesians 4:1–16

I therefore, the prisoner in the Lord, beg you to lead a life worthy of the calling to which you have been called, with all humility and gentleness, with patience, bearing with one another in love, making every effort to maintain the unity of the Spirit in the bond of peace. There is one body and one Spirit, just as you were called to the one hope of your calling, one Lord, one faith, one baptism, one God and Father of all, who is above all and through all and in all. (Ephesians 4:1–6)

I'm covered head to toe in mud. The run is called "Dance with Dirt," and it's certainly fitting. The torrential downpour that lasted barely fifteen minutes has turned everything into a swamp. This was not what I expected when I signed up two months ago. At the time, I thought trail race? It'll be tranquil—sunlight streaming through the trees—and I'll run with birds and deer, with a babbling brook marking the course. About two miles in we come to a dead stop. The pack I've been in for the first two miles of the course has stopped to look for the little white flags and ribbons telling us where to go and turn on the trail. We are scattering a bit like sheep, looking everywhere, backtracking, running ahead, running through the trees. Half the group eventually decides to go back up the insanely horrible hill we just stumbled down, and the other half goes toward the road in front of us.

I hesitate, with a few others, and we look at each other briefly before choosing the road. We introduce ourselves. Small talk. I'm Mihee. I'm Abby. I'm Heather. Do you go to Penn State? How long have you been in Bloomington? Is this your first time doing DWD? I remember seeing that house. Look, there's an aid station there. There's a volunteer. We eventually cut through a field of high grass, hoping that this hasn't totally cut into our mileage and time, only to find out it has added about a quarter mile and twenty-five minutes, and now we have to climb up that old ski hill?

Yet I can't remember the last time I had so much fun. I am smiling the entire time. I'm laughing, talking, and making jokes. We're cheering each other, we're waiting for each other, we're all covered in mud and grime, struggling along the path together, and I'm thinking, why isn't church more like this?

The body of Christ described in Ephesians 4 sounds a little more like my muddy running buddies than our typical church experience. Humility. Patience. Bearing with one another in love. It's so much easier said than done. We all have a tendency to think we know best, to insist on our own way, to be intolerant of others' quirks and weaknesses. Yet in the church we are called to be unified as one body.

This is clearly not to say that by being "one body and one spirit," with "one hope . . . one Lord, one faith, one baptism, one God and Father of all," our differences fade away. The second half of today's reading is devoted to the various gifts we have and functions we perform. The writer celebrates the different qualities everyone brings to the table but emphasizes that the calling of Christ requires we be mature and loving enough to work together as a unified body, "joined and knitted together . . . building itself up in love."

Like the impromptu community I found on that swampy trail, we disciples have our strengths and our struggles, but by humbly accepting one another (mud and all) and being willing to listen and learn from one another, we can find the energy and strength to persevere toward our common goal.

Proper 14: Making Peace
Ephesians 4:25–5:2

Put away from you all bitterness and wrath and anger and wrangling and slander, together with all malice, and be kind to one another, tenderhearted, forgiving one another, as God in Christ has forgiven you. Therefore be imitators of God, as beloved children, and live in love, as Christ loved us and gave himself up for us, a fragrant offering and sacrifice to God. (Ephesians 4:31–5:2)

Here in the second half of Ephesians, the writer of this letter continues to instruct the church at Ephesus on how they should live as a Christian community. Central to that is how they should avoid conflict—a difficult thing for any group of people attempting to live and work together. The section we read today offers some very practical advice for how to keep the peace: speak the truth, speak positively, avoid bitterness, forgive one another. By doing these things, we can be "imitators of God," "beloved children."

I am struck by that term "beloved children." There's another place in the Scriptures that connects peacemaking with one's status as children of God; it's in the Beatitudes. Jesus says, "Blessed are the peacemakers, for they shall be called children of God."

Given that we are all children of God, there is something interesting happening here. Jesus' blessing may be interpreted to mean "only certain people are peacemakers, so therefore only certain people are God's children." Ephesians, on the other hand, considers anyone who might read this letter a child of God, necessarily called to be a peacemaker.

Working for peace isn't optional for Christians, yet sometimes we seem to be the most negative, hostile, and unloving people around, stirring up and perpetuating conflicts rather than resolving them. The comment threads on Facebook and online articles come to mind as the venue of particularly vicious arguments! It's understandable, perhaps, that debates over moral and ethical issues raise the stakes and arouse the passions of faithful people. There is such a thing as righteous anger, but as Ephesians 4:26 makes clear, it's not the anger itself that is the problem. It's what we do with it.

"Be angry but do not sin." That's somewhat vague, if you're not sure what constitutes a sinful response to anger, but the following verses help to clarify a bit.

"Do not let the sun go down on your anger." I think a lot of married people can testify this isn't always the best advice; when one partner is tired and cranky, it's sometimes best to press the pause button on an argument until everyone is in a better frame of mind. The point here seems to be to resolve conflicts as quickly as possible, not holding a grudge or letting your anger stew and grow.

"Let no evil talk come out of your mouths, but only what is useful for building up." How many arguments resort to low blows and name-calling? This is not helpful. If you are legitimately angry, choose your words carefully so that your point can be constructive and more likely to be heard.

"Be kind." It sounds so simple, but we all know that resisting bitterness and slander, being "tenderhearted" and forgiving, is often the hardest thing to do when we're angry. The writer's entreaty to be "imitators of God" hinges on this radical forgiveness, "as God in Christ has forgiven you." That is the key to making peace in spite of our anger: being like Christ, who sacrificed himself in the face of an angry mob of undeserving people.

Being a peacemaker requires a kind of sacrifice. It means a giving up of yourself. Give up your need to be right, your need to feel superior, your need to nurse your anger into a bitter grudge. This is how we can live in Christian community, loving as Christ loved us.

Proper 15: Overflow
Ephesians 5:15–20

But be filled with the Spirit, as you sing psalms and hymns and spiritual songs among yourselves, singing and making melody to the Lord in your hearts, giving thanks to God the Father at all times and for everything in the name of our Lord Jesus Christ. (Ephesians 5:18b–20)

Natalie Merchant's "These Are the Days" came on over the radio as we sat and sipped wine in the brightly lit kitchen that first night. "Ministers Gone Wild" is what Jim, one of our hosts, would call the weekend as his wife, Heidi, filled up our glasses. The conversation flowed, conversations about church and about raising kids and lamenting the exhaustion and hearing how that does change a little when the kids go to school.

"When they go to college?!" I shrieked, thinking there's no way I'm going to make it.

"No, no, no, when they go to kindergarten," Heidi laughed. Oh, thank God.

We talked more about these ordinary, extraordinary days, how these days go by so unbelievably fast, and how despite the struggle and uncertainty, these are the days.

The writer of Ephesians tells the people, "Be careful then how you live . . . making the most of the time." Assuming, as they did in the days of the early church, that the end was near, his exhortation urged them to live wisely, live cleanly, and be "filled with the Spirit."

In my days of parenting young children, the end feels anywhere but near, and my cup feels anything but full. It feels as if someone is always whining, screeching, crying over one small thing or another. It's exhausting, and by the end of the day, I feel emptied of all my energy, everything I have to offer.

Then those loud little feet come running into the kitchen and . . . I stop and release all the stress with a loud exhalation. I close the laptop, plug in the phone up on the shelf, and pull out all the pots and pans, big mixing bowls, spoons and measuring cups, toss barley rice into each one and soon they are squealing, shouting, and down on the floor with me, running their fingers through the rice, scooping and shaping, transferring and spilling, smelling and tasting the dry rice, and I'm laughing. I'm laughing at the pandemonium, I'm laughing at how mortified my mother would be if she saw me wasting that rice (though I likely would use what didn't fall on the floor), and I'm laughing at how maybe it's OK that some days I'm just a housewife. I'm being filled in ways I never imagined, and I see it happening in the family, in the church, in my neighborhood, and in my town. There's promise here.

Maybe this is what it means to be filled with the Spirit, not just when we're singing hymns and praying together, but when the joy of ordinary days "makes a melody to the Lord in our hearts," as Ephesians says. When we are "giving thanks to God at all times and for everything."

As the body of Christ, we are no longer strangers, but a community responding together to the wonderful things God has done. It's often difficult, not often glamorous, but as we live these ordinary days together, we can be filled to overflowing with the gracious, powerful, loving Spirit of God.

Fall Series 1:
A Faith That Works

Five Parts: Proper 17 through Proper 21

The book of James shows us how to live our faith in action.

MAGREY R. DeVEGA

Series Overview   The book of James stands unique in the New Testament for its no-nonsense, practical, proverbial wisdom. There is very little cryptic language or mysterious imagery in the way that it calls people to live out their discipleship. For James, faith is neither radically privatized nor solely personal. It is to be expressed outwardly, to improve one's relationships with others and to help those in need. This series challenges those in a congregation who believe that faith is something that should be kept to one's self and challenges a culture that sees very little value in religion at all.

Tips and Ideas   There are many visual metaphors that can be useful in tying together
for This Series   the themes for this series. Whereas other books in the Bible are informative (the head) or emotive (the heart), James is uniquely practical,

	Sermon Title	Focus Scripture	Theme
Proper 17	Just Do It!	Jas. 1:17–27	Be doers, not just hearers, of God's commands.
Proper 18	Body and Soul	Jas. 2:1–17	The body matters: using our physical means to meet physical needs.
Proper 19	Taming the Tongue	Jas. 3:1–12	The tongue is a small organ that can do great damage.
Proper 20	The Good Life	Jas. 3:13–4:3, 7–8a	Gentleness and wisdom are the keys to contentment.
Proper 21	Powerful Prayer	Jas. 5:13–20	Prayer is a healing balm for physical suffering and broken communities.

so the image of hands might be appropriate. Images of people in your congregation living out their faith could be especially inspiring and highlight opportunities for discipleship and service that are already available. Musically, songs that reinforce the idea of living out one's faith, making a difference, and offering one's whole life to God would fit nicely with the weekly themes.

Proper 17: Just Do It!
James 1:17–27

But be doers of the word, and not merely hearers who deceive themselves. For if any are hearers of the word and not doers, they are like those who look at themselves in a mirror; for they look at themselves and, on going away, immediately forget what they were like. But those who look into the perfect law, the law of liberty, and persevere, being not hearers who forget but doers who act—they will be blessed in their doing. (James 1:22–25)

The temptation in reading this text is to focus on the negative commands it contains, much like the way some perceive the Ten Commandments to be little more than a series of "Thou Shalt Nots": Don't be quick to speak. Don't be angry. Don't let your life be sordid, or rank, or wicked. It is easy to imagine this text as waggling a giant index finger in our faces, reprimanding us for wrong behavior.

However, let us remember how this text begins: with a gift. The capacity to live generously comes as a gift to us from a faithful God who remains steadfast even through the chaotic changes of life. In that light, the call to live righteously becomes less a rigid obligation, and more a grateful response to God's grace. James suggests to us that gratitude is a much purer motivation for the holy life than fear of punishment or retribution.

To reinforce the idea of gratitude, James introduces the metaphor of a mirror. Imagine a mirror that reflects back to the viewer all of God's grace, love, peace, and joy that have been working in and through a person's life, the fullness of a person's salvation in Christ. The inappropriate response would be to turn from that mirror and immediately forget what was experienced in that mirror (or, in the language of this passage, "heard.") The appropriate response instead would be to live in grateful response and to express that gratitude outwardly. To be a "doer" rather than just a "hearer."

But James has one more positive note to add here. Not only should expressing one's faith emanate from gratitude for God's blessings. It will lead to further blessings: "being not hearers who forget but doers who act—they will be blessed in their doing." James does not subscribe to the notion that blessings come to those who wait, or that there is virtue in simply "letting go and letting God." Instead, James endorses an active faith, and one can almost hear echoes of biblical heroes whose active risk taking was rewarded by God:

- Abraham, who relocated his family to a far country and became the patriarch of a great people;
- Moses, who boldly confronted Pharaoh and led the people of God to liberation;
- Esther, whose risk-taking sacrifice saved her people from massacre;
- David, whose remembrance of God's past saving activity empowered him to slay a giant;
- Mary, who courageously said yes to God and became a blessing to the world by giving birth to the Messiah.

Over and over again, people of God became blessings to others through their willingness to obey God, regardless of the sacrifice or the cost. This is most fully expressed and embodied through the example of Jesus Christ himself, who willingly gave his own life so that others might live. He became a blessing so that we, by living an active and open faith, can become a blessing to others.

Proper 18: Body and Soul
James 2:1–17

What good is it, my brothers and sisters, if you say you have faith but do not have works? Can faith save you? If a brother or sister is naked and lacks daily food, and one of you says to them, "Go in peace; keep warm and eat your fill," and yet you do not supply their bodily needs, what is the good of that? So faith by itself, if it has no works, is dead. (James 2:14–17)

James speaks specifically about the mistreatment of the poor at the hands of the rich, so the most obvious topic for the preacher would be to address economic injustices at work today. Where are the poor throughout the community you serve? The text speaks of "a brother or sister who is naked and lacks daily food." In what ways are the poor in your community not receiving the basic human services they need to survive? What are the systemic forces at work that have created such poverty in the first place? How might the church offer a prophetic witness to correct those injustices?

In a way, James offers a direct challenge to the first-century heresy of Gnosticism, which claimed that our earthly bodies are irredeemably sinful and therefore do not matter to our faith. We see this expressed today by those whose evangelistic efforts focus solely on what happens to us after we die and whether or not we are going to heaven. James elevates to equal importance what happens to human bodies, because if we do not supply their bodily needs, "what is the good of that?"

It is in this context that we hear the hallmark phrase of the entire book: "So faith by itself, if it has no works, is dead." Much has been said over the years about the apparent contradiction between this verse and the idea that salvation is by faith alone. But James is not interested in a debate between works-based and grace-based righteousness. He is less interested in the source of salvation and more committed to its effects. God's grace ought to prompt us toward good works, not as a way of earning our salvation, but to demonstrate its power for those in need. In this regard, James is one of the most evangelistic books in the whole New Testament.

But this text goes even further than simply focusing on the dichotomy between the rich and the poor. It contextualizes this injustice in the broader issue of favoritism and partiality, which are the sources of a myriad of problems in the world today. It would therefore take little effort to translate this passage into contemporary news events that are affecting people in this country and around the world, and it beckons us to speak directly and boldly about the barriers that we build to divide us from each other.

Prejudice takes many forms today, including discrimination based on race, gender, social status, class, age, and sexual orientation. James identifies the source of these divisions as being a matter of the heart. He identifies the propensity humans have to carry private judgments against certain types of people, in a way that impacts our behaviors and reactions toward them.

And he carries the indictment to the strongest level possible: If we are open minded and tolerant of one group of people but discriminate against another, we are still violating the law of liberty. We cannot pick and choose whom we love with acceptance and tolerance, for we should love our neighbor as ourselves.

Proper 19: Taming the Tongue
James 3:1–12

For every species of beast and bird, of reptile and sea creature, can be tamed and has been tamed by the human species, but no one can tame the tongue—a restless evil, full of deadly poison. With it we bless the Lord and Father, and with it we curse those who are made in the likeness of God. From the same mouth come blessing and cursing. My brothers and sisters, this should not be so. (James 3:7–10)

James uses some playful but powerful metaphors to illustrate the power of our words. The tongue, he says, is a like a horse's bridle, or a ship's rudder, or a small fire, in its ability to generate great impact on the lives of others. This text invites us to consider the many ways that our words can cause great harm if not held in check by responsible thoughts and motivations. Here is just a sampling of examples, in the format of a Top Ten List:

10. *Slander and Lies:* This is an easy place to start, because, after all, this one is listed in our Ten Commandments. "Thou shalt not bear false witness." James puts it another way later in this book when he says, "Let your 'Yes' be yes and your 'No' be no." Yet hearing the commandment and actually carrying it out are two different things.

9. *Gossip:* This one is a particularly tough one for many people. We have developed crafty ways to gossip without calling it gossip, such as cleverly disguising the sharing of prayer requests in a way that actually spreads gossip instead. It is a slippery slope, indeed.

8. *Insults:* That old adage "Sticks and stones may break my bones, but words can never hurt me" is simply untrue. Words do cause harm. They can hurt. And the bruises can last a very long time.

7. *Grumbling and Complaining:* This one cuts right to the heart of what it means to be a Christian. Christians need to be people of joy and enthusiasm and hope. Yet it is easy to let our words and our actions suck the joy and life out of the world around us. There is often little room for that in the body of Christ.

6. *Speaking Rashly:* This is one of James' most vital pieces of advice. He says, "Everyone must be quick to listen, but slow to speak and slow to become angry." The principle here is simple: try listening more. In each of our conversations, particularly ones that get tough or heated, listen first. Hear the other person out. It is amazing how much more sensible and more productive one's responses will be.

5. *Cursing:* Our language must be kept pure, as it is a window to the purity of our own hearts. Profane words might communicate a flavor of meaning that adds color to our language, but we must never cross a line that identifies us as nonbelieving, faithless, or anything less than followers of Jesus Christ.

4. *Not Using Encouraging Words:* "Bear one another's burdens," Paul writes, "and in this way you will fulfill the law of Christ" (Gal. 6:2). Elsewhere, in Romans 12:15, Paul says, "Rejoice with those who rejoice, weep with those who weep." Yet how many times do we put our own needs and our own emotions before others?

3. *Not Practicing Patience:* Being in control of our words must be rooted in a spirit of patience. Often we are quick to let our emotions take over, and we pay the price.

2. *Hypocrisy:* This one was Jesus' favorite accusation against the

religious leaders of his time. Too much talk, and not enough action. Too much talking about the law, and not enough acting in love. As the old saying goes, "Your walk talks, and your talk talks, but your walk talks louder than your talk talks."

1. *Not Speaking the Truth in Love:* Taming the tongue is more than just keeping your mouth shut when you feel like saying something you shouldn't. It also means saying something you don't want to say but needs to be said. Our speech can be used to speak the truth to others, even when the truth hurts. Sometimes it is costly to do so, and it can be very painful. But when done in love and genuine concern for other people, in the long run, speaking the truth is for the benefit of all involved.

Proper 20: The Good Life
James 3:13–4:3, 7–8a

Who is wise and understanding among you? Show by your good life that your works are done with gentleness born of wisdom. But if you have bitter envy and selfish ambition in your hearts, do not be boastful and false to the truth. Such wisdom does not come down from above, but is earthly, unspiritual, devilish. For where there is envy and selfish ambition, there will also be disorder and wickedness of every kind. (James 3:13–16)

With surgical precision, this passage takes a scalpel to the soul and makes an exact diagnosis of the human condition. All the various ways that humans live in broken relationships with each other can be located in one source: envy. "You covet something and cannot obtain it; so you engage in disputes and conflicts," James says.

Of course, the most obvious manifestation of this kind of envy is in material possessions. We compare what we lack with what those around us have, and it becomes easier to crave a bigger house, a fancier car, a fuller stock portfolio, finer furniture, and better clothes. All the while, we tend to believe that better goods constitute a better life.

But James fervently disputes that notion. The better life is not found in amassing more material goods. Instead, it is found in works that are done with "gentleness born of wisdom." This is the only place in the entire Bible where this phrase is found. One does not usually associate gentleness with wisdom, as it is not often assumed that the two necessarily go hand in hand. It is possible, for example, for someone to have a gentle disposition but do things that are foolhardy. And it is equally possible for wise people to be arrogant and domineering in the way they relate to others.

But this passage is clear: to live the best kind of life, one needs to have both, for they offer an important balance to each other. When one is truly humble, self-giving, and kind, then the wisdom that one gains will be used for the benefit of others and in service to the world. When one seeks genuine wisdom from God, then one is able to be self-composed, content, and disciplined in the way one relates to others.

Ultimately, having a "gentleness of wisdom" provides the clearest, most effective antidote to the problem of envy: contentment. To be content is to believe (wisdom) that one has all that one needs and, therefore, to refuse to mistreat or demean others (gentleness). When one is truly content with what one has, then there is a freedom that is unlike any other in the world. It truly is the best life.

In the children's classic *Harry Potter and the Sorcerer's Stone*, there is an important conversation between the young student wizard Harry Potter and the headmaster of the school, Albus Dumbledore. Harry had discovered a peculiar artifact called the Mirror of Erised, which reflected back to the observer that which they most deeply and most desperately desired in their lives. For Harry, it was the image of his long-deceased parents. For friend Ron, it was an image of himself holding the house trophy. Dumbledore explained the power of the mirror to Harry in this way: "The happiest man on earth would be able to use the Mirror of Erised like a normal mirror; that is, he would be able to see himself exactly as he is."

James suggests to us that the best life can be defined in precisely that manner. It is a life in which contentment, rather than envy, is the rule of life. That can be achieved only when one has gained two important personal attributes: gentleness and wisdom.

Proper 21: Powerful Prayer
James 5:13–20

Are any among you suffering? They should pray. Are any cheerful? They should sing songs of praise. Are any among you sick? They should call for the elders of the church and have them pray over them, anointing them with oil in the name of the Lord. The prayer of faith will save the sick, and the Lord will raise them up; and anyone who has committed sins will be forgiven. Therefore confess your sins to one another, and pray for one another, so that you may be healed. The prayer of the righteous is powerful and effective. (James 5:13–16)

This final text from James is the most prescriptive of all of them. The writing is pithy and proverbial and eminently clear: if you are sick, pray.

Skeptics might criticize the text for being much too simplistic and dismissive of modern medicine as a viable treatment to illness. But the passage is not intended to be an affront to medical science (just as the creation story in Genesis does not need to contradict evolution). To try to read contemporary scientific truths into this ancient text would be a sore misreading of the Bible, as well as a glib treatment of science.

In fact, there have been many scientific and medical studies conducted over the past several years chronicling the power of faith to bring about physical healing. One's belief in God and trust in a power beyond oneself can reduce stress, lower blood pressure, and bring a sense of serenity that can enable the body to naturally fight off diseases. Again, this is not to say that this biblical text is true because it can be proven scientifically; it is simply to affirm that there need not be an inherent contradiction between faith and reason.

But it is not just prayer that is efficacious for healing. Verse 14 reminds us that it is also critical for a community to surround a person in need and bring solidarity to their suffering. James knows little about any notion of being "spiritual but not religious" or being a person of faith without being part of a faith community. The mere sense that a person is not alone can be therapeutic.

In this context of the importance of community, James expands the definition of illness to include more than the physical. James is equally interested in the deterioration and brokenness of human relationships, evidenced by verses 16a, 19, and 20. Sin, in a sense, is the ultimate disease, though it is not explicitly defined as such here. Sin not only destroys the bonds of human kinship but also prevents the efficacy of corporate prayer.

This is why the act of forgiveness is one of the most significant deeds a person can perform. Forgiveness participates in God's global redemption effort and contributes to the transformation of this whole broken world back to God's intended goodness. This idea is beautifully embodied by the reference in verse 17 to Elijah, whose singular act contributed to the replenishing rains on the earth. In this light, a single prayer for healing and a single act of forgiveness can trigger a shower of God's redeeming love throughout the earth.

Ultimately, this text covers a lot of ground—healing prayer, solidarity in community, forgiveness of sins—but it is all tied together into a common theme: prayer really works. This is in line with the theme of much of the rest of the epistle. Prayer is most efficacious not simply when it is understood or when it is believed but when it is practiced.

Fall Series 2:
The Upside-Down Kingdom

Four Parts: Proper 22 through Proper 25

Shocking reversals lead to true discipleship,
the Gospel of Mark tells us.

MAGREY R. DeVEGA

Series Overview   The tenth chapter of Mark is a critical transition between the transfiguration of Jesus and the triumphal entry into Jerusalem. After Peter named Jesus as the Christ, the Son of the living God, at the transfiguration, Jesus elaborated on what following him would require. This ensuing journey toward Jerusalem contains a collection of teachings about the nature of true discipleship. It is based on a life contrary to the perspectives and priorities of the world and is more in line with the kingdom of God. In a sense, the values of the kingdom seek to turn the world upside down. Each of these texts reveals a different way that God inverts the culture at large and requires us to live a life "upside down."

	Sermon Title	Focus Scripture	Theme
Proper 22	Where the Children Are Blessed	Mark 10:2–16	Jesus welcomes children, the lowest in society, and calls them great.
Proper 23	Where the Last Are First	Mark 10:17–31	A rich man asks Jesus how to inherit the kingdom and is saddened by Jesus' answer.
Proper 24	Where the Least Are the Greatest	Mark 10:35–45	James and John argue over who will be first in the kingdom.
Proper 25	Where the Blind Can See	Mark 10:46–52	Bartimaeus shows honor where there would be shame; Jesus brings light to the darkness.

Since reversals and inversions are the key aspects of these Scripture passages, the central visual metaphor could be an item or image that is flipped upside down. Song selections might focus on aspects of life in the kingdom of God, such as "I Love Thy Kingdom, Lord" or "Seek Ye First the Kingdom of God." Publicity for the series might include an invitation for people to come and "have their world turned upside down" or "learn how to live right side up in an upside-down world."

Proper 22: Where the Children Are Blessed
Mark 10:2–16

People were bringing little children to him in order that he might touch them; and the disciples spoke sternly to them. But when Jesus saw this, he was indignant and said to them, "Let the little children come to me; do not stop them; for it is to such as these that the kingdom of God belongs. Truly I tell you, whoever does not receive the kingdom of God as a little child will never enter it." And he took them up in his arms, laid his hands on them, and blessed them. (Mark 10:13–16)

We often associate this passage with placid scenes of Jesus surrounded by children at his feet, lovingly caring for them. One such depiction is in one of the stained glass windows of our church sanctuary. During one of my confirmation classes, I led the students around the sanctuary to ask them if they recognized the stories represented by the stained glass. When they got to this scene, one student said, "Oh, I know what this story is. It's Jesus running a preschool."

As popular as this interpretation of this story might be, it misses the deeper point. This is not only about the love Jesus had for little children but also about communicating a polemical countercultural truth about the kingdom of God.

In the ancient Roman world, there was an understood hierarchy of power and authority. At the very top, of course, was Caesar, followed by members of the upper class, including senators. Below was the lower class, made up of commoners and most families. Families were led by the father, with women and slaves below them. The children had no rights in society and were often treated as commodities or worse. When a child was born out of wedlock or with a physical or mental handicap, the father had the right to give the child away or even have the child killed. Children's value was primarily economic, as workers and heirs, not sentimental.

So here was Jesus, telling his listeners to let the children come to him, for it is to such as these that the kingdom of God belongs. In one bold stroke, Jesus took the entire Roman establishment and flipped it upside down. Those who are at the bottom are at the top; those who are disregarded by society are favored by God. Those who are on the outside are welcomed into the kingdom.

This interpretation broadens the text to include anyone who has been shunned by society due to economic injustice and discrimination, and the preacher might identify specific examples of such people within the community. It is also appropriate to still make connections to the rights of children today, especially given the dire conditions in which many children in the world live. According to the Children's Defense Fund's State of America's Children 2014 Report:

- One in five children was poor in 2012. That's 16.1 million American children, the most vulnerable among us.
- Nearly 1.2 million public school students in 2011–12 were homeless, 73 percent more than before the recession, and more than one in nine children lacked consistent access to adequate food in 2012.
- A child is abused or neglected every forty-seven seconds.
- More than 4,000 children are arrested each day—one every twenty-one seconds; close to 2,000 children are serving sentences in adult prisons.
- In 2011, guns killed 2,694 children and teens and injured 15,576; guns killed more infants, toddlers, and preschoolers than law-enforcement officers in the line of duty.

This Scripture passage compels us to look for ways for the church to be a prophetic agent for change and to address these serious concerns. To pray, "Thy kingdom come, Thy will be done," is to work actively to invert the power structures of our country today and ensure the life, health, and vitality of the least among us, especially our children.

Proper 23: Where the Last Are First
Mark 10:17–31

Then Jesus looked around and said to his disciples, "How hard it will be for those who have wealth to enter the kingdom of God!" And the disciples were perplexed at these words. But Jesus said to them again, "Children, how hard it is to enter the kingdom of God! It is easier for a camel to go through the eye of a needle than for someone who is rich to enter the kingdom of God." (Mark 10:23–25)

Having surprised the crowds in the previous passage with a polemical word against the culture's understanding of power and human value, Mark goes one step further and tells a story about the inversion of economic priorities. If money indeed "makes the world go 'round," Jesus in this story effectively reverses the direction of the earth's rotation.

We are told little about the man that comes to kneel before Jesus and ask him this question about eternal life, except that he has many possessions. That in itself is no reason for concern; how closely he chooses to hold on to them is the problem for Jesus. This text reminds us that of all the topics that Jesus preaches about throughout his ministry, money is the second most frequent, second only to the kingdom of God.

Jesus knew that one's relationship with money is, for many people, the greatest obstacle to living a life of full commitment and faithfulness. How much of not just our money but our time is spent in the procurement and upkeep of our possessions? Whether we like it or not, what we own has a tendency to define, or at least influence, who we are. If people can get their economic priorities right before God, then they can give their entire lives to God. And this point is punctuated by the well-known image of the camel and the eye of a needle.

Meanwhile, let us not forget the rather troublesome context in which this conversation begins in the first place. The man begins by asking a question that, by every measure of Protestant doctrine, should be disregarded: "What must I do to inherit eternal life?" We would naturally want to say, "Nothing! Nothing at all!" But that is not how Jesus answers the question. Instead, he lists the commandments, with which the man is not only familiar but also fully obedient. In verses 19 and 20, the man has gone an apparent six-for-six in keeping those commandments, which is a far-better record than most people these days.

Still, we may be puzzled as to whether Jesus is at first advocating for something other than a grace-based salvation, since he apparently states that eternal life is something that can be inherited with one's good works. Ultimately, this question becomes moot, since this man—and, presumably, all of us—have not sold all we have and given the proceeds to the poor. Even if it is permissible for human beings to earn their salvation with their deeds, this story reminds us that it is ultimately impossible to do so.

Verse 27 then sets the entire doctrine of salvation by grace alone back in right standing: "For mortals it is impossible, but not for God; for God all things are possible." This caveat does not let us off the hook in our need to right our relationship with money, but it reminds us that another relationship is the key to making everything else right.

Proper 24: Where the Least Are Greatest
Mark 10:35–45

So Jesus called them and said to them, "You know that among the Gentiles those whom they recognize as their rulers lord it over them, and their great ones are tyrants over them. But it is not so among you; but whoever wishes to become great among you must be your servant, and whoever wishes to be first among you must be slave of all. For the Son of Man came not to be served but to serve, and to give his life a ransom for many." (Mark 10:42–45)

Most of us who grew up with brothers or sisters know what it is like to be involved in what has become popularly known as sibling rivalries. The Bible is full of examples: Cain and Abel, Jacob and Esau, Joseph and his brothers, Rachel and Leah, Mary and Martha. The list goes on and on and on. This Scripture text has another example, with the family of the twelve disciples arguing among themselves about who would get to sit at the right hand of Jesus in glory. It is a conversation that echoes Mark 9:34, in which the disciples were arguing among themselves about who would be the greatest.

Imagine. The disciples were in the presence of Jesus Christ. He had been disclosing to them the mysteries of the kingdom and giving them a glimpse of the future God had in store for the world. But instead of relishing his teaching and hanging on his every word, they were completely fixated on their own agendas. Competing for Jesus' attention. Debating who would get to be second in command. Trying to one-up each other for greatness in the kingdom. This was sibling rivalry on a cosmic scale.

There is a great truth here for all of us, since we are all brothers and sisters in Christ: we too can be prone to sibling rivalries. Any time we get swept up into petty arguments over who is great and who is more worthy of attention, or whose opinions count more and who should be in charge, we succumb to those divisions.

Whenever that happens, we miss a chance to see Jesus in glory. We miss an opportunity for God to share with us something bold and exciting, a vision of the future, and hope for tomorrow. Every time we get caught up in ourselves, we miss a chance to hear God's voice.

Jesus said to the disciples, and says to us today: "Whoever wishes to become great among you must be your servant, and whoever wishes to be first among you must be slave of all." If you want to be truly great in the kingdom, it is not about how many people are below you; it is about how many people are above you. If you truly want the attention of our heavenly Parent, it is not about how many people serve you, but about how many people you serve. If you want to be first, you must be last. It is not about the glory you get. It's about the glory God gets through you.

Sibling rivalries occur when spiritual brothers and sisters fail to recognize that there is enough of God's love and attention to go around and choose instead to replace a sense of God's love with a sense of selfishness. But the truth is, there is enough of God's love for all of us. It is we who have tried to convince each other that there is a hierarchy of God's love in the church. We are victims of our own folly. When we fight, everyone loses. When we serve each other, we help bring God's kingdom to earth.

Proper 25: Where the Blind Can See
Mark 10:46–52

They came to Jericho. As he and his disciples and a large crowd were leaving Jericho, Bartimaeus son of Timaeus, a blind beggar, was sitting by the roadside. When he heard that it was Jesus of Nazareth, he began to shout out and say, "Jesus, Son of David, have mercy on me!" . . . Then Jesus said to him, "What do you want me to do for you?" The blind man said to him, "My teacher, let me see again." Jesus said to him, "Go; your faith has made you well." Immediately he regained his sight and followed him on the way. (Mark 10:46–47, 51–52)

In many other healing stories in the Gospels, the name of the one being healed is not given. But for some reason Mark wants us to be very clear about the name of the blind beggar. He gives it to us not once, but twice, in rapid succession. He is Bartimaeus, which literally translates as Bar ("son of") Timaeus. And then Mark says it again. "Bartimaeus, son of Timaeus."

What's in a name? Well, in this case, plenty of mystery. The clearest, cleanest translation of Timaeus would be the Greek word for "honor" and "reverence." It would seem an odd, almost ironic, juxtaposition to put blindness with honor, and perhaps that is Mark's point. Those with honor in our society—those who are great by the world's standards—are actually spiritually blind to the greatness of God's kingdom. This would certainly be in keeping with the running theme throughout the rest of Mark 10.

But another intriguing—although less plausible—alternative would be to translate Timaeus as "ritually unclean" and "impure." This would make sense to some degree, as those who were blind were often treated as impure in that society. It would underscore how desperate the situation of this man really was. He was not only physically impaired but also societally shunned. And it would underscore the running theme of Mark 10 to remember those who were less fortunate and pushed to the fringe of society.

The other peculiar aspect of this story is the way Jesus responds to him. Whereas in other miracle stories Jesus heals the individual immediately or is at least moved to compassion, here Jesus instead first asks a question: "What do you want me to do for you?" We might wonder why Jesus would even ask that. Isn't it obvious what the man needs?

But Jesus' question actually affords the man the opportunity to demonstrate his faith: "My teacher, let me see again." His words are both personal and confessional, naming Jesus as "my teacher." Then Jesus immediately heals the man, not with the touch of his hand, as he has in other miracles, but with the mere sound of his voice. It reminds us of the way the voice of God eviscerated darkness at the beginning of creation, when God's first act was to say, "Let there be light."

This is a story that therefore reminds us of the ways that God is still in the business of eliminating blindness and bringing light to all creation. The preacher might acknowledge the many ways that people are experiencing darkness today. What is the deep, impenetrable haze that fogs our eyes and blocks our vision? How are we facing a kind of blindness today?

On a systemic level, our blindness may be to the many ways that people are experiencing economic, societal, or political injustice. Those who are "revered" and "honored" by our culture are actually spiritually unclean by kingdom standards, while those who are suffering receive little attention.

On a personal level, there may be those in our congregation who are suffering physical, emotional, or relational blindness, as they struggle with brokenness in their bodies, their minds, and their relationships with others. How might a renewed trust in God and a commitment to the way of love and faithfulness bring healing from God?

Fall Series 3: Gifts of Love

Four Parts: Proper 26 through Proper 29
(Reign of Christ)

A stewardship series on giving from the heart.

MAGREY R. DeVEGA

Series Overview

This sermon series coordinates well with a church's fall stewardship initiative, as these texts all explore different dimensions of giving in love. It begins with Christ's call to love God and love one another, especially recognized in the lives of the saints. It continues with the extravagant generosity of the poor widow, whose contribution made a sizable impression on Jesus. It offers a compelling view of Christian community in Hebrews, in which all members are responsible for the encouragement and nurturing of one another. And it concludes with the grand vision of Jesus as the king of all creation, whose return and ongoing presence call us to love, courage, and persistence.

Tips and Ideas for This Series

This sermon series considers different dimensions of the love of God; so a central metaphor of a heart would certainly be appropriate.

	Sermon Title	Focus Scripture	Theme
All Saints *(observed in place of Proper 26)*	The Greatest Commandment	Mark 12:28–34	We love God and others with our whole selves.
Proper 27	The Greatest Gift	Mark 12:38–44	The widow in her offering gives sacrificially.
Proper 28	A Community of Love	Heb. 10:11–25	In response to Christ's sacrificial love, we gather to encourage one another in love.
Proper 29 (Reign of Christ)	The King of Love	Rev. 1:4b–8	We live and love in the now-and-not-yet kingdom of God.

That heart might be rendered in some way to illumine the four aspects of love chronicled in these texts: (1) love of God and others, (2) love through financial generosity, (3) love in Christian community, and (4) love in the reign of Christ the king. Stewardship campaign materials (pledge cards, etc.) should reflect this same imagery, emphasizing the heart as the source of our giving.

All Saints' Sunday: The Greatest Commandment
Mark 12:28–34

One of the scribes came near and heard them disputing with one another, and seeing that he answered them well, he asked him, "Which commandment is the first of all?" Jesus answered, "The first is, 'Hear, O Israel: the Lord our God, the Lord is one; you shall love the Lord your God with all your heart, and with all your soul, and with all your mind, and with all your strength.' The second is this, 'You shall love your neighbor as yourself.' There is no other commandment greater than these." (Mark 12:28–31)

Many religious and philosophical traditions claim that there are three centers of human nature and experience. They are the mind (which is the capacity for thinking, intellect, and understanding), the body (which governs one's actions, behavior, and strength), and the heart (which guides one's emotions and the capacity to be in relationships with each other). These three poles are quite common archetypal characters in some of our favorite works of art. Think about Dorothy's three traveling companions to Oz: a lion (who wanted strength, or the courage to perform the right deeds), a scarecrow (who wanted a brain, to master intellect and reason), and a tin man (who wanted a heart, and the emotional capacity to sympathize and feel).

In essence, when Jesus summarized this commandment as the "first of all," he was saying that we needed to offer God the entirety of who we are. The heart, soul, mind, and strength of a person compose the totality of a person, and God deserves to have all of who we are, in obedience and surrender. When the scribe responded affirmatively (albeit leaving out "soul" in his response), Jesus said, "You are not far from the kingdom of God."

This text is an appropriate way to begin a sermon series that might serve as a church financial stewardship campaign, which is often conducted during this time of year. It refocuses one's perspective on financial giving, from simply giving to church budgets and expenses to giving that is based on love—love of God and love of neighbor. Recalibrating stewardship in this way requires the totality of one's life, including the mind (the way one perceives one's relationship with money), the heart (the way one associates possessions with pleasure and interpersonal relationships), and the body (the way one spends, saves, and gives money). If all of this is done out of a motivation of love, then we are indeed "not far from the kingdom of God."

That phrase might serve as a unique connection to the other observance of this day, which is All Saints' Sunday. On this day the church remembers those who have gone before us and demonstrated through their witness and example the kind of total love advocated in this text. As we recall the way the saints have embodied love for God and others, we recognize that they are now close to the kingdom themselves, in a very real and cosmic way, as the "cloud of witnesses" described in Hebrews. And as we choose to live out their example through our own lives, the saints become the channels through which we too might be "not far from the kingdom of God."

The passage concludes with the curious statement, "After that no one dared to ask him a question." This might suggest that Jesus' response was so thorough, cunning, and complete that no one chose to press him further. But in the context of All Saints' Sunday, we might say in the context of awe and reverence for God and for the saints, our response is not to question but simply to give thanks—generously, with heart, soul, mind, and strength.

Proper 27: The Greatest Gift
Mark 12:38–44

A poor widow came and put in two small copper coins, which are worth a penny. Then he called his disciples and said to them, "Truly I tell you, this poor widow has put in more than all those who are contributing to the treasury. For all of them have contributed out of their abundance; but she out of her poverty has put in everything she had, all she had to live on." (Mark 12:42–44)

The gospel is driven by people with unknown names, whose contributions seem so insignificant, and whose words and deeds seem so miniscule. Yet they set in motion an incredible spirit-driven domino effect that causes the world to be changed right before our very eyes.

Think of the unnamed visitors from the east who came first to spy on—and ultimately to worship and offer gifts to—the newborn baby Jesus. Or the little boy who had but a small bag lunch to offer Jesus and whose mere five loaves and two fish became enough to feed a massive crowd. Or the woman who gave the best she had to Jesus—a jar of expensive ointment that she used to anoint Jesus' feet—as an act that touched Jesus at the deepest level.

What do all these stories have in common? Extravagant generosity. A kind of sacrifice and persistence that is remarkable not only for its impact but also because of the seemingly anonymous nature of its origin. And this story from Mark 12 is a perfect example.

Imagine this scene. Jesus was at the temple one day, with people watching. He focused squarely on the part of the temple called the treasury, where people brought their offerings in support of the temple. And many rich people were putting in large sums.

We might imagine a line of people, each one dressed in fine linens, adorned with expensive jewelry. Each one is hoisting a large bag of gold coins, or a large coffer of copper and silver, or a satchel full of jewelry and gems. We can hear the rushing sound of an avalanche of coins pouring in from bag after bag, crate after crate, into the ever-bulging temple treasury. Many rich people put in large sums. We might even hear a bit of applause from gawking onlookers.

Then something else caught Jesus' attention. Not a rich person, but a poor widow. Maybe it was the way she was dressed. Maybe it was the look on her face. But something about her communicated to Jesus that she was not like those other people. She was poor, alone, and left with little. Her contribution to the temple treasury barely made a clink, let alone an avalanche. She pulled out two copper coins, worth about a penny, about 1/64 of the average person's daily wage. She walked up and dropped her two coins into the treasury.

I bet there wasn't any applause. I bet nobody turned their heads. But this unnamed woman, unknown to the world, caught the attention of the Son of God. Jesus turned and said to his disciples: "Truly I tell you, this poor widow has put in more than all those who are contributing to the treasury."

Now some of us with CPA minds might say that Jesus made an accounting error. After all, this long procession of wealthy people were giving many times more money than this poor widow. How could Jesus say that the widow was giving more? How could he say, "For all of them have contributed out of their abundance; but she out of her poverty has put in everything she had, all she had to live on"?

The widow's offering made a bigger difference than the offerings of the wealthy. No, not a bigger difference in the finances of the temple. It didn't buy more animals or supply more candles. But it did make a bigger difference—in the life and heart of the giver.

When the wealthy gave their sums, they didn't miss it. They had plenty left over, to live their fast lives, to wear their fine clothes, and to take their big vacations. They didn't have to give up any luxuries, sacrifice any ambitions, or give up any greed. Their offering made no difference to them at all.

But not so for the widow. The moment she heard her coins plunk into the coffer, she knew she would feel the effects of that for a long time. She would have to do without a luxury for that day. She would have to wait until the next time she had money before she fed her own ambitions, succumbed to her own greed. She would, as a result of her gift, have to do some serious reprioritizing, reassessing of her commitment to God. And she would have to do it soon.

But somehow she knew she was doing the right thing, because she recognized that her offering was a reflection of her commitment to God. Somehow, the money she left in the box that day was emblematic of her love for God, her gratitude for God's blessings, and her desire to see the work of God continued in her community. She gave painfully, but she gave joyfully. And in return, her little two-cent gift would impact her forever.

Jesus called her gift greater because it made a bigger difference in her life and was a better indication of the sincerity of her commitment than any of the other gifts from any of the wealthy people.

Proper 28: A Community of Love
Hebrews 10:11–25

And every priest stands day after day at his service, offering again and again the same sacrifices that can never take away sins. But when Christ had offered for all time a single sacrifice for sins, "he sat down at the right hand of God," and since then has been waiting "until his enemies would be made a footstool for his feet." For by a single offering he has perfected for all time those who are sanctified. (Hebrews 10:11–14)

This Sunday might serve as the climax of your financial stewardship campaign, before next week's celebration of Reign of Christ Sunday. It may also be the Sunday before Thanksgiving, which would be an appropriate time to observe a service that focuses on gratitude and thankfulness to God. This text from Hebrews would be quite suitable to tie these observances together.

It begins with an acknowledgment of the great offering that God has made to the world through Jesus Christ. It is only by recognizing God's generous grace that we can truly be grateful for the many things we have in life that we cannot earn and do not deserve. It is through Christ's single offering that we have been perfected in love for all time. But God has also given us the gift of the Holy Spirit, which assures us of the forgiveness of our sins by writing a new covenant on our hearts.

These two gifts alone—salvation through Christ and the strength in the Holy Spirit—are motivation enough for giving generously to God out of a sense of irrepressible gratitude. But Hebrews reminds us that the work of God is not merely individual but communal. Jesus, who is our high priest, presides over "the house of God," suggesting that we are part of a family whose relational ties are forged in our mutual kinship in Christ. Most of the time in the New Testament, whenever the Holy Spirit is mentioned, it is in the context of the body of Christ and the communal life to which all believers are responsible.

It is no wonder then that this passage ends with the reminder that all of us in the church are called to care and serve for each other, by (1) provoking each other to good deeds, (2) gathering together, and (3) encouraging one another.

"Provoking each other to good deeds" acknowledges that we grow most effectively in our faith when we are surrounded by others who are interested in challenging themselves and others toward spiritual growth. Forget any nonsense about being "spiritual but not religious." Hebrews understands that spiritual maturity comes only in the context of Christian community.

"Gathering together" simply recognizes that there is power in "showing up." Isolation can breed selfishness, and separation from each other wrongly suggests that we can grow in our faith on our own. Instead, there is power in the act of joining together in solidarity with our like-minded believers in gatherings of worship, small-group discipleship, and service.

Finally, "encouraging one another" means nurturing those who are downtrodden and offering fellowship to others, regardless of whatever differences there might be among believers. Encouraging someone who needs comfort and assurance is one of the most precious, most sacred gifts we can give to someone. And it requires risk, vulnerability, and persistence.

In the end, this passage reminds us that we are all called to be responsible stewards of God's church. Not out of a sense of duty or obligation but out of gratitude: for the gift that God has given us in salvation through Christ and through the strength of the Holy Spirit that creates and nurtures Christian community.

Proper 29 (Reign of Christ): The King of Love
Revelation 1:4b–8

Grace to you and peace from him who is and who was and who is to come, and from the seven spirits who are before his throne, and from Jesus Christ, the faithful witness, the first-born of the dead, and the ruler of the kings of the earth. To him who loves us and freed us from our sins by his blood, and made us to be a kingdom, priests serving his God and Father, to him be glory and dominion forever and ever. Amen. (Revelation 1:4b–6)

There are many reasons that today is of special significance in the life of the Christian church. It is the last day of the Christian year, as next Sunday begins Advent, the start of a new year. It is also widely observed as Reign of Christ Sunday, the day that the church affirms the universal and eternal rule and reign of Christ as Lord and King of all creation.

Ultimately, this day contains a sort of paradoxical dichotomy. On the one hand, today is about anticipating the eventual return someday of Jesus Christ. But it is also about acknowledging the Christ who is already here and whose rule and reign governs our very lives in the present moment. In other words, we live in the tension between the Christ who is to come again and the Christ who is already here.

It is our job, therefore, to live in both expectation and responsibility. To live in the hope of the establishment of God's kingdom through Christ, and to live in the present reality of seeking and doing the work of Christ in our day and time. We live with eyes fixed on the future and hands active in the present.

That important dichotomy disappears if we simply interpret Revelation predictively and make it speak only about the future. It also leads to apathy and laziness in the face of many world crises today. After all, if one believes that all the violence and chaos in the world today are merely signs of the end times, as "wars and rumors of wars," then what is the motivation for the church to try to stop it? If we believe that mounting crises in the environment, global poverty, AIDS, and suffering of all kinds are simply part of the end game of human history, then why try to fight it?

God has not called the church to be spectators of global chaos. Instead, we are called to be agents of love, healing, hope, and justice, over and against the forces of evil and destruction.

The community to which Revelation was written was a community under intense persecution by the Roman Empire. They were people who died as a result of their profession of faith in Christ, who had to meet in seclusion, gather in fear, and live out their commitment as disciples of Christ under threat of death. The book of Revelation is filled with veiled language acknowledging the terror of the empire, naming Caesar, the Roman military, and the government establishment with colorful, dream-like, terrifying language. In contrast to this vivid imagery, a simple theme runs throughout the book to the Christian church: Don't give up. Hope is coming. Victory will be yours in the end. Have patience. Endure suffering. Persevere.

Read in that light, the book of Revelation becomes less a book about the end of time and more a word of comfort for disciples in all times. In a time when demonic forces of violence, injustice, and oppression assault us from all sides, in a time when we are tempted to mute our convictions about peace and forgiveness, and when prophetic words of justice and social change become muffled, the book of Revelation calls the church to persevere as witnesses to Christ's gift of love.

Revelation has a stirring, challenging word for today's church and today's Christians: Do you identify more with the persecuted church or the Roman persecutors? Are you in a position of privilege, prestige, and self-made power, or are you in the position of self-sacrificial, self-giving love?

Year C

Advent/Christmas Series: Living "In Between"

Six Parts: First Sunday of Advent through
First Sunday of Christmas, including Christmas Eve

*We wait in the liminal state between Christ's first
and second comings.*

ROBERT S. DANNALS

Series Overview

Advent is an in-between time of year. It is not just between Thanksgiving and Christmas, though that is when it occurs. Advent is all about what was and what is to be, about what has already happened and what has yet to occur. It's a time of anticipation, of expectancy. To live the Christian journey with expectancy at a most basic level is to be a resident of two worlds. We live fully in the here and now, with all the joys and sorrows, victories and setbacks of incarnate life. We love, laugh, get tired, make mistakes, hurt, rejoice, and grieve in the journey through this wonderful creation and re-creation given us by God. *And* we live with anticipation in the life to come, having entered into the near end of the eternal journey through the waters of baptism and

	Sermon Title	Focus Scripture	Theme
First Sunday of Advent	Looking for the Fig Tree	Luke 21:25–36	The coming kingdom means new life.
Second Sunday of Advent	Repent and Follow	Luke 3:1–6	Shifting our direction and priorities enables reception of new life.
Third Sunday of Advent	What Then Should We Do?	Luke 3:7–18	Repenting means choosing to live differently.
Fourth Sunday of Advent	Can They Hear Us Singing?	Luke 1:39–55	We magnify the Lord in our own day.
Christmas Eve	Salvation from the Margins	Luke 2:1–20	As God meets us on the margins, we're compelled to meet others there too.
Christmas 1	The Sounds of Silence	Luke 2:39–52	Thinking about Jesus' silent years reminds us how God works slowly in us.

belief, faith, and practice. We are in between the coming of Christ and his coming again, living the "now" with hopeful expectancy that empowers us and sustains us.

Tips and Ideas for This Series

As you explore what it means to live "in between," help your congregation to connect the "here and now" of celebrating the Christ child's birth with the "kingdom come" work serving those Christ came to serve and committing ourselves to a more just world. Choose an important cause to support during the season: homelessness, human trafficking, domestic violence, income inequality, and so forth. You can also use Advent as a way of heightening outreach to visitors. Print a list of alternative Christmas giving, volunteer opportunities, participation in advocacy for the poor. Offer family activities at the church and for at home. Judy McMillan's *Advent Activities for the Family* is an old standard.

Advent 1: Looking for the Fig Tree
Luke 21:25–36

And then he told them a parable: "Look at the fig tree and all the trees; as soon as they sprout leaves you can see for yourselves and know that summer is already near. So also, when you see these things taking place, you know that the kingdom of God is near." (Luke 21:29–31)

Today is the First Sunday of Advent, the very beginning of the Christian year . . . and the day we consider the end of the Christian story. Our readings invite us into anticipation, expectancy. Not the kind that all the department stores have been promoting since Halloween and not even the kind focused on a baby in a manger, but expectancy of the end time, the end of my time, your time, and the fulfillment of all that God has made and redeemed.

We hear a lot these days about a destructive apocalypse. Like the magi searching for a star announcing the Christ child, many seek signs that our risen Lord is about to return. Look: see the droughts in west Texas, earthquakes in Nepal, floods in the Mississippi valley, famine in northwest Africa, dreaded diseases like Ebola. People say things like "Life just isn't like it used to be"; "Things seem to be getting worse"; "Right here in 'River City', in the heart of my city, my neighborhood, within my church community, we no longer can move about with sure safety, with a trusting confidence."

"Look at the fig tree and all the trees," Jesus said. "As soon as they sprout leaves, you can see for yourselves and know that summer is already near."

Listen again to Jesus. He did not say, as the destructionists declare, "When the fig tree loses its leaves, you will know that winter is coming." Describing an anticipated kingdom, he spoke of summer and new life, not winter barrenness and death. We miss that subtle detail when we concentrate only on what is passing away, being torn down, and being lost. What about the things that are sprouting and being built up?

Look at the schools in our town or city, for instance. We can choose only to see students who aren't learning and teachers who are about to give up. Or we can notice and affirm the children whose minds and hearts are growing, fed by so many bright and dedicated teachers and tutors.

There are other budding leaves that are easy to overlook. Sections of town are decaying, but dedicated people of faith are also building new homes for people in need. Our jails are full of prisoners, but hundreds of their children receive gifts from caring groups during these weeks. Across the world, people are cold, hungry, and dying, but communities of faith are reaching out with sustainable provisions, food sources, clean drinking water, heat, and safety.

Look carefully this Advent, because we can't help but participate in the coming kingdom of new life. Welcome to Advent, a season to celebrate such signs of new life. Among the mantras of pessimism and doomsday prophecies, the Lord who will return in a glorious appearing is already bringing us signs of peace, of sustainable community, of mutual care and generous inclusion, of hope and promise, of fulfillment.

Advent 2: Repent and Follow
Luke 3:1–6

In the fifteenth year of the reign of Tiberius . . . The word of God came to John son of Zechariah in the wilderness. He went into all the region around the Jordan, proclaiming a baptism of repentance for the forgiveness of sins. (Luke 3:1–3)

Today John the Baptist joins the story of expectancy. He asks us to check our spiritual reservoir and to evaluate the direction of our lives. He implores us to make sure that we recognize two core imperatives in baptism: repentance and following, helping to "prepare the way of the Lord." John the Baptist knows that we need a period of in-between time to consider the condition of our world, the wrongdoing, our regret, the damage caused by the human condition, what we've said and done, and what we've left unsaid and undone.

Many people stream into houses of worship wishing to hear messages that merely flatter, to sing hymns that simply warm the heart, to be baptized into settled paths that justify, and to enact rituals without challenge.

You may remember an October when a World Series game was disrupted by a powerful earthquake. The scenes on the news were of burning buildings and collapsing bridges. In the midst of the wreckage of split earth and jagged concrete, residents in one neighborhood were shown having a block party, adults joking and drinking and children riding bikes up and down the fault line. Then without warning we saw a police officer emerge on the scene with a voice of warning: "What are you doing? Do you people not know what has happened? Go to your homes and prepare!"

John emerged on the scene to rattle the status quo. The kingdom earthquake was shaking the old mores. The fault line now ran down the middle of history. God was announcing a new order, one that would require a new heart, a fresh, new path.

Repentance begins with a profound change in the way we see reality. It is not blubbering and self-loathing. It is insight. John is not inviting us into Christianity lite—a journey without challenge, a pilgrimage of pampered, ineffective comfort. He invites us to change direction, to ask ourselves tough but life-giving questions: How's the depth of my faith? What about the actions of my life? Am I expectant, alert, growing, serving? Or is my faith journey small, tired, tepid, dull, unresponsive? Yes, today John speaks uncomfortable words to us—during a season when we yearn to be comfortable.

Most of us are not fans of sermons that do little more than scold us like a bad dog. But I wonder if Shakespeare might not remind us that "we protest our innocence too much." Or, as Anselm wrote: "In your self-centeredness you have not yet considered the seriousness of sin and, thus, have not received the boundless forgiveness of God."

If repentance is the *no*, the stop, the be quiet, the appraisal, the change of direction; then the second reality of baptism, the following, is the *yes*, the discernment for action, the taking stock of our gifts and resources, the heart, passion and muscle of conviction and mission. In our following, we claim assurance of forgiveness, pardon, and a fresh start. Advent is the liminal space in which we pause and prepare for the following.

The promise on this Second Sunday of Advent is that God forgives sins and equips souls that repent with a new life and inclusion in God's mission. John invites us into participation—to help "prepare the way of the Lord" in our own day, so that the world may see God's salvation.

Advent 3: What Then Should We Do?
Luke 3:7–18

John said to the crowds that came out to be baptized by him, "You brood of vipers! Who warned you to flee from the wrath to come? Bear fruits worthy of repentance. Do not begin to say to yourselves, 'we have Abraham as our ancestor'; for I tell you, God is able from these stones to raise up children to Abraham. Even now the ax is lying at the root of the trees; every tree therefore that does not bear good fruit is cut down and thrown into the fire." And the crowds asked him, "What then should we do?" In reply he said to them, "whoever has two coats must share with anyone who has none; and whoever has food must do likewise." (Luke 3:7–11)

It's hard to perceive it at first read, but John is hopeful, even in the midst of an encounter when he calls some in the crowd a "brood of vipers." He is talking to the naysayers, the joyless cynics who have come out from Jerusalem to see a sideshow in the desert. They have come out to the Jordan River to judge this prophet and to slander his message. John's challenge is about the poison of cynicism, the denial that God is working in us and around us, even in the grimmest and darkest parts of human existence.

Vipers are poisonous snakes who latch on to whatever they bite and continue to inject venom. They are often small and hard to notice, and in the Middle East they are likely to congregate in the same places where human beings go looking for refuge—a cave out of the sun, the shady side of a rock where you go for cool respite. To call the religious leaders—then and now—vipers is to name them as people capable of injecting poison into, and sucking the joy out of, the human community, the folk who find something wrong with every new idea or attempt to build up the kingdom of God. You have heard them in our day: "That won't work; we've never done it that way before. . . . You are doing it all wrong. . . . Those people cannot come in here. . . . we cannot bless their relationship, their culture, their tradition!" In response, John invites repentance, turning around, moving in a new direction, and bearing fruit that gives evidence of this change.

John's announcement of judgment is pretty stark—it includes axes falling and trash burning. But this cutting away, this pruning, this chastening action of God, brings new fruit, new vision, new life. Joy comes in building justice. And when pressed about how to act on repentance, John turns lovingly practical: "Whoever has two coats must share with anyone who has none; and whoever has food must do likewise." In short, three simple but profound words: share, fair, and care.

Share generously; give freely. Be fair in your dealings with others. Care for young and old alike, sick and poor, women and men, gay and straight. Don't steal time away from your spouse, your children, or your friends. Stop complaining; be gracious and honor your commitments. Be content with what you have. Accumulating stuff beyond reason means that others are likely to go without.

John's point is that repentance involves change toward greater justice and healing of everybody. And this repentance will bring forth new fruit. It will deepen and encourage the ability to turn toward a loving and just God who is coming into the world, and it will strengthen us and open our hearts and our generosity.

In receiving the gift of forgiveness, we are enabled to spring forth in generosity and concern. We have time to share. There is time to worship God—to direct worth to the source and not to your most recent whim. In our communities of faith, there is time to reflect on how far we have come, where we have grown, where we have fallen short, and always to give thanks for the Spirit that abides with us and surprises us and enables us to bear fruit that befits our repentance.

Advent 4: Can They Hear Us Singing?
Luke 1:39–55

And Mary said, "My soul magnifies the Lord, and my spirit rejoices in God my Savior, for he has looked with favor on the lowliness of his servant. Surely, from now on all generations will call me blessed. . . . He has brought the powerful down from their thrones, and lifted up the lowly." (Luke 1:46–48, 52)

Christians have historically been uncomfortable with Mary's Magnificat. When Luther translated the Bible into German, he left the Magnificat in Latin because the German princes took a dim view of the mighty being brought low. Similarly, when Thomas Cranmer translated the old Roman Latin missals into English, he left all the canticles, including the Song of Mary, in Latin because the royals didn't care for its imagery.

Continuing our Advent journey of the in-between space, we back up from the apocalyptic, future-focused prophesies of adult Jesus and John. We go back to the first two chapters of Luke, where some strange works unfold in the lives of the two men's mothers. Elizabeth, barren and advanced in years, receives the divine surprise of pregnancy. Then her cousin Mary is visited by the angel Gabriel, announcing "that she too would bear a son, who will be called Jesus."

After Mary says her unmistakable yes, after her insemination by the Spirit of God, "the angel left her," seemingly alone in silence. But like all our individual promptings, our experiences need to be manifested in community. She begins with her cousin. Elizabeth's greeting is *eulogetos*—"Blessed are you among women," a greeting of favor, of worthiness, of tenacious faithfulness and humble service. The other blessing conferred by Elizabeth is to call Mary's encounter an event of *makarios*—"a life full of God." Mary is to be full of divine life, love, and action. What's her response? Holy wonder, marvel, spiritual rejoicing, singing aloud to God with a prophetic message not unlike that which her son will preach in the years to come.

What about our context? Do we notice people singing God's song, magnifying God's presence? How about us? Can they hear us singing?

A Lutheran pastor, one of eight children who lived in Austria as a child during the Nazi occupation, tells this story. It was Christmas Eve, and his father was away at the war. So his mother gathered the children around her to read about Mary giving birth to Jesus. As she did, they could hear soldiers outside their windows, patrolling the curfew and enforcing the orders forbidding religious celebrations. The family was very quiet.

When the mother finished reading, the youngest sister asked, "Mama, aren't we going to sing?" With only a moment's hesitation, his mother answered, "Of course we are going to sing. Tonight we celebrate the coming of the Christ child into our world." She gathered the children about the piano, and they sang "Joy to the World." Hearing footsteps in the stairway, the mother didn't stop but launched into "Hark! The Herald Angels Sing." As the soldiers appeared at their door, to their great surprise and delight, the soldiers didn't arrest them. Instead, they all sang.

How about us? Can they hear us singing? Whether with our voices or our actions, we can sing a song that magnifies God. Like Evelyn in Haiti, who runs a daycare center for children with HIV/AIDS. Or Henry, who quietly makes a monthly meal for those in the homeless shelter. They are each singing the Magnificat in their own way, and we're invited to join them.

Christmas Eve: Salvation from the Margins
Luke 2:1–20

While they were there, the time came for her to deliver her child. And she gave birth to her firstborn son and wrapped him in bands of cloth and laid him in a manger, because there was no place for them in the inn. (Luke 2:6–7)

The inn mentioned in Luke's birth narrative has received a great deal of attention through the generations, as it brings to mind the image of a cozy B and B. In a first-century context, it just means there was no place in the front of the cave where guests bedded down, but there was a place in the back with the animals—and that was enough. The place and the meaning turned out to be just right! The birth happened in obscurity; the night-shift shepherds visited the manger; and the mysterious magi offered their gifts.

Jesus started his saving purpose anonymously and on the margins. If the "in between" we've been talking about is a matter of time, Jesus' place on the margins is an "in between" of space. God's mission thrives on the edge. While there wasn't room for Jesus in the center of life and commerce, there was a starting place on the margins. And, as we learn throughout his lifetime, Jesus fulfilled his purpose from the margins. Even at the end, his life ended outside the city gates in the garbage dump, the landfill. The Epistle to the Hebrews states, "Jesus suffered for the world outside the city gates in order to sanctify the people by his own blood."

One of my all-time favorite Christmas stories is Charles Dickens's "A Christmas Carol." The story pulls on our heartstrings as the selfish old miser, Scrooge, is shown the truth about how so much of humanity lives on the margins. Then he discovers the joy of sharing and caring. Scrooge is afraid, he has lost hope, and in his selfishness he has marginalized himself. Over the years he has become hardened to the struggles of others, indifferent to anyone else. As he has withdrawn from others, he has failed to see that he is shrinking inside and that his capacity for love is dying. In losing his ability to acknowledge the worthiness of others, he too loses any sense of worth, even though he is the richest person in the village.

That's not so very far from many in our world. Much of the running over one another—to buy, to visit, to party, to decorate—evolves out of an elemental need to know God, to seek meaning and purpose, to face our fears and uncertainties, and to discover love and belonging. But in so much running around, agonizing over the "stuff" of the holidays, we marginalize ourselves from true connection.

It's all right to be on the margins; it's only wrong to pretend we're not. It's all right to be vulnerable, it's only empty to play as if we're always strong. Most of us are tired of clanking around in our armor, of bumping into masks. It's all right to admit that we need more connection, more love, more forgiveness; it's only wrong to pretend that we don't.

Into this world in which there is very little room for God to dwell, Christ comes uninvited. His primary place is with those for whom there is no place. His place is with those who do not belong, who are rejected, who are discredited, who are denied status, who are tortured, terrorized, and exterminated. Christ is present to the whole world, from the margins.

First Sunday of Christmas: The Sounds of Silence
Luke 2:39–52

When they had finished everything required . . . they returned to Galilee, to their own town of Nazareth. The child grew and became strong, filled with wisdom, and the favor of God was upon him. (Luke 2:39–40)

Today's Gospel text tells us all we know about Jesus as a child. After Mary and Joseph take their infant to the temple for dedication, we have one little story about Mary and Joseph taking the boy Jesus to the Passover festival in Jerusalem, and the next chapter begins with John the Baptist preaching in the wilderness. During the silent years in between, Jesus grows up. As if in a split second, he jumps from age twelve to age thirty.

What went on during that time? What lies behind that one too-short sentence: "The child grew and became strong"?

Consider what these thirty years really mean. Can you sense how incredible it is that we Christians believe that almighty God lived among us in human form? Can you imagine God as one of us, playing tag in the streets of Nazareth? Can you imagine Jesus complaining to Mary about the evening meal or running so hard that he runs out of breath? Can you picture him falling and skinning his knee, or tearing up when his girlfriend broke up with him?

Let's put some flesh on the bones of those silent years. Let's think about God as one of us, needing everything that we have needed. Like a mother to dress him and bathe him and put him to bed. A mother who urged him to eat more fruit and drink more milk. Who reminded him to stay out of the heat at midday and wear an extra cloak when winter came.

Can you see God as one of us, living with a human father? A father who scolded him when he stayed behind to teach in the temple. A father who taught him the skills of a craftsman, cutting rock and sawing wood. Can you imagine him grieving at his father's death and then being exhausted by running the business and supporting the family by himself?

All of this—and many more everyday, ordinary experiences— slowly unfolded during the thirty years between chapter 2 and chapter 3 of Luke's Gospel.

Those silent years have much to say about how God works. They say that God has embraced and made holy every moment of ordinary, everyday life. They mean that God has sanctified washing the dishes, taking out the garbage, doing algebra homework—and even failing to balance the family bank account.

Those silent years say that God spent the majority of time on earth finding out what it's like to be an ordinary human being. There's a message there for us who live in this quick-fix, immediate-results, instant-computer kind of world, a message we should keep in mind this week as we are tempted to make big resolutions to change our habits and lives. These silent years in between the promise and the fruition say that God takes time before acting. God's movements in human history are rarely sudden. God does not create change overnight, and God rarely changes people that quickly either. Salvation is never a quick fix, a dumbed-down liturgy, a simplistic reading of Scripture.

Behind the silence is the sound of silence, God slowly growing within the silence. The promise for this Christmas Sunday, as we look toward a new calendar year, is that God will be present to us in our silent years, slowly growing and growing until Christ fills in all our gaps.

Epiphany Series: A Light to Enlighten the Nations

Nine Parts: Epiphany through
Transfiguration Sunday

Christ shines as a light beyond Israel, to the whole world.

ROBERT S. DANNALS

Series Overview "For my eyes have seen your salvation, which you have prepared in the presence of all peoples, a light for revelation to the Gentiles and for glory to your people Israel." These lines from the Song of Simeon (Luke 2:29–32) speak of the season of Epiphany, of the light of Christ for all the world. Seeing Jesus born in Bethlehem, dedicated at the temple, and baptized in the River Jordan, it's easy to focus on his life as a first-century Jew. But the audacity of the gospel is that the light shining in Jesus shone far beyond Israel to illuminate the whole world. Through the Gospel readings of this season, we see how the light of Christ reached outsiders from the beginning and continued to grow, lighting the dark places throughout our world and in our own hearts.

	Sermon Title	Focus Scripture	Theme
Epiphany[1]	Outsiders Becoming Insiders	Matt. 2:1–12	Christ's love and light draws the whole world in.
First Sunday after Epiphany	Saved to Serve the Whole World	Luke 3:15–17, 21–22	A baptism empowers mission.
Second Sunday after Epiphany	The Illumination of New Wine	John 2:1–11	At Cana, Jesus began his work of illuminating the dark places.
Third Sunday after Epiphany	A Mission to Light Your Way	Luke 4:14–21	We define Jesus' mission, and our own.
Fourth Sunday after Epiphany	Hometown Boy	Luke 4:21–30	Jesus' good news for the world isn't a threat, but an invitation.

1. The congregation can observe Epiphany on the Second Sunday of Christmas if January 6 does not fall on a Sunday.

	Sermon Title	Focus Scripture	Theme
Fifth Sunday after Epiphany	Called and Sent	Luke 5:1–11	We hear and accept our own call to be part of Jesus' work.
Sixth Sunday after Epiphany	Fullness and Emptiness	Luke 6:17–26	Only by emptying ourselves will we experience true fullness.
Seventh Sunday after Epiphany	Unlimited Love	Luke 6:27–38	Jesus' unconditional love opens the boundaries of our love.
Transfiguration Sunday[2]	Listen to Him	Luke 9:28–43a	Don't box Jesus in; shine his light for all to see.

2. Transfiguration Sunday is observed on the last Sunday before Lent begins. Depending on the date of Ash Wednesday, the season after Epiphany can range from four to nine Sundays. This series can be shortened or lengthened as needed.

Tips and Ideas for This Series

Invite Christmas visitors to return for a Feast of Light or Twelfth Night celebration the night before Epiphany (January 5 being the twelfth and final day of the Christmas season). Using light and darkness, the worship might include the lighting of candles and the saying of prayers. A drama enacting the magi coming to manger can be a special feature. If you used real greenery to decorate during Advent and Christmas, have a "burning of the greens" bonfire and dinner afterward. Coming as this series does in the genuine quiet of January and February, it may be a better time than Advent for achieving some measure of quiet and reflection. So consider offering a take-home daily devotional booklet or scheduling a weekly gathering for contemplative prayer.

The Epiphany: Outsiders Becoming Insiders
Matthew 2:1–12

In the time of King Herod, after Jesus was born in Bethlehem of Judea, magi from the East came to Jerusalem, asking, "Where is the child who has been born king of the Jews?" . . . they set out; and there ahead of them, went the star that they had seen at its rising, until it stopped over the place where the child was. (Matthew 2:1–2a, 9)

Luke's version of the nativity is good news, full of sweet, pleasant scenes and glowing metaphors. On the other hand, Matthew's version is full of challenge and terror. Exit the stable (or cave), enter the king's palace; exit the shepherds and angels, enter the magi and King Herod; exit Mary and enter Rachel; close the music box playing sweet

Christmas carols, enter the screams of Rachel and the other parents of murdered children. If made into a movie, one version would be rated G for comfortable family entertainment; the other version would be rated R for violence.

We call the celebration of the magi's visit to the Christ child the Epiphany. The word means "manifestation," an unveiling of sorts, when something that is hidden is revealed. God makes divine glory known to all the world in Jesus. The world finally gets to find out what God is like. Light is the traditional symbol for this season. The people who walked in darkness have seen a great light.

The magi's journey could be any of our own. We know about deserts and dry places and thirst, if not of the body, then of the soul and the heart. We know about looking into the stars and, in a thousand other places, searching for hope and love and meaning. We know about wanting to find someone who can be trusted to guide us on our journey. We know about dark places and the ruthlessness that can take hold of people when they are threatened and afraid. We know about being on the outside looking in, the times when we've been left out in the cold or when we were not included, and we know when we've done that to others.

We suppose the magi are mysterious astrologers who have been prompted by a star—what scientists now think was a manifestation in the heavens, a conjunction of the planets Jupiter and Saturn. Regardless of the details, Matthew has another subtheme: they were outsiders, likely Arab Gentiles, shattering religious tradition by showing up to give homage to the new baby king whose light was being revealed beyond Israel to the whole world. Before the story is over, of course, Jesus is going to continue to shatter boundaries of race, class, and gender. Those who are cultural and/or religious outsiders are brought into belonging and purpose.

Christ's birth shows forth God's glory in at least three ways. First, it is about belonging and inclusion. All people are equally under the light of Christ. Epiphany then has to do with any place or event when the realities of racism and exclusion are addressed with justice, belonging, and hospitality.

A second dimension has to do with the competition that will dog Jesus every place in the world. Who is sovereign in this world? There is a Herod-like darkness deep inside people that craves power and possession. Jesus enters this world with a message of mutuality, of equitability, of democratic, unconditional love and light for all people.

The third way is about the light that shines from the incarnation. This light is born not from a star but from a life. That life was lived in first-century Palestine, but its light still warns and warms us in our day. That life was buried just outside of the Old City of Jerusalem, yet its resurrected light still shines. As Jesus said years later: "I am the light of the world. Whoever follows me will never walk in darkness but will have the light of life" (John 8:12).

First Sunday after Epiphany: Saved to Serve the Whole World
Luke 3:15–17, 21–22

As the people were filled with expectation, and all were questioning in their hearts concerning John, whether he might be the Messiah, John answered all of them by saying, "I baptize you with water; but one who is more powerful than I is coming; I am not worthy to untie the thong of his sandals. He will baptize you with the Holy Spirit and fire." . . . Now when all the people were baptized, and when Jesus also had been baptized and was praying, the heaven was opened, and the Holy Spirit descended upon him in bodily form like a dove. And a voice came from heaven, "You are my Son, the Beloved; with you I am well pleased." (Luke 3:15–16, 21–22)

John the Baptist is one of the most dramatic and unforgettable characters in the New Testament. Dressed in unusual clothes, with a wild look in his eye and a strident urgency in his voice, rugged and unkempt, he burst on the scene in the Jordan River wilderness, exhorting people to be baptized. No one was more surprised than John when Jesus came south from the Galilee and presented himself for baptism. Jesus—the one John had just been saying would baptize all of them, not with water but with the fire of the Holy Spirit.

John protested! According to Mark's account: "I need to be baptized by you, and do you come to me?"

Why would Jesus of Nazareth, the only one who has walked this earth without sin, present himself for baptism? Why would the blazing light of a baptism by fire be put on hold in favor of a cool, comparatively ordinary baptism by water? That was John's question, and it is a question we still ask. I offer two stories that may help us with the answer.

Several years ago I received a nice letter of thanks from one of our bishops for our congregation's contribution for flood relief in the Mississippi delta. He told me of one family we helped—a mother and her four children. It seems that her husband was swept away by the floodwaters. As rescue workers tried desperately to save him by throwing a line from the sandy bank, this man kept passing the line to others until the surge of water swept him away. "He was a brave man," said the rescue workers. "He could have grabbed the line first, but he put everyone else ahead of himself. He repeatedly passed the lifeline to others."

The other story, told by C. S. Lewis, is of the lawyer in London who stood by watching as a young woman drowned in the River Thames. He was haunted and tormented all his life by his failure. It drove him to the brink of suicide. One night he found himself standing once again on the bridge where he had failed to act years before, and he said aloud: "Oh, young woman, throw yourself into the river once again, so that I might save the both of us."

Jesus was not baptized because he had sinned; nor was this a coronation of him as a Davidic monarch. Jesus' baptism was God's anointing of him, God's commissioning of him to a mission of serv-anthood. Jesus was appointed, born to be among us as One who saves and serves the whole world, as One who passes the lifeline to others . . . and calls us to do the same.

In his role as servant king, Jesus flew in the face of all of Israel's expectations of a victorious, conquering Messiah. Instead, the world received One who washed feet, touched lepers, befriended sinners, and passed the lifeline to all.

Second Sunday after Epiphany: The Illumination of New Wine
John 2:1–11

Jesus said to them, "Fill the jars with water.'" And they filled them to the brim. He said to them, "Now draw some out, and take it to the chief steward." So they took it. When the steward tasted the water that had become wine, and did not know where it came from, the steward called the bridegroom and said to him, "Everyone serves the good wine first, and then the inferior wine after the guests have had plenty. But you have kept the good wine until now." Jesus did this, the first of his signs, in Cana of Galilee, and revealed his glory; and his disciples believed in him. (John 2:7–11)

The Galilee in which Jesus had grown up was relatively fertile country, at least in comparison with some of the neighboring regions. Its resources enabled many of the people to be self-sufficient. But taxation was oppressive, transportation was difficult, and almost no one had discretionary income. Feasting and celebration took place only when there was a great occasion; one of the hallmark events in the life of a family was the wedding of a son or daughter. Very often a wedding festival would last a full week.

Well before the week was out, a miscalculation became evident. Not enough wine had been secured. Word of the mistake was passed to Mary, Jesus' mother, and she passed this news to Jesus. By the grace of God, the common water was changed into the uncommon; the ordinary was made extraordinary. Jesus unmasked God's glory working in him. He suddenly shouldered the kingship predicted by the magi when they asked Herod: "Where is the child who has been born king?" At Cana, Jesus began his work of "kinging."

"Kinging" is a word and practice that I learned in Puerto Rico. Latin American Christians take the noun "king" and turn it into the verb form "kinging." How does God king someone? Jesus reveals God's glory and provision making in turning water into wine. Wine is a symbol of joy, lighting up a room with laughter and friendship.

In Latin America they envision the kingdom ruled by Christ as a place filled with singing, dancing, and feasting. They believe the first responsibility of kinging is to allow God to turn the water of sadness, anxiety, stress, and emptiness into the wine of new life. As they begin the new year, they invite each person in the community to make a new start. But it is not enough to have your own water changed into wine. A second feature is that you must seek the same for others. The second aspect of kinging is to seek the welfare of others, to increase their station and joy of life. It means to have direct responsibility for the least, the lost, and the last of one's community.

What would kinging look like in your community and mine?

In an interview a number of years ago, Madeleine L'Engle was asked about the art of wine hosting. She said at a most basic level, the job of the wine host, or the everyday Christian, is to serve lavishly what you have been given:

> The point is to be ready at all times to give and serve what God has given us, to manifest God's glory by reaching out with the ordinary . . . to manifest God in your own givenness through everyday opportunities. It may be that turning six jars of water into wine will be your given task, but I doubt it. On the other hand, it could mean turning your jar of peanut butter into sandwiches for the homeless, or turning your voice into corporate praise on Sunday morning.

Jesus' ministry began with the reillumination of a celebration that had gone dark. How can we light up the dark places of our world, playing our part as servants of the king?

Third Sunday after Epiphany: A Mission to Light Your Way
Luke 4:14–21

When [Jesus] came to Nazareth, where he had been brought up, he went to the synagogue on the sabbath day, as was his custom. He stood up to read, . . . "The Spirit of the Lord is upon me, because he has anointed me to bring good news to the poor. He has sent me to proclaim release to the captives and recovery of sight to the blind, to let the oppressed go free, to proclaim the year of the Lord's favor." (Luke 4:16–19)

Following on the heels of his baptism and his experience in the wilderness for forty days, with its attending understanding of his vocation, Jesus stands in his hometown synagogue and gives his inauguration address by quoting from Isaiah. He concludes his oration with the stirring words: "Today this scripture has been fulfilled in your hearing."

I don't know about you, but it seems to me that at any new beginning—a marriage, a birth, a new job—there is a moment of truth. It is a moment that overshadows and flavors and gives meaning to all the other moments. A moment when declarations are made, commitments sealed, mission statements shaped, and inauguration statements publicly proclaimed.

When Jesus concluded his reading of Isaiah, he sat down and gave a one-sentence homily: "Today this scripture has been fulfilled in your hearing." In one powerful sentence he summed up his life's purpose. What you and I have before us is a moment of truth: we can decide to leave this statement alone, or we can choose to imitate it in living out our baptismal covenant. If only we would let his voice light our way, instead of attending with great energy and devotion to the many other voices and promptings we receive.

Knowing your mission helps keep your priorities straight. I bought a boat once. I was much younger and idealistic. I was influenced by my friends at church and the incredible allure of the water. I spent way too much of my income for that boat. But I thought it would be life giving. I was wrong!

Every time I had a day off, or even a half day away, I would leave my house by the side door, and that boat would speak to me: "You paid too much for me. You and others are doing without so that you can have me. Therefore, it is your responsibility to use me whenever you have any spare time. Now, go get your bathing suit on, hook me up to the trailer, and let's go have fun, fun, fun." I didn't possess the boat; it possessed me. I'd let other voices guide me, and I chose the wrong path.

In the winter of 1947, the abbot Pierre, who was known as the modern Apostle of Mercy to the poor of Paris, found a young family on the streets one night. They were homeless and destitute, nearly frozen to death. He gathered them up and brought them to the monastery, which was already full of other poor and outcast. As he looked for a place for their makeshift beds, there wasn't room in the regular rooms, so the abbot took them to the chapel. He promptly removed the reserved sacraments from the altar area and placed them in an unheated attic. He placed the family's bedding on and around the altar. The other monks expressed shock at such irreverence. The abbot replied, "Jesus Christ is not cold in bread and wine, but he is absolutely cold in the body of a little child."

That priest knew that his mission was not to be a protector of the church building and its rituals, but to open the church doors to those whom Christ made it his mission to serve. Know your mission, and it will light the path you are intended to take. What is your mission?

Fourth Sunday after Epiphany: Hometown Boy
Luke 4:21–30

When they heard this, all in the synagogue were filled with rage. They got up, drove him out of the town, and led him to the brow of the hill on which their town was built, so that they might hurl him off the cliff. But he passed through the midst of them and went on his way. (Luke 4:28–30)

The story of Jesus returning to his hometown synagogue began with so much promise. He stood up and read Isaiah's description of the messiah: one who would bring good news to the poor, sight to the blind, and freedom to the captives. Then he claimed that this old prophecy is being fulfilled in their midst. His neighbors, friends, and family looked at each other and smiled. The year of the Lord's favor, right here in Nazareth of Israel. How nice.

But then things took a different turn. Jesus couldn't leave well enough alone. He told them how the ancient prophets Elijah and Elisha didn't focus on the widows and lepers of Israel but brought good news and healing to outsiders—a widow in Sidon and Naaman the Syrian. The people began to shift uneasily in their seats. They began to have second thoughts. The craziness, the audacity of what Jesus said began to sink in. This good news wasn't just for them? The people sprang to their feet, drove him out of town, and tried to push him over the cliff. What a homecoming!

Luke's description of this situation has at least two levels: the one located in Nazareth, the other the tensions that existed in the postresurrection church out of which Luke was writing. One element is the open affirmation of the Jewishness of Jesus and his message. He was a Galilean Jewish rabbi, but he was also the Messiah for the world. His mission was global and trans-Jewish. On this score, some of the early churches had tension between the Jewish Christians and the converted Gentiles, between those who worshiped on Friday nights and those who observed the Sabbath on Sundays.

Some of the Jewish Christians of Luke's day felt like the Nazarenes listening to Jesus read Scripture. They were pleased with the idea of "hometown boy makes good" ("hometown" in their case meaning "Jewish like us") but were not so comfortable with the idea that the glorious prophesies of their tradition, the "good news," the "year of the Lord" Isaiah spoke about, would apply to everyone. They wanted to hold back this light that Jesus wanted to share with the whole world.

This whole encounter makes me think of Dorothy in *The Wizard of Oz*. I see her sitting in her backyard in Kansas, singing "Somewhere over the Rainbow," longing to fly beyond the ordinary, the obvious, the dimness of her own surroundings. Her fellow Kansans tell her to get her head out of the clouds and focus on the here and now, where work needs to be done and storms threaten to rage.

When Dorothy is blown out of Kansas and into Oz, her dream is suddenly fulfilled, her black-and-white world suddenly illuminated with brilliant Technicolor. That amazing world isn't perfect, but there are forces at work she's never before imagined. When she wakes up back in her black-and-white home, she tells her disbelieving friends and family of the wondrous light she's seen "out there." She's in awe, but the biggest realization is that all that glory was right there the whole time—she just couldn't see it.

Jesus' revelation that the good news is for the whole world, not just those of us who have known Jesus all our lives, shouldn't offend us or make us want to run Jesus off a cliff. It's not a threat but an invitation. Jesus is indeed bringing good news to the poor, sight to the blind, all of this, today in our midst—and we can be a part of it, spreading his good news all over the world.

Fifth Sunday after Epiphany: Called and Sent
Luke 5:1–11

But when Simon Peter saw [the catch of fish], he fell down at Jesus' knees, saying, "Go away from me, Lord, for I am a sinful man!" For he and all who were with him were amazed at the catch of fish that they had taken; and so also were James and John, sons of Zebedee, who were partners with Simon. Then Jesus said to Simon, "Do not be afraid; from now on you will be catching people." (Luke 5:8–10)

For the last few weeks, we've been talking about the beginnings of Jesus' ministry: his baptism, his first miracle, and his declaration of his mission as a light to the whole world. Today we see Jesus calling the first disciples to be part of his mission.

For anyone responding to God's call, there is a time when it all began. Sometimes it's a flash of understanding, a revelation after which you know life will never be the same. Other times it's gradual, and you can't necessarily pinpoint any particular day when you finally knew what God was asking you to do.

Isaiah's ministry began in the year that King Uzziah died. Jeremiah's prophetic mission began in an era that led to exile. Paul's evangelistic work began in a particular moment when a light from God struck him blind on the road to Damascus. In our own day, our story of calling might begin the year 9/11 happened, the year after graduation, the week you lost your job, the day that your child got sick, the moment a mentor affirmed your talent.

For Peter, James, and John in today's Gospel text, it was the day Jesus showed up and got into their fishing boat. Peter's response was similar to many of us who begin to suspect God has a job for us; he declared himself unworthy: "Go away from me, Lord, for I am a sinful man!" But Jesus called him anyway.

God's call is rooted in everyday life, and the promptings to serve usually happen during our regular routines. In the midst of the ordinary, our calling emerges; and no person is good enough, or strong enough, or pure enough. No tongue is clean enough. But we are called anyway. The Zenith Television Company used to have a familiar slogan to sell their product: "The quality goes in before the name goes on." In the work of the kingdom, God seemingly calls us to be in the group before there is any evidence of quality.

This Gospel text is about finding our God-given purpose and acting on it. What happens in the story of call by that lake 2,000 years ago continues to ring true in our own day. Acting in spite of their insecurity, the first thing they do is "launch out." They cast off from the shore; they begin to leave behind their carefully arranged security, the sure routines, reliance on merely their own ingenuity. We too are invited to launch out into deeper waters.

The second thing that happens is that they "let down the nets." Peter and his mates expect nothing but get a huge catch. What would it mean for you and me to "put out into the deep and let down the nets"? It might mean investing ourselves in the exact place where we're most afraid or intimidated. God might be asking us to take bigger risks, to step beyond our comfort zones. It might mean that we have to ask for help more often or perhaps for forgiveness.

The third action in the story of call is that "leaving behind the nets, they followed him." What must we leave behind in order to answer Jesus' call?

Jesus called his disciples to leave their nets and follow him. He called them, not because of who they were, but because of who they could be.

Sixth Sunday after Epiphany: Fullness and Emptiness
Luke 6:17–26

Then he looked up at his disciples and said: "Blessed are you who are poor, for yours is the kingdom of God. Blessed are you who are hungry now, for you will be filled. Blessed are you who weep now, for you will laugh. . . . But woe to you who are rich, for you have received your consolation. Woe to you who are full now, for you will be hungry. Woe to you who are laughing now, for you will mourn and weep." (Luke 6:20–21, 24–25)

I have long been both fascinated and repelled by ants. Several months ago, I happened onto the Discovery Channel. My screen was swarming with ants: endlessly foraging for food, darting single file along invisible trails, scrambling over bridges made of grass blades and twigs.

But not all the ants were so active. Somewhere deep within the ant hill was a chamber filled with what are known as the cows. The chamber looked like a hanger of tiny blimps, for the cow ants clinging to its walls had enormous bellies swollen with a form of nectar. The cow ants were living storehouses, filled with the ant hill's surplus food. They were filled to overflowing, condemned to being endlessly stuffed, eternally immobilized by the very weight of their awesome fullness. I kept wondering if they were at least dimly aware that, for them, this is all there is, has ever been, and ever will be. The cow ants never see daylight; they never know anything except getting full, the kind of fullness that is actually empty.

Jesus spoke about fullness as he stood on a level place somewhere in Galilee, surrounded by a great multitude. His Sermon on the Plain began with a shortened version of the Beatitudes. He started by preaching about the fullness that feels empty—and also the richness that feels like poverty, the laughter that feels like weeping, and the power and prestige that ultimately feel weak and inadequate.

We are not readily encouraged to favor meekness and hunger and poverty. In fact, quite the opposite: we are hard wired to look out for self. But Jesus' mission to be a light, not just to a privileged inner circle but to the whole world, requires that we embrace his mission and prioritize the "other," those outside the circle of privilege.

Jesus is clear: the things with which we fill up our lives often leave us empty; and when we are left empty by a disregarding world, God will fill us up with that which sustains. Are you going to be eternally full in God's kingdom, Jesus asked, or are you going to be full and satisfied in this world? If you hoard the world's goods, then you are going to swell up like a cow ant, and you will have already received all you're going to get for your efforts—emptiness.

There is a better way, Jesus said.

More than seventy years ago, on a bitterly cold February night, aboard the U.S. transport ship *Dorchester*, the ship carrying a thousand troops to battle in World War II was struck by a torpedo and sank. Four Army chaplains—two Protestants, a Jewish rabbi, and a Roman Catholic priest—worked to distribute life jackets, calm the men, and help them into the lifeboats. There were not enough life jackets or lifeboats to go around, so the chaplains took none for themselves. They gave away everything they had and then joined hands and prayed together as the ship sank.

These men did something crazy by the world's standards, but they lived the reality of the Beatitudes. They gave us a living parable of how to shine Jesus' light to the whole world, entering into the fullness of God's kingdom with hands and hearts wide open—and empty, but full.

Seventh Sunday after Epiphany: Unlimited Love
Luke 6:27–38

"But I say to you that listen, Love your enemies, do good to those who hate you, bless those who curse you, pray for those who abuse you. If anyone strikes you on the cheek, offer the other also; and from anyone who takes away your coat do not withhold even your shirt. Give to everyone who begs from you; and if anyone takes away your goods, do not ask for them again. Do to others as you would have them do to you." (Luke 6:27–31)

This Sunday's Gospel continues Luke's version of Matthew's Sermon on the Mount, with teachings requiring unconditional, unlimited love and the prohibition of retaliation. The love that discipleship in the kingdom of God requires, that is consistent in the behavior of Jesus' earthly pilgrimage, extends to all persons, regardless of merit or deservedness. The love of the disciple, like the love of God, goes out even to the enemy: those who do us wrong, those who curse us, and those who do damage.

Jesus is teaching *agapē*, a love that is so deep and forgiving that it breaks through normal barriers and becomes open hearted and radically generous in its operation. This unlimited love does not come from a moral "should" but from an infused vision, a holy, enlightened view of all people that only God can give. Thus it goes beyond mere daily justice, the norm that says that if you harm a neighbor, you are to compensate him or her on an equal basis. This love is to be expressed even when there is no loving response!

Like many of you, I grew up in a "Christian home," with parents who taught me the stories in the Bible, especially the life and teachings of Jesus. I was instructed in moral living, to respect others, to mind my manners, and to "do to others as I would have them do to me."

When I started school, I began to discover that the world didn't always behave in the manner that I was taught. I learned this new lesson in the person of Jimmy Burgan. Jimmy was the school bully, and he chose me for his sport. I had been taught in Sunday school not to fight and to "turn the other cheek," and for several weeks in the second grade I received a daily beating. My older brothers and my cousins began to exert another teaching on me: "Stick up for yourself, and pay him back slug for slug. . . . Only sissies don't defend themselves. . . . You've got to be a tough guy and take him down." During the first week of this new teaching, I looked for my opportunity and learned several things during our tussle. I was stronger than Jimmy; the first time I drew blood, it was a sweet feeling and a pleasant sight. And the experience of satisfaction didn't last. I knew there was a better, more complicated way.

"Love your enemies and do good to those who hate you." Can you and I come close to fulfilling this expectation? If we want it to be more than just a well-known teaching, then we must ask God to help us with its precepts, to take some steps in its direction. We do this by asking: who are my present enemies? We can begin this process by praying for them. It's hard to hate anyone for whom we pray. Secondly, we might probe why they are enemies: threat, jealousy, abuse, insecurity, violence, cultural or political differences, crime? Thirdly, we can consider what steps we can take to bridge the gap: what is realistic, what is doable, what is within my time and resource limits?

As coworkers in Christ's mission, we are called to imitate Jesus' radical, all-encompassing love. We don't always succeed. All of us fall short. But when we take some steps, we are on our way to coming very close to the very heart of God.

Transfiguration Sunday: Listen to Him
Luke 9:28–43a

And while he was praying, the appearance of his face changed, and his clothes became dazzling white. Suddenly they saw two men, Moses and Elijah, talking to him. They appeared in glory and were speaking of his departure, which he was about to accomplish at Jerusalem. . . . Just as they were leaving him, Peter said to Jesus, "Master, it is good for us to be here; let us make three dwellings, one for you, one for Moses, and one for Elijah"—not knowing what he said. While he was saying this, a cloud came and overshadowed them; and they were terrified as they entered the cloud. Then from the cloud came a voice that said, "This is my Son, my Chosen; listen to him!" (Luke 9:29–35)

The story of the transfiguration is always read on the Sunday before Ash Wednesday. In this story, at the conclusion of our series "A Light to Enlighten the Nations," we see not only another message of Jesus' light metaphorically going out to all people but also a literal, physical light, as Jesus himself starts to glow! Like others we've read about who want to box Jesus in and keep his good news for themselves, here we see Peter and the others wanting to build "dwellings" on Mount Tabor for the glorified Christ and the prophets with whom he appears, grounding them in this one place.

Like Peter, our first instinct is to build "booths" (as it is phrased in many translations) around our view of Christ and hold on to a view of Jesus we're comfortable with, which ironically looks a lot like us, rather than the more expansive view of the Scriptures. No, we are invited by the transfigured Christ to hold our images lightly, not to limit the expansive love and light of Christ.

Long ago in a small European village, there lived an old man whom everyone considered infinitely wise. Whenever the villagers needed advice, they came to the old man's door and knocked. In the same village lived a number of rough young men. The young adults came to resent the old man, for he had so often been correct in his counsel. So, for once, they were determined to prove him wrong.

The young ruffians caught a bird and decided to ask the old man whether the bird was dead or alive. If he said it was dead, the one holding the bird would let it fly away. If he said it was alive, then the one holding it would squeeze it to death before opening his hands. They went to the old man's house and said, "Old man, we have an important question to ask you. Is this bird dead or alive?" The old man thought for a minute, then answered: "It's all in your hands."

I once had a spiritual director who said little, but what he said counted. Of the wisdom he offered me, I most often draw on one piece of advice: "Hold all things lightly, or you will leave no room for God to work." I would add: Hold all things lightly, for you have the power to crush or to give life.

The one time I visited the top of Mount Tabor, my own understanding of holy places was expanded by a short homily at morning prayers. The service was led by one of my fellow travelers, an African American seminarian from Los Angeles. Ken's church had been damaged during the Watts riots in the 1960s. Ken's life experience had taught him something important. "Every encounter with another human being has the potential to be destructive or to be holy," he said.

When two people or groups encounter each other, they either deal death or give life. We deal death when we criticize, belittle, misunderstand, ignore, boast, and insist on our own way. We give life when we notice, affirm, thank, listen to, rejoice with, and encourage others. We are transfigured and transformed by God's grace when we are able to extend life to others.

As we begin our Lenten pilgrimage, we are bid to listen to Jesus and imitate his life, reflecting and expanding God's glorious light to all the nations.

Lenten Series: God on the Move

Seven Parts: First Sunday in Lent through Easter Sunday

Exploring God's work through the travels and teachings of Jesus.

JESSICA LaGRONE

Series Overview
Jesus didn't stay in one place for long. His earthly ministry was one of moving from one place and encounter to the next. He also moved through every part of the human experience, encountering everything from temptation, to joy, to suffering and even death. This series helps us reclaim the movement of Jesus' ministry from temptation to condemnation, through his teaching and miracles and finally through the story of his death and resurrection. As we encounter the life and ministry of Jesus, we cannot stay the same. We ourselves are moved to grow and change as followers and imitators of the gospel.

The comforting truth of Lent is that as we delve deeper into our own self-examination, we find that we are not alone. God is still on the move in our lives, walking with us every step as we travel the road to Easter.

	Sermon Title	Focus Scripture	Theme
Lent 1	God Moves . . . into the Desert	Luke 4:1–13	Jesus' temptation in the desert shows us that God has moved fully into human flesh and can identify with our every experience.
Lent 2	God Moves . . . past All Obstacles	Luke 13:31–35	Jesus won't let Herod's threats or the people's opposition keep him from fulfilling his loving purpose.
Lent 3	God Moves . . . over the Fence	Luke 13:1–9	Instead of gazing at the grass on the other side of the fence, Jesus brings us back to focus on realities that will bring change and growth in our own backyard.

	Sermon Title	Focus Scripture	Theme
Lent 4	God Moves . . . down the Road	Luke 15:1–3, 11b–32	God is always running to meet us, even when we have squandered his grace.
Lent 5	God Moves Us . . . to Empty Ourselves	John 12:1–8	As Mary anointed Jesus with the scent of sacrifice, we are called to pour out ourselves for him.
Lent 6	God Moves . . . to the Cross	Luke 23:1–49	Throughout his story Jesus has been moving in one direction—to the cross.
Easter Sunday	God Moves . . . out of the Tomb	Luke 24:1–12	Even the grave could not still Jesus. He is alive and active and moving in our lives and our world.

Tips and Ideas for This Series

The Gospels show Jesus' movement in many different ways: across the land of Israel, through the human experience, and toward the cross. With the emphasis on moving in this series, you could use graphics that portray moving vans or decorate the front of the worship area with moving supplies like boxes and packing tape or old suitcases covered in travel stickers. Invitation cards for the series could mimic a change-of-address card "We're moving!" to catch people's attention.

Lent 1: God Moves . . . into the Desert
Luke 4:1–13

Jesus, full of the Holy Spirit, returned from the Jordan and was led by the Spirit in the wilderness, where for forty days he was tempted by the devil. He ate nothing at all during those days, and when they were over, he was famished. The devil said to him, "If you are the Son of God, command this stone to become a loaf of bread." Jesus answered him, "It is written, 'One does not live by bread alone.'" (Luke 4:1–4)

How many of you have moved to a new city? How about out of state? Has anyone moved to another country? Unless we live in the house we were born in, most of us have experienced the transition of packing up our things and moving from one place to another.

You may have experienced that moving creates both opportunity and stress. Along with the opportunity to begin again in new jobs, schools, and friendships comes the stress of loading up your belongings, trying to find a new place to live, and starting over in a brand-new community. We often discover things about ourselves that we didn't know before: our tendency to accumulate things, how much the friends we leave behind have meant to us, and how we react in the face of new experiences. Moving brings us new realizations about ourselves as well as our new environment.

The season of Lent brings us a chance to move inward as we move toward the cross. During Lent we move deeper into the biblical story of Jesus' journey on earth, as well as into our own inward landscape to see things God wants to show us about ourselves.

When God took on flesh in the person of Jesus Christ, God moved into a whole new neighborhood and set of experiences. Today we look at Jesus' brand-new first move in his ministry, his move into the desert. After being baptized, Jesus went immediately into the desert and fasted for forty days, where he was tempted by Satan. This move, into some of the most physically and spiritually demanding experiences humans can go through, showed that God in Jesus wasn't here for the tourist's view of earth, one where he would casually drive by our struggles and gaze out the tinted windows of his air-conditioned limo. No! Jesus actually walked through the toughest struggles you and I face.

Jesus' forty-day move into the desert also mirrors the experience of God's people when the Israelites moved through the desert for forty years. In those forty difficult years, God's children "grumbled for bread, flirted disastrously with idolatry, and put God continually to the test," as Tom Wright puts it in his commentary *Luke for Everyone*.[1] Jesus faced these exact temptations, but instead of letting his appetites and desires rule him, he leaned on his Father, responding with God's Word immediately and decisively.

You and I probably won't ever be tempted in the same ways Jesus was, but every single one of us moves through desert times of loneliness, emptiness, and temptation to sin. When we do, we know we can rely on Jesus to walk with us and show us the way. He's been there before and conquered the most difficult experiences we could imagine. Moving is hard, and our move to Easter will bring new and unique challenges, but we have a Savior who has promised to walk beside us every step.

1. Tom Wright, *Luke for Everyone* (Louisville, KY: Westminster John Knox Press, 2004), 43.

At that very hour some Pharisees came to Jesus and said to him, "Get away from here, for Herod wants to kill you." He said to them, "Go and tell that fox for me, 'Listen, I am casting out demons and performing cures today and tomorrow, and on the third day I finish my work. Yet today, tomorrow, and the next day I must be on my way, because it is impossible for a prophet to be killed outside Jerusalem.'" (Luke 13:31–33)

It shouldn't surprise us that as Jesus' ministry progresses, major obstacles begin to stand in his way. The most obvious are the members of the political and religious establishments, both feeling threatened by him for different reasons. The Pharisees (spiritual leaders) show up with a warning about Herod (the political leader), but can their warning be trusted? Do they have Jesus' best interests in mind? Herod wants to kill him, a warning that sounds pretty sobering for one moving in on Herod's territory in Jerusalem. Surely this is an obstacle that Jesus should take seriously in his planning to move forward!

Jesus' determination is clear: I will keep on. . . . I will reach my goal. . . . I must press on. For Jesus, there is no turning back. He is on a course that cannot be interrupted, not even by a dangerous and murderous leader. "You tell that fox," he says, "that I will reach my goal." We associate foxes with being clever, cunning. But the truth is that a fox is deceptive and wily, a small animal reduced to chasing weak animals like chicks in the chicken yard, because it has no intrinsic power. Basically, Jesus is calling Herod a varmint.

And what of the chicks themselves? The city on Jesus' radar, the one at the end of his unstoppable course, is Jerusalem. Jesus compares his love for Jerusalem to a mother hen's love for her chicks and her desire to gather, protect, and cherish them. But Jerusalem, this cherished city, has responded to God's clear love for them with rebellion, selfish ambition, and violence. Jesus holds these two facts in tension. He loves Jerusalem, but ultimately his love for her will be the death of him. In this way Jerusalem is a stand-in for all of us here. Jesus' love for us is so strong that it leads to his death.

Which is the bigger obstacle? Herod's murderous plot to stop Jesus before he reaches Jerusalem or the cherished city itself, loved by the Messiah whom it will ultimately kill upon arrival? Jesus' answer to both obstacles is that nothing—even his own death—can stop him from reaching the goal of loving his children. Jesus' love is opposed from the outside, and he keeps moving toward the object of his love. Jesus' love is rejected, and he still keeps on track to give that love away.

It's Lent, and that means we've set a course for ourselves, a course that will end in Jerusalem, at the cross and the tomb. We need to prepare ourselves to arrive in Jerusalem, to face the cross, or we won't be able to take it all in. We need to ask if our course is set as resolutely as that of Jesus. Do we have a commitment to set our faces to Jerusalem, to the place where we meet God face-to-face and give our lives up for him? Will we be stopped by the people on earth who might not be pleased with the goal we have chosen? By the obstacles outside of us? By the obstacles that arise within our own hearts?

Jesus is on an unstoppable course toward Jerusalem, but that also means that he's on an unstoppable course toward us, toward our hearts, with tenacity and determination that will not be blocked, not even by the obstacles we put in his place.

Lent 3: God Moves . . . over the Fence
Luke 13:1–9

Then he told this parable: "A man had a fig tree planted in his vineyard; and he came looking for fruit on it and found none. So he said to the gardener, "See here! For three years I have come looking for fruit on this fig tree, and still I find none. Cut it down! Why should it be wasting the soil?" He replied, "Sir, let it alone for one more year, until I dig around it and put manure on it. If it bears fruit next year, well and good; but if not, you can cut it down." (Luke 13:6–9)

We've all heard the phrase "The grass is always greener on the other side of the fence." There's a reason it's so well known. Our human nature often compels us to look around and compare our own lives with those we see in person, on TV, even on Facebook and Twitter. When we do, we either come out on top and feel superior, or we find some inadequacy in ourselves that makes us feel our lives are inferior. This tendency prompted someone to quip defensively, "The grass may be greener, but boy, have you seen their water bill?"

Jesus was a master of helping pull people back across the fence to look at their own property. When people asked him, who is my neighbor?, he challenged them (through the parable of the Good Samaritan) to look at ways they could self-sacrificially give even to those they didn't consider neighbors at all. When a group of men in the temple tried to force Jesus publicly to judge a woman who had committed adultery, he encouraged them to look inward first and see what sins they found in themselves (then released her with gentle encouragement to sin no more).

When a group of people brought up to Jesus a tragedy that had happened and asked if those who died deserved it because they were more wicked sinners, Jesus saw through the comparison, right to the heart of the issue. Disasters do not come to those who are disobedient, but imagining that those who are facing them somehow deserve misfortune makes us feel a bit safer and better about ourselves.

Jesus didn't let these fence gazers keep their vision in the distance for long. He immediately challenged them with these words: "Unless you repent, you will all perish just as they did." That kind of language will bring your view back into your own yard pretty quickly!

Jesus followed the challenge with a story about a barren fig tree that was not bearing fruit. Feeling it had served its purpose, the owner wanted to cut it down, but the gardener pleaded for just one more year to water, fertilize, and nurture it in an effort to bring it to the fruitfulness for which it was created. Because of the gardener's commitment to work to bring out the best in it, the tree was allowed one more year to change its ways and become fruitful, or it would be cut down.

Isn't it amazing that on Easter morning Mary mistook Jesus for a gardener just outside his tomb? Jesus not only calls us to stop looking over the fence at others, and instead notice the dead spots in our lives; he actually promises to care for us until those places come to life again. Gazing over to the other side of the fence helps us only avoid confronting our issues, but Jesus brings our gaze to the truth, and that truth is the beginning of being set free. We are, every one of us, living in the season of second chances, having been saved from the ax by Jesus' desire to restore us to our best. We may climb over the fence from time to time, wondering about the lives lived on property surrounding our own, but Jesus brings us back over the fence to the place we find healing and change—right in our own backyard.

Lent 4: God Moves . . . down the Road
Luke 15:1–3, 11b–32

"So he set off and went to his father. But while he was still far off, his father saw him and was filled with compassion; he ran and put his arms around him and kissed him. Then the son said to him, 'Father, I have sinned against heaven and before you; I am no longer worthy to be called your son.' But the father said to his slaves, 'Quickly, bring out a robe—the best one—and put it on him; put a ring on his finger and sandals on his feet. And get the fatted calf and kill it, and let us eat and celebrate; for this son of mine was dead and is alive again; he was lost and is found!' And they began to celebrate." (Luke 15:17–24)

In 2007 a woman in Oregon won $1 million on a scratch-off lottery ticket. Two weeks after collecting her money, when she had already spent $30,000 of her winnings, authorities discovered that she had bought the ticket under a false identity, using the credit card of her boyfriend's deceased mother. They took away her winnings and prosecuted her, of course. But how did they find out about the crime? Only because, after she had won the million, she had continued to use the fraudulent credit card! She had a million dollars in hand, but she was still charging credit on a dead woman's credit card.[2]

Why would someone risk a fortune that was certain, only to gamble on risky behavior? That might be the question we would ask the prodigal son, if we could meet him face-to-face and shake him by his robes before he made his grand exit, trying to knock some sense into him. This young man has a loving home and family, his physical needs provided for, and an inheritance "in the bank," waiting for a day when he's mature enough to handle it wisely. Why does he take his father's money and run? Why do any of us turn from the goodness of God? For a lifetime or a momentary lapse? It's hard to say why we continue to gamble when the fortune is already ours.

The focus on the son in this story has been often contested. He may be the one with the most action, but the father is the most compelling character. Rebellious sons are a dime a dozen, but it's the father whose behavior surprises us. His graciousness begins long before the closing arc of the story. He hands over the fortune that his son demands, even though that premature request for an inheritance means the son is rejecting his identity and his family and wishing that his father were dead. Then he stands on the porch and watches the boy go out into the world, knowing his son well enough to know what he will do with the money, knowing the world well enough to know how it will respond.

The son goes down the wrong road, but the father stays put, always staring at the spot where he saw his son disappear, watching the road for a day when things will be different. When the son appears on the horizon, prepared for chastisement, servanthood, even banishment, the father stands still no longer. He runs. It's hard for us to understand what an incredible picture this is unless we know that in those days the men wore long robes, and men of age and stature did not run. It was not dignified. But this father loved his son more than his dignity, hiked up his skirts, and sprinted off to reach him.

The son in the story experienced exactly what the book of James describes: "Draw near to God, and he will draw near to you" (Jas. 4:8). But it could say, "He will run to you." Even when we squander the incredible fortune that is God's love and gamble on pleasure that never lasts, God does not stay stuck frozen in anger or resentment.

---

2. "Oregon Woman Loses Her $1 Million Jackpot," *Seattle Times*, August 10, 2007; http://seattle times.nwsource.com/html/localnews/2003830331_weblottery10m.html.

No, he runs up the road to meet us, again and again, propelled by grace.

Lent 5: God Moves Us . . . to Empty Ourselves
John 12:1–8

Mary took a pound of costly perfume made of pure nard, anointed Jesus' feet, and wiped them with her hair. The house was filled with the fragrance of the perfume. But Judas Iscariot, one of his disciples (the one who was about to betray him), said, "Why was this perfume not sold for three hundred denarii and the money given to the poor?" . . . Jesus said, "Leave her alone. She bought it so that she might keep it for the day of my burial. You always have the poor with you, but you do not always have me." (John 12:3–5, 7–8)

It's easy to recognize memories bound up in visions of old photographs or the familiar melody of an old song. But our sense of smell is also closely tied to memory. A perfume can evoke a lost memory of someone you haven't seen in years. A whiff of a sharp cleaning fluid or a rotting dumpster can transport you to a place you'd forgotten. The smell of a certain baked good rising in the oven can bring you right back to a holiday when you were a child or to the presence of your grandmother. (You might consider exposing your congregation to a scent during worship: bread machines baking bread if you're taking Communion, fresh baked cookies or cinnamon rolls greeting them in the gathering area, or popcorn as they leave. Mention it here and remind them of how smells evoke emotions and memories. Avoid using perfume, as it may aggravate people's allergies.)

In this story a strong scent brings up strong emotions in the people who surround Jesus. When we find him, he is on the move again, on his final route to Jerusalem, where we know his story will end with the tragedy and victory he's been proclaiming all along. But first, Jesus stops at the home of some good friends. We're familiar with the family of Mary, Martha, and Lazarus from the encounters they've had with Jesus before—sibling struggles over work in the kitchen and Lazarus's being brought back to life by Jesus.

This time they're at the table once again, but the scent of good food is overcome by the strong stench of controversy as Mary breaks open an expensive vial of perfume and begins to use it to anoint Jesus' feet. Judas strenuously objects, supposedly out of sensible charity: the money for that perfume could have been given to the poor. (But we can never read any of Judas's story without thinking of its ending, and we are narrowing our eyes knowingly even as he feigns selfless motives.)

I wonder what that perfume smelled like. Does sacrifice have a scent? Is there a unique aroma to the greatest loss we've ever known, a life given for the sake of gain for the whole world? Mary pours out the treasure she has saved and wipes her Savior's feet, and he praises her actions. In the next few days he will turn around and wash the feet of his disciples before pouring out his life for them and us.

Not only were the sick anointed for healing and the dead anointed for burial, but kings were anointed as a consecration to set them apart for leadership and authority. Mary's anointing carried with it the scent of brokenness and death but also ironically the scent of power, a king coming into his kingdom. This is the strange paradox of Jesus' act of giving of himself for us: anyone who wants to save his life will lose it, but anyone who loses his life will save it. Sacrifice as victory, loss as gain: Do you and I dare to wear the same perfume as our Lord? When we are with people, do they catch a hint of the scent of sacrifice on us?

Lent 6: God Moves . . . to the Cross
Luke 23:1–49

The soldiers also mocked him, coming up and offering him sour wine, and saying, "If you are the King of the Jews, save yourself!" There was also an inscription over him, "This is the King of the Jews." (Luke 23:36–38)

Jesus' whole life has been filled with paradoxes. How can an immortal God with no beginning and no end have a birthday? How does his father go looking for him and find him in his Father's house? How does the creator of the world, the owner of the cattle on a thousand hills, have no place to lay his head? Finally, as Charles Wesley wrote, "'Tis mystery all, the immortal dies."

Nowhere is the irony of Jesus' life stronger than in the expectations of his royalty. He is descended from David, the greatest king Israel had known. He is the Messiah, or anointed one, who is expected to rule and reign. Mary has anointed him as kings are anointed, and now we come to the point of his coronation, but it's nothing like what anyone following his story of royal aspirations would ever have expected. He is moving to his kingdom . . . via a cross of torture.

Kings are not martyrs. They do not die self-sacrificial deaths. In the fairy tales they live happily ever after with their queen by their side. In the history books they die at the hands of an enemy or a rival, but always self-protectively, not self-sacrificially. Here the King of Kings is given a crown to wear and a placard is placed over his head: "This is the King of the Jews." Instead of a royal cupbearer he is offered sour wine. Instead of commanding an army he is surrounded by soldiers who mock and beat him.

There is only one in the story who uses his title unironically. Jesus does not die alone: with one criminal on his right and one on his left, he finally hears a single voice of sincerity among the jeers of the crowd: "Jesus, remember me when you come into your kingdom." He is truly hailed as king at last—and it's by a petty thief.

Jesus spent so much time explaining and demonstrating what the kingdom of God looks like, and we still have a hard time understanding. Is it a mustard seed? A pearl? Yeast working its way through dough? If his kingdom, which he took such pains to describe, was so hard to grasp, it is no wonder we have a hard time recognizing him as king at the end.

Jesus' whole life was a paradox, his actions unexpected, his choice of followers startling, his path to power the path of defeat and death. The cross is the final moment of confusion for the royal watchers among us. This can't be it? Can it? Can this be what he was intending to do with his reign?

If God met our expectations, how small would the kingdom be? If the kind of king we anticipated had begun to rule, wouldn't that have been just as short lived a kingdom as that of any other earthly king, surrounded by wealth and glory and power for just as long as a single human life could grasp those things? Instead, we have this unexpected king, his final throne a cross, his final words a proclamation of forgiveness, his final act one that ensured this kingdom would not end.

Easter: God Moves . . . out of the Tomb
Luke 24:1–12

But on the first day of the week, at early dawn, they came to the tomb, taking the spices that they had prepared. They found the stone rolled away from the tomb, but when they went in, they did not find the body. While they were perplexed about this, suddenly two men in dazzling clothes stood beside them. The women were terrified and bowed their faces to the ground, but the men said to them, "Why do you look for the living among the dead? He is not here, but has risen." (Luke 24:1–5)

A bank in Binghamton, New York, had some flowers sent to a competitor who had recently expanded their business into a new building. There was a mix-up at the flower shop, and the card sent with the arrangement read, "With our deepest sympathy." The florist, who was greatly embarrassed, said he couldn't imagine how this mix-up happened, and he apologized. It was halfway through the day before he sat up, with a horrified look on his face, realizing that at some funeral somebody was opening a note that read, "Congratulations on your new location!"[3]

When the women approached the tomb on Easter morning, it was with the grief and devastation of Good Friday. They were bringing spices and oils to anoint a body—the dead body of their Savior and friend. They were stuck in a world proclaiming a message like the card: "With our deepest sympathy." Those who opposed Jesus, both the Roman and religious authorities, had worked hard to stop him and silence his message. They saw a man who sparked a movement—whose ministry moved throughout that country with power and authority—and they knew the movement had to stop.

What they didn't know was that even death could not stop Jesus, who was God-on-the-move among us. The women arrived to see a stone that had rolled and a world that had changed, even though they didn't know it yet. They expected to encounter a continuation of the message of grief and sympathy that had begun on Friday; instead they found Sunday's message of congratulations and a Savior who would not be contained to one location.

Throughout his ministry Jesus encountered profound brokenness in the world and went about reversing that brokenness. Where he found sickness he healed people, where he found hunger he fed people, where he found sin and death he brought forgiveness and resurrection. The question of the tomb is this: would he be strong enough to reverse even the brokenness the world had inflicted on him? We have encountered stories of resurrection in Scripture before, but no one has ever resurrected themselves! God is always in the business of stopping evil, bringing wholeness, and defying death, and this was the ultimate occasion to prove that mission.

What a beautiful thing that even the tomb cannot stop Jesus. Just when evil thinks they've stopped him, he's on to a new location! It's no accident that in Luke's telling, the story that immediately follows his resurrection is the story of the road to Emmaus, where Jesus is on the move again, walking with his followers. Two of his disciples are on their way home, broken in grief by the events of Jesus' death, and there he is with them! They think they're going home to lick their wounds in sadness and grief; but Jesus shows up, and they are so moved that they change their direction and run back to Jerusalem to share the news.

3. *Our Daily Bread*, May 25, 1992.

This is just the first instance of how the empty tomb, the rolling stone, the Savior breaking the chains of death move his followers. Wherever you are feeling stuck or trapped, wherever your past has told you that you will never change, wherever you encounter a world that seems to be lost in grief and pain—you will find a moving Savior. Today is a day of congratulations for God's people. For new locations and second chances. For new hopes and dreams. Death tried to stop our Jesus and did not succeed. He is alive and moving in our world and our lives today. Hallelujah!

Easter Series: Surprise! The Unexpected Acts of God

Seven Parts: Second Sunday of Easter through Pentecost

The unlikely, ironic, and surprising stories in the book of Acts.

JESSICA LaGRONE

Series Overview This series beginning with the Sunday after Easter focuses on surprising acts of God in the book of Acts. We all know the excitement and disquiet that come with the sudden reversal of our expectations. The early Christians whose stories are told in the book of Acts have no shortage of surprises. The resurrection sets off a host of unexpected events and changes for Jesus' followers, even changes within themselves. If our own spiritual lives have come to seem humdrum and everyday, these stories will awaken in us a new desire for God's work in the lives of unsuspecting, ordinary people like ourselves. As we explore the journey of surprises in these texts, we will learn the spiritual habit of welcoming an unpredictable God and coming to expect the unexpected.

	Sermon Title	Focus Scripture	Theme
Second Sunday of Easter	A Surprising Turnaround	Acts 5:27–32	The resurrection can spark changes in our beliefs and behavior that surprise even ourselves.
Third Sunday of Easter	An Unlikely Friendship	Acts 9:1–20	God often brings us the surprising gift of friendships we never expected.
Fourth Sunday of Easter	An Astonishing Imitation	Acts 9:36–43	By imitating Christ we become more like him and bring other people's attention to his glory.
Fifth Sunday of Easter	An Unexpected Change of Menu	Acts 11:1–18	When we think we have God figured out, he surprises us by revealing his heart for the unexpected.

	Sermon Title	Focus Scripture	Theme
Sixth Sunday of Easter	An Amazing Detour	Acts 16:9–15	The power of conversion is still God's building block to change the world one person at a time.
Seventh Sunday of Easter	An Ironic Escape	Acts 16:16–34	Sometimes those who seem free are truly enslaved, and those who seem to be in chains are truly liberated.
Pentecost	Pentecost: The Ultimate Surprise Party	Acts 2:1–21	All the astonishing events in Acts (and in the church since) can be traced back to this one surprising moment.

Tips and Ideas for This Series

Include stories of surprises in every sermon: surprise parties, times God surprised you by bringing good in the midst of hardship, times you surprised yourself by having courage, times you were surprised by the goodness of others. Encourage your congregation to create surprises for others during the series and share their stories: paying for a stranger's coffee or meal at a restaurant, for example. As a community you could surprise someone who has had a difficult time or who is simply underappreciated (your church's custodian or secretary might be a good start). The final week of this series is Pentecost, the birthday of the church, so go all out with a surprise birthday party for the congregation to enjoy, complete with cake, streamers, and balloons.

Second Sunday of Easter: A Surprising Turnaround
Acts 5:27–32

When they had brought them, they had them stand before the council. The high priest questioned them, saying, "We gave you strict orders not to teach in this name, yet here you have filled Jerusalem with your teaching and you are determined to bring this man's blood on us." But Peter and the apostles answered, "We must obey God rather than any human authority." (Acts 5:27–29)

Last week was Easter Sunday, the Sunday we celebrated the biggest surprise the world has ever known. Jesus Christ, arrested, tortured, and executed in plain sight, surprised everyone by defeating death and escaping alive from the tomb. This single surprise changed human history forever, but it also set in motion a series of surprising adventures for Jesus' followers recorded in the Acts of the Apostles.

During Holy Week we saw Jesus' disciples become so intimidated and terrified by the horror of watching what their rabbi went through on his journey to the cross that they scattered in fear. Can we blame them? They knew that even to associate with Jesus during this terrible week could mean a cross for them as well.

Peter in particular was scared into denying Jesus in his greatest hour of need, just as Jesus had predicted. Far from being an isolated event, this is the same Peter who doubted Jesus when he told him (after fishing all night) to try throwing the nets out on the other side of the boat. The same Peter who, with the other disciples, told Jesus to send five thousand people home from a hillside because there just wasn't enough to feed all of them.

Imagine Peter's surprise when there were nets full of fish, people full of food (and twelve full baskets left over!), and then, finally and most importantly, the tomb empty of the body of his Savior. God surprised Peter again and again by doing the impossible, the wonderfully unexpected, the miraculous.

In today's reading from the book of Acts, we meet Peter again, but this time he's the one surprising us! The apostles have boldly been proclaiming the news about the resurrection, and as a result they are thrown in prison. But during the night an angel releases them and tells them to go and publicly share the good news right in the temple court! This is the boldest possible move: they've been arrested by the high priest, but they return to the public center of religious activity and do again what they were arrested for doing. Instead of running away or hiding, Peter and the others are faithful to obey what God has told them to do and then stand up to the high priest and the other leaders. When confronted with doing exactly what they've been told not to do, Peter and the other apostles replied: "We must obey God rather than human beings!"

What a turnaround! From running away from the cross to standing in the temple courts telling the story of the resurrection. Peter has been surprised by God for so long he's learned a lesson—that you can bet God will surprise you. No matter how grim the circumstances look, God always has something up his sleeve. Peter has learned to bank on it, and it has turned him into a new person. He is an example of a complete turnaround in faith.

Sometimes the unexpected work of God in our lives leads us to surprise even ourselves. Have you ever surprised yourself by acting in faith instead of in fear? God leads us to lean on his unseen potential for surprise rather than to obey the seen expectations of this world.

Third Sunday of Easter: An Unlikely Friendship
Acts 9:1–20

But the Lord said to [Ananias], "Go! This man is my chosen instrument to proclaim my name to the Gentiles and their kings and to the people of Israel. I myself will show him how much he must suffer for the sake of my name." So Ananias went and entered the house. He laid his hands on Saul and said, "Brother Saul, the Lord Jesus, who appeared to you on your way here, has sent me that you may regain your sight and be filled with the Holy Spirit." And immediately something like scales fell from his eyes, and his sight was restored. Then he got up and was baptized, and after taking some food, he regained his strength. (Acts 9:15–19)

Ron Hall and Denver Moore had one of the most unlikely friendships you could imagine. They were about as different as two men could be: Denver was a homeless African American man living on the streets of Fort Worth, Texas. A former sharecropper from Louisiana, he had gone to prison for trying to rob a bus at gunpoint. Ron was a bond trader turned art dealer, a married college graduate living in suburbia with his wife and two kids. When Ron and his wife, Deborah, met Denver at a mission where they volunteered, an unlikely friendship began.

While their relationship began as the haves sharing with the have-nots, it quickly turned into a friendship between equals. When Deborah was diagnosed with liver cancer, Denver became her most faithful prayer warrior, pouring his heart out to God for her. Her death was the catalyst for Ron and Denver to become more like brothers than friends. Each man discovered something in the other that he needed, something God had put there as a surprise gift, one that could be discovered only when each of them opened himself to a friendship with someone as different as they could be.[1]

God often places people in our lives who we might not have chosen as friends for ourselves. Maybe you've met someone in your own life who may be different from you in background, profession, beliefs, or other ways. You may not have sought them out, but God gave you a chance to receive the gifts he placed in them.

Ananias and Saul were natural enemies. They were headed for a collision course, not a bromance. Saul had stood guard over the execution of Stephen, the first Christian martyr and one of Ananias's brothers in faith. When Ananias is told to go to Saul and lay hands on him in healing prayer, it's no surprise that he balks, wondering if Saul will instead lay hands on him in a different way. God assures him that this Saul is "an instrument whom I have chosen to bring my name

---

1. This story is told in the book *Same Kind of Different as Me* by Ron Hall and Denver Moore (Nashville: Thomas Nelson, 2008).

before Gentiles and kings and before the people of Israel." Only God knows how he can use someone, no matter how lost or antagonistic they seem to us.

God is full of surprises. Saul will become Paul, an apostle whose witness will forever change the spread of faith in Christ around the world. We should keep our eyes open to those around us, asking if God has called us to enter their lives in improbable but holy friendship. After all, the most unlikely friendship that could have developed is the one between the Creator of the universe and us, his creations. Who could imagine that our Creator and Lord would long to become our friend, even as antagonistic as we may have originally been to the idea. Ananias and Saul show us that God can call us to put aside our differences and serve him together.

Fourth Sunday of Easter: An Astonishing Imitation
Acts 9:36–43

So Peter got up and went with them; and when he arrived, they took him to the room upstairs. All the widows stood beside him, weeping and showing tunics and other clothing that Dorcas had made while she was with them. Peter put all of them outside, and then he knelt down and prayed. He turned to the body and said, "Tabitha, get up." Then she opened her eyes, and seeing Peter, she sat up. He gave her his hand and helped her up. Then calling the saints and widows, he showed her to be alive. (Acts 9:39–41)

Great artists aren't just born, they are made. They practice, toil, paint, and sculpt over and over until they produce something worthwhile; but there are many first drafts the world never sees. One of the techniques artists have learned over the years to improve on their talent is the art of imitation. *Harper's Weekly* ran an article in the late 1800s about Americans flocking to the famous Louvre museum in Paris to copy the work of the masters found there. The article claimed that "the true artist, the real one, copies the picture of some great master, and follows it out not only with his eyes and hands, but with his heart and soul."[2]

If imitation is the most sincere form of flattery, then what better way to give praise and glory to God than by imitating Jesus? Our story today from the book of Acts tells about a time when someone's life was profoundly changed by the imitation of Christ.

Tabitha (also called Dorcas) is introduced to us in this story with two surprises right from the beginning: (1) she's dead before we have

2. http://www.rockwell-center.org/essays-illustration/artists-learning-by-copying/.

a chance to know her, and (2) she's called a disciple (an unusual title for a woman to be known by in those days). But why not? She is a follower of Jesus, not just in name, but in the goodness of her life that has become her reputation, known to all through her good works and acts of charity. She's been an imitator of Jesus in life, and now she has died. It's significant that she is surrounded by widows who are mourning her death. These widows may have been recipients of Tabitha's goodness, as they show off garments that she made for them, the physical remnants of a life filled with caring for others.

When the believers in Joppa hear that Peter is close by, they send for him, believing that one who was so close to Jesus will know exactly what to do. But do they expect that Peter will raise her from the dead? Does Peter expect it himself? Sometimes we don't know what to expect, but we do know that we can turn to God for help and trust God to determine the rest.

When Peter walks into the situation, he does the only thing he knows how to do: he imitates Jesus. The whole situation is an uncanny replication of a story he once witnessed while looking over Jesus' shoulder where a young girl died and was raised to life (Mark 5:35–43). Peter is summoned by messengers and finds weeping bystanders. He imitates Jesus so closely when he asks mourners to leave the room, commands Tabitha to arise in the same language Jesus once used, and takes her by the hand. I wonder, is he as surprised as everyone else when it works?

You and I may not ever witness a resurrection, but it's clear that Jesus wants us to imitate him, to do what he did, on a daily basis. Ephesians instructs us to "be imitators of God, as beloved children, and live in love, as Christ loved us and gave himself up for us, a fragrant offering and sacrifice to God" (Eph. 5:1–2). Tabitha was a disciple, a follower of Jesus, because she imitated him in love and service to others. Peter spent so much time with Jesus that he couldn't help but imitate what he'd seen Jesus do—even to the point of raising someone from the dead. Our lives should be imitations—not cheap ones—but imitations that show off the glory of the original as we work on copying the Master.

Fifth Sunday of Easter: An Unexpected Change of Menu
Acts 11:1–18

"I was in the city of Joppa praying, and in a trance I saw a vision. There was something like a large sheet coming down from heaven, being lowered by its four corners; and it came close to me. As I looked at it closely I saw four-footed animals, beasts of prey, reptiles, and birds

of the air. I also heard a voice saying to me, 'Get up, Peter; kill and eat.' But I replied, 'By no means, Lord; for nothing profane or unclean has ever entered my mouth.' But a second time the voice answered from heaven, 'What God has made clean, you must not call profane.'" (Acts 11:5–8)

Imagine a big celebration you've had in the past with those you love all around you—maybe a graduation, a wedding, a Thanksgiving or Christmas. Do you have the scene set in your mind? Is it clear whose faces are around the table? Friends? Family? Now—quick—what are you eating? You probably don't have to think about that one for long. Our celebrations often revolve around food, and our recollections of those events often contain as many memories of flavors and smells as they do of conversations and relationships.

Now imagine that someone changed the menu. You arrived at the next celebration expecting the traditional fare: turkey and dressing, or wedding cake, or your favorite lasagna or apple pie—and SUR-PRISE! You ended up with something completely different on your plate. Would you be startled? Disappointed? Upset?

Peter's attention to detail of menu went far beyond tradition and expectation. For him it was a matter of faithfulness to God and God's commands. To eat the things lowered on the sheet in his dream would mean more than a change of menu. In his understanding, it was just as much of a sin as lying or adultery or murder. So for Peter to come to terms with these menu changes, enough to tell the believers of Judea that the items on the sheet are clean and acceptable to eat, is life changing. But he has been told by a voice from heaven: "What God has made clean, you must not call profane."

Just as astounding as Peter's announcement of what is OK to eat is his announcement of whom to expect around the table. For us, "You are what you eat" is a mantra we all know, but those in Peter's day would have found it even more important to say, "You are whom you eat with." Jews did not eat with Gentiles, did not accept their hospitality, and believed to do so would mean they would become culturally and spiritually polluted. Now the menu has changed, and so have the table companions, and this radical change is causing quite a stir among the followers of Christ who were first Jewish.

There are three surprisingly filling moments in this story: First, Peter receives orders to fill himself with all kinds of foods he has pre-viously thought off limits. Second, he receives an equally surprising order to fulfill an invitation to the house of non-Jews. Third, suddenly his new Gentile friends are filled with the Spirit of God. It's the move-ment of the Holy Spirit into the new Gentile believers that finally convinces Peter's critics, those who believed you had to follow Jewish law to follow Jesus. After all, if entering these believers hearts is good enough for the Holy Spirit, who are they to say that they are unclean or unworthy?

The shocking truth they have to accept is this: Gentiles are on God's menu of acceptable converts. In fact, everyone is on God's menu as a person fit for his love and grace. As we look around us, we should ask: who out there have we assumed is off God's menu?

Sixth Sunday of Easter: An Amazing Detour
Acts 16:9–15

On the sabbath day we went outside the gate by the river, where we supposed there was a place of prayer; and we sat down and spoke to the women who had gathered there. A certain woman named Lydia, a worshiper of God, was listening to us; she was from the city of Thyatira and a dealer in purple cloth. The Lord opened her heart to listen eagerly to what was said by Paul. When she and her household were baptized, she urged us, saying, "If you have judged me to be faithful to the Lord, come and stay at my home." And she prevailed upon us. (Acts 16:13–15)

Michael Billester visited a small town in Poland in the late 1930s, shortly before World War II began. He met a man in the village and gave him a single Bible. The man read it and was converted to faith in Christ. He then passed the Bible on to others who were also converted, until two hundred people had become believers through that one Bible.

When Billester returned to the little town in 1940, this group of Christians met together for a worship service in which he was to preach the Word. He thought of asking them to give testimonies, but this time he suggested that several in the audience recite verses of Scripture. One man stood and asked, "Perhaps we have misunderstood. Did you mean verses or chapters?"

These villagers had not memorized a few select verses of the Bible but whole chapters and books. Thirteen people knew Matthew, Luke, and half of Genesis. Another person had committed to memory the Psalms. That single copy of the Bible given by Billester had sunk deeply into the community and the hearts of those who received it. The surprising results of that one small Bible had born fruit of hundreds of lives changed.[3]

With all the big surprises found in the book of Acts, perhaps we're surprised to find the little old story of Lydia recorded here. Her story begins with a detour: Paul has a vision that a man from Macedonia

3. "Only One Bible," Bible.org, February 2, 2009, https://bible.org/illustration/only-one-bible

is pleading for his help. When he arrives, he finds not a man but a group of women who listen to his teaching (a surprising event, given the times and the culture, but not surprising in the context of the rest of Luke and Acts, where women are honored and elevated in faith). When Lydia opens her heart to receive the words about Jesus and becomes a follower of Christ, we learn that her own life will take a major detour as well. She and her entire household are baptized, and a new spark is ignited in Macedonia that could spread into a blaze.

Why, in a book of big miracles and major events, do we find the story of one woman coming to faith? Why bother to give her story top billing here among dramatic and stunning events? Because God has always worked to change the world one life at a time. Lydia, just like the rest of us, has a choice of whether to listen and follow when she hears God's Word for the first time. And she does open her heart and then her home to the message of the gospel. Who knows what will happen in her town because of her?

Michael Billester's story of the little town in Poland reminds us that the faithfulness of one person's life changed, one little Bible shared, one faithful risk taken for God's kingdom can be a tiny change that surprisingly shakes the foundations of entire communities. As we look at the big surprises God has brought into being in Acts and in our world today, we need to remember that changed hearts are major events and big victories as well.

Seventh Sunday of Easter: An Ironic Escape
Acts 16:16–34

About midnight Paul and Silas were praying and singing hymns to God, and the prisoners were listening to them. Suddenly there was an earthquake, so violent that the foundations of the prison were shaken; and immediately all the doors were opened and everyone's chains were unfastened. When the jailer woke up and saw the prison doors wide open, he drew his sword and was about to kill himself, since he supposed that the prisoners had escaped. But Paul shouted in a loud voice, "Do not harm yourself, for we are all here." The jailer called for lights, and rushing in, he fell down trembling before Paul and Silas. Then he brought them outside and said, "Sirs, what must I do to be saved?" (Acts 16:25–30)

In the movie *The Shawshank Redemption* prisoners exercise by pacing the yard at Shawshank Prison, making plans for what they will do once they're released, and even scheming about how to escape. One of the older prisoners, Brooks, is released after spending most of his life behind bars. You'd think after a life of imprisonment he'd look forward to freedom. Instead there's fear and anxiety about whether he can make it in such a different kind of world. After trying to make it on the outside, he carves his name into a beam in the boarding house where he's staying and then sadly takes his own life, hanging himself from the same beam. He had become so accustomed to captivity that the free world seemed too much to bear.

In Acts, there is a story full of surprising contradictions between freedom and imprisonment. First, we meet someone whose freedom is compromised: a slave girl. This girl may be free to follow Paul and Silas around, but in truth she is not free at all. In fact she is doubly enslaved: bound by the evil spirit that inhabits her and taken advantage of by the slave owners who use her to make money off of her fortune-telling. She is calling Paul and Silas slaves (of the Most High God), for she knows slavery well, and declaring that they are proclaiming salvation. Paul frees her of her evil spirit, more because of annoyance than compassion, and promptly finds himself immediately in trouble with her owners, who are too much slaves to their own financial gain to appreciate her newfound emancipation.

What do Paul and Silas get for their generosity in freeing the girl? They are dragged to the authorities, attacked by the crowd, stripped, beaten, and thrown into prison—a bad day at the office, to say the least. So what do they do once in prison? At midnight they are still praying and singing hymns to God while the other prisoners listen incredulously. Their bodies are in chains, but their spirits are free to worship.

Then an earthquake remedies the problem of the chains. The visible manifestation of God's power shakes the foundations, not only of the prison but of the earthly powers as well. Nothing can keep his servants locked up forever, and Paul and Silas are now free to go. The jailer, on the other hand, while he seems to be a free man, is so enslaved to his authorities that he is about to attempt suicide rather than face what they will do to him if he has lost his prisoners. Paul and Silas reassure him that they are still there, and he ironically does what he was afraid the earthquake had done—liberates them from prison and brings them out to his own home, where he now becomes a joyful follower of Jesus himself. After washing the physical wounds of the prisoners, he is washed in the waters of baptism, and he and his whole household become believers in Jesus.

This jailer and his entire newly baptized household—mentioned here again and assumed to include adults, slaves, and children—are rejoicing in their new faith as the story ends, despite the problem of the magistrates punishing him for having let such high-profile visitors go free. This is a great story of reversals: everyone whom we assume to be free (the jailer, the magistrates, the owners of the slave girl) is really in bondage, and everyone whom we assume to be enslaved (Paul and Silas and the slave girl) has been freed.

Having the key to lock someone up doesn't make you a free person. Being on the inside of prison bars doesn't necessarily mean you aren't free. The determiner of freedom is so available, so accessible, so immediate, that we don't have to wait for a key to unlock it or an earthquake to experience it. "If the Son makes you free, you will be free indeed" (John 8:36).

Pentecost: The Ultimate Surprise Party
Acts 2:1–21

When the day of Pentecost had come, they were all together in one place. And suddenly from heaven there came a sound like the rush of a violent wind, and it filled the entire house where they were sitting. Divided tongues, as of fire, appeared among them, and a tongue rested on each of them. All of them were filled with the Holy Spirit and began to speak in other languages, as the Spirit gave them ability. (Acts 2:1–4)

Bringing surprising results from lost causes is God's specialty. Take, for example, George Frideric Handel. His life was filled with debt and despair, loss and infirmity. A cerebral hemorrhage left him paralyzed on one side, and for four years he couldn't walk, much less write. Then, at age sixty, after attempting several mediocre compositions for opera, he fell even deeper into debt and hopelessness and assumed his life was over. At this point a friend challenged him to write a sacred oratorio, a work dedicated to God.

For twenty-four days Handel sequestered himself, read God's Word, and passionately worked nonstop, hardly stopping even to eat. His new work was far more ambitious than anything he had attempted before, a more grandiose production with all its lyrics taken straight from Scripture. At his lowest point he took the biggest risk. What emerged many consider the greatest oratorio ever written, *Messiah*. Millions of people have heard the inspiring melody and had their hearts lifted by the lyrics declaring God "King of Kings and Lord of Lords" and ending with a chorus of Hallelujahs that could have been sung straight from heaven.

Think this was a stand-alone event? A happenstance?

- Abraham and Sarah gave up after hoping for a child long into old age, until God made them a promise.
- Peter fished all night without a catch before Jesus told him to throw the nets on the other side.

- A woman who had been suffering with bleeding for twelve years walked in a crowd, feeling invisible and alone until she caught sight of Jesus and reached out for him.
- The body of the Savior of the world was placed in a tomb and sealed off with a stone . . . until the third day brought a surprise like the world had never seen.

Why are we surprised when God shows up and reverses circumstances that are stacked against him? Being astonished again and again by God's intervention is a bit like having friends who throw you a surprise party year after year on your birthday, but yet you are still thrown off guard in true shock when you open the door and the lights all come on to the tune of "Surprise!"

A different kind of surprise party was in store the day Jesus' followers were gathered together, waiting, fifty days after Easter. It wasn't someone coming in the door who would be surprised, but those gathered behind closed doors. They didn't know what to expect, but they certainly didn't anticipating anything like what happened; no one could have.

When we think of the strange events that happened in the room that Pentecost day, we often focus on the unusual occurrences: the tongues of fire, the violent wind, and the sudden ability to speak other languages. Those things certainly must have been the greatest shock of the moment for the disciples and their friends. But the hidden surprise, the truly astonishing outcome that occurred, is the change in the followers of Jesus—not just at the moment, but from that point on. Once they received the Holy Spirit, they were different. Bolder, more able to minister with power from above, less afraid of human retribution, more unified and certain of their purpose to spread the gospel. These were a few of the characteristics of a new body of believers born that day, one we call the church.

All of the surprising, amazing, unexpected events that happened throughout Acts, stories we've told throughout this series, would never have happened without the day of Pentecost, the day the church was born. Every Pentecost since then has been a celebration of the church's birthday, the day we remember with awe how the Holy Spirit took a ragtag band of followers (I'm talking about us here, not just those first disciples!) and made them into something powerful for God's kingdom. My prayer is that God will continue to surprise the world and us!

Summer Series 1: Intervention

Four Parts: Proper 6 through Proper 9

We serve a God who sees, cares, and—at times—intervenes in human affairs.

CLEOPHUS J. LaRUE

Series Overview In our contemporary age some people are uncomfortable with the notion of a God who intervenes from time to time in the earthly affairs of humankind. Yet the Scriptures are filled with such stories of God doing exactly that—intervening in human affairs to make right those things that are wanting and to bring to completeness those things that help us to be the kinds of people God is calling us to be. In this short series, we explore times in the Old and New Testaments when God intervened to correct injustice, spiritually free a demon-possessed man, instruct the disciples, and bring healing to

	Sermon Title	Focus Scripture	Theme
Proper 6	The God Who Sees and Sets Things Right	1 Kgs. 21:1–10, (11–14), 15–21a	Humans may temporarily thwart God's will for humankind, but ultimately God acts to make things right.
Proper 7	A Change of Heart, Not a Change of Scenery	Luke 8:26–39	The Lord's intervention may empower us to live with faithfulness and conviction in our current situations in order to transform them.
Proper 8	Intervening to Enlighten His Own	Luke 9:51–62	Often the Lord's intervention is intended to guide and direct his own as much as the people to whom our ministries are directed.
Proper 9	A Humbling Intervention for a Proud Commander	2 Kgs. 5:1–14	The way God chooses to intervene in our lives often surprises us in its simplicity.

a proud and powerful man. So let the record be clear, the Scriptures often portray God as a God who intervenes.

Tips and Ideas for This Series

As our usual connotations of the word "intervention" may include difficult family dynamics or military action, be wary of making God's intervention seem too frightening. Imagery for the series might be primarily typographical, with something bisecting the word "Intervention" or the word itself bisecting an image. Personal testimonies of times when God has intervened in the lives of congregants can be especially powerful alongside the stories of God's actions in Scripture.

Proper 6: The God Who Sees and Sets Things Right
I Kings 21:1–10, (11–14), 15–21a

As soon as Jezebel heard that Naboth had been stoned and was dead, Jezebel said to Ahab, "Go, take possession of the vineyard of Naboth the Jezreelite, which he refused to give you for money; for Naboth is not alive, but dead." As soon as Ahab heard that Naboth was dead, Ahab set out to go down to the vineyard of Naboth the Jezreelite, to take possession of it. Then the word of the LORD came to Elijah the Tishbite, saying: Go down to meet King Ahab of Israel, who rules in Samaria; he is now in the vineyard of Naboth, where he has gone to take possession. (1 Kings 21:15–18)

Here we have before us a story of power being abused in the worst way. King Ahab had ambitious plans to acquire the family vineyard of Naboth the Jezreelite. Ahab was willing to give him a larger plot of land in an even better place. The king's offer was exceedingly generous, so it did not occur to him that Naboth would be foolish enough to refuse it. Mortified and humiliated, Ahab, sulking, lay on his bed and turned his face to the wall when people spoke to him or offered him food. The villain in this passage at this point is not Ahab but his wife Jezebel, who was determined at all costs to get Naboth's vineyard for the king. Jezebel did not openly take the vineyard or kill Naboth outright; she devised a royal cover-up, but completely within the law, whereby Naboth could be framed and condemned for treason and blasphemy. The ruse worked! Naboth was condemned and stoned to death, just as Jezebel had ordered.

When Jezebel boastfully reported to Ahab that Naboth was dead, Ahab headed out to claim Naboth's property for the crown. There was nothing to stop him now!

Nothing, that is, but the word of the Lord—this Lord of power and might who sits high but looks down low.

Just as Ahab was about to claim his ill-gotten gains, the word of the Lord came to him through Elijah the prophet. Elijah forcefully opposed the royal practice of injustice and the arrogant use of power against the weaker members of society. Injustice is not simply an offense against human beings but an offense against God as well. God intervened on behalf of the slain Naboth.

In the end, the truth will out. Unjust powers will not have the last word in our broken world. Though innocents may suffer and die, God speaks through prophetic voices still today, taking up and adjudicating their cause. The God who intervenes is the God who is determined to act with justice and might on behalf of the oppressed.

God has promised never to leave or forsake the weaker members of any society. A theme that runs through the whole of Scripture is the willingness of this God to intervene on behalf of the downtrodden and abused. Though we may despair over pain and injustice in our world, we can trust that God sees what is happening and is working through his people to bring justice. God is indeed the God who sees and sets things right. Humans may temporarily usurp and thwart the just purposes of God, but in the end God will prevail.

Proper 7: A Change of Heart, Not a Change of Scenery
Luke 8:26–39

Then people came out to see what had happened, and when they came to Jesus, they found the man from whom the demons had gone sitting at the feet of Jesus, clothed and in his right mind. And they were afraid. . . . The man from whom the demons had gone begged that he might be with him; but Jesus sent him away, saying, "Return to your home, and declare how much God has done for you." So he went away, proclaiming throughout the city how much Jesus had done for him. (Luke 8:35, 38–39)

From the territory of the city of Gerasa, Luke describes a man from the town who was possessed by demons. His condition was one of melancholy associated with extreme antisocial and suicidal frenzy. This deranged man had fled from home and human society and found a ghoulish pleasure in living among the rock-hewn graves on the hillside. Night and day he cried out and gashed himself with stones. He was clearly disturbed, for it was considered to be a sign of madness when anyone spent the night in a place of graves. But when he saw Jesus he fell down before him and shouted at the top of his voice, "What have you to do with me, Jesus, Son of the Most High God?" It was in his encounter with the sovereign Lord that the demoniac's life was changed forever.

Jesus intervened and took a proactive stance on behalf of this troubled individual. He commanded the unclean spirits to come out of the man. He permitted them to enter a herd of swine feeding on the hillside where they plunged to their deaths. Soon thereafter Jesus had the man sitting at his feet, clothed and in his right mind.

Still uncertain of what to do with his newly restored life, the man begged Jesus to let him go with him. We are not sure why he wanted to follow Jesus. Maybe it was out of a sense of deep appreciation, or the thrill of a new challenge, or simply a desire to move on from a sordid and messy past. Whatever the reason, Jesus answered him in the negative. "No," said Jesus, "go home to your family and friends, and tell them what great things the Lord has done for you and how he has had compassion for you."

Return home! Return to the people who know you best and saw you at your worst. Jesus' no came in the interest of the demoniac's spiritual development. How easy it would have been for the healed demoniac to put his past behind him and head out with Jesus to new vistas far removed from the confused and sordid life he once lived before his community. The intervention of Jesus granted the man a new life but not necessarily a new direction.

Jesus intervenes in our lives to bring wholeness and completeness. However, his intervention does not always lift us out of difficult situations but instead empowers us to live with faithfulness and conviction in the midst of the ordinary and the familiar; in the midst of past failures and painful memories, in order that we may transform them with the promised aid and comfort of the Lord. To leave would be easy, but to return is both affirming and redemptive.

It was the demoniac's change of heart, not change of scenery, that served as a powerful witness to the power of God to make whole again; to make what had been useless useful once again. It is our changed lives once we return home that serves as a potent witness to what God is like and what God can do *to* and *for* our lives.

Proper 8: Intervening to Enlighten His Own
Luke 9:51–62

On their way they entered a village of the Samaritans to make ready for him; but they did not receive him, because his face was set toward Jerusalem. When his disciples James and John saw it, they said, "Lord, do you want us to command fire to come down from heaven and consume them?" But he turned and rebuked them. Then they went on to another village. (Luke 9:52b–56)

In the opening scene of this passage, Jesus sets his face to go to Jerusalem. "Set his face" echoes the song of the Suffering Servant of Isaiah 50:7: "Therefore I have set my face like a flint, and I know that I shall not be put to shame; he who vindicates me is near." Quoting from this Isaianic passage, Jesus seems to indicate that he expects strong opposition in Jerusalem. The direct way from Galilee to Jerusalem led through Samaria, but most Jews avoided it. For Jesus to take the road through Samaria on his way to Jerusalem is unusual. He understands full well that he is entering hostile territory. That notwithstanding, he sends his disciples ahead of him, and they enter a village of the Samaritans to make ready for his arrival.

Not necessarily to the disciples' surprise, but most certainly to their dismay, the villagers do not receive Jesus, because "his face was set toward Jerusalem." His attempt and subsequent rejection to find hospitality in a Samaritan village is a precursor of the opposition Jesus will face in Jerusalem. Jesus purposely injects himself into a historically messy situation. In his deliberate decision to pass through Samaria he is extending a hand of friendship to a people who are long-standing enemies of the Jews. In this case not only is hospitality refused, but the offer of friendship is spurned.

No doubt James and John believe they're doing a most praiseworthy thing when they offer to call in divine aid to blot out the villagers who reject Jesus. But Jesus saves his disciples from themselves and teaches them a lesson on tolerance and the fullness of the saving power of God! Jesus purposely goes through Samaria because he has every intention of taking his ministry to these despised, half-Jewish heretics. He has ministered to Jews and Gentiles, to social, ritual, and political outcasts, and now he makes an effort to extend that ministry in Samaria. Why? Because Jesus understands that there are many ways to God and that no person, no church, no denomination has a monopoly on the truths of God. Jesus' ministry to the outcasts and despised must become our own.

In a day of diversity, competing narratives, and differing contextual realities, the wideness of God's mercy must be seen in our ministries to people who are other and different. We may ask or expect God to intervene on behalf of "those like us," against those in whom we find fault. But God does not see as we see. Sometimes, when God intervenes, it is to correct and redirect us. It takes some humility to accept that kind of correction.

James and John desire to rain down fire on the villagers—much as we probably would, in response to that kind of rejection—but Jesus desires love, forgiveness, and mercy, and asks that we follow his example, difficult as it may be. It may be especially difficult when we have approached a situation with the best of intentions, aiming to show compassion and reconciliation, and our efforts are rebuffed. But Jesus checks his disciples' misguided anger by simply moving on to another village. In what situations might we need to humble ourselves today and accept that we may be the object, not the beneficiary, of God's correction?

Proper 9: A Humbling Intervention for a Proud Commander
2 Kings 5:1–14

Elisha sent a messenger to him, saying, "Go, wash in the Jordan seven times, and your flesh shall be restored and you shall be clean." But Naaman became angry and went away, saying, "I thought that for me he would surely come out, and stand and call on the name of the LORD his God, and would wave his hand over the spot, and cure the leprosy! . . . But his servants approached and said to him, "Father, if the prophet had commanded you to do something difficult, would you not have done it? How much more, when all he said to you was, 'Wash, and be clean'?" (2 Kings 5:10–11, 13)

From time to time we all stand in need of a divine intervention that will bring hope and healing into our lives. No matter how many accomplishments and accolades come our way in life, no one is absolutely free of difficulty. Naaman, commander of the army of the king of Aram, was a great man with a problem. Naaman suffered from leprosy. He, like all of humanity from time to time, had to contend with a humbling negative in his life, for which he seems not even to dare hope for healing.

When God stepped in to make his situation better, we don't see an intervention on par with Elijah's gruesome condemnation of Ahab or Jesus' dramatic exorcism, complete with pigs running over a cliff. No, what we see is God working through plain, ordinary people. Though Naaman's restoration came *from* God, it came *through* a servant girl and then through a prophet's errand boy. This slave girl could have kept her knowledge of healing to herself. She was after all a captive, enslaved by the Aramean army. Yet, when she saw the suffering of Naaman, she empathized with him and volunteered that there was a prophet in Israel who could heal him. With this unpretentious word of advice, this young Israelite captive brought hope to one of her captors.

We are often surprised at the ways in which God chooses to intervene in our lives in order to bring healing and restoration. So surprised, in fact, that we find the way forward hard to imagine. Naaman was too proud to believe the simplicity of his cure ("Go wash in the Jordan seven times"), and the king of Israel was too fearful to believe himself to be a conduit of Naaman's blessing ("Am I God to give death or life?").

Although Naaman's visit brought grave anxiety to the king of Israel, the prophet Elisha was unfazed by the visit and was sure of his place in God's providential healing of Naaman. So sure was Elisha that he did not even bother to come out of his house when Naaman arrived, but sent a messenger instead. The prophet's confidence in God was perceived as a slight by Naaman. Naaman's national pride was hurt, because if he had to wash himself in a river, he did not understand why he couldn't stay home and wash himself in one of the great rivers of Damascus. His healing, however, was not in a river but in obedience to the command of the prophet. Naaman had originally expected the prophet to stand before him, but on the heels of his obedience to the simple commands of the prophet he now stood before Elisha, helped and healed.

We talked last week about being humble enough for God to correct us. We must also be humble enough to accept God's blessings in the simple, surprising ways they may come. Oh for a faith that will be open to the action of God and obedient to God's will and God's way!

Summer Series 2: Action Required

Four Parts: Proper 10 through Proper 13

God has done so much for us. Luke's Gospel shows us what God expects of us in return.

CLEOPHUS J. LaRUE

Series Overview

Many people of faith have no problem talking about what God has done *for* us and for our salvation, but have a problem when it's time to talk about what God *requires* of us. God's claim on our lives calls on us to engage in a radically different way of loving, seeing, and doing in the world. Each text of this series involves a story of people being challenged to discover the importance of acting on what they believe in a fitting manner. It is also the case that acting faithfully in service to God's commands often involves paradoxes and reversals that make it more difficult to discern how best to act in keeping with God's will.

Tips and Ideas for This Series

Like the attention-grabbing stamp one sees on bills and office communications, a bold, red "Action Required" graphic would make a

	Sermon Title	Focus Scripture	Theme
Proper 10	Love Unconditionally	Luke 10:25–37	The Good Samaritan: Love others, no matter who they are.
Proper 11	Stop and Listen	Luke 10:38–42	Mary and Martha: Those who would serve must also sit and learn.
Proper 12	Be Persistent in Prayer	Luke 11:1–13	The Persistent Friend: Ask and you will receive.
Proper 13	Look beyond Yourself	Luke 12:13–21	The Rich Fool: Self-interest is to lose perspective of God's greater desire for us.

simple and compelling visual for bulletins and screens. Though Micah 6:8 is not among the texts for this series, using those familiar words "What does the Lord require of you?" would make a powerful addition to liturgy and musical choices for the series. Consider using the hymn by that name composed by Jim Strathdee.[1]

Proper 10: Love Unconditionally
Luke 10:25–37

"But a Samaritan while traveling came near him; and when he saw him, he was moved with pity. He went to him and bandaged his wounds, having poured oil and wine on them. Then he put him on his own animal, brought him to an inn, and took care of him. The next day he took out two denarii, gave them to the innkeeper, and said, 'Take care of him; and when I come back, I will repay you whatever more you spend.' Which of these three, do you think, was a neighbor to the man who fell into the hands of the robbers?" He said, "The one who showed him mercy." Jesus said to him, "Go and do likewise." (Luke 10:33–37)

Though we are unsure of the precise circumstances that give rise to the lawyer's question, we do know that immediately after addressing his disciples with a blessing (Luke 10:21–24), Jesus is confronted by a lawyer. The lawyer, supposedly well versed in the Pentateuch, attempts to embarrass Jesus. He tries to show him up before the public. It is clear both from verse 25 ("a lawyer stood up to test Jesus") and verse 29 ("But wanting to justify himself") that this man's motives were far from honorable. The lawyer inquires about eternal life, and Jesus' explanatory parable about the exemplary Samaritan shows that one's obligation to engage in acts of mercy and love should include all, not just certain people.

The lawyer asks his question about who his neighbor is, in hopes of having the strong ethical demand of the law qualified. But in his answer, Jesus demonstrates that the real issue is not *whom* we should serve but *that* we serve. The issue is not how we *see* others but how we are to *act* toward them. We are not to ask who our neighbor is; we are to be a neighbor. Thus Jesus answers the question by turning the onus back on the lawyer, saying in effect, "Do not worry about the other guy, but focus on being a neighbor yourself."

Jesus answers the lawyer's question by teaching about the practical love of God and of one's neighbor. The Samaritan lifted up by Jesus in this parable is ceremonially unclean, socially outcast, and religiously a heretic. In other words, he is the very opposite of the lawyer—as

1. Jim Strathdee, "What Does the Lord Require of You?" in *Glory to God* (Louisville, KY: Westminster John Knox Press, 2013), 70.

are the priest and the Levite. The Samaritan is the last type of person the lawyer would expect to be the climactic figure who resolves the story. This parable must have been a shocking one to its first audience, shattering their categories of who are and are not the people of God. What this narrative powerfully presents to us is an example of acting in love without preference or partiality, and expecting nothing in return.

The parable is intended to provoke. The violence done to the traveling Judean is overt: he is stripped, beaten, and left half dead. However, the priest and Levite, out of concern for safety and ritual purity, pass by on the other side. Most shocking, however, is the discovery that a despised Samaritan, himself most at risk in this dangerous no-man's-land of deserted territory, takes the chance of stopping, looking, and—increasing his own vulnerability—leading a man on his beast to an inn. It is the hated enemy, according to Jesus, who is the hero with a human heart—who puts his money where his mouth is, in a manner of speaking.

The point of this parable is not who deserves to be cared for but rather the action required of us, to treat everyone we encounter—however frightening, alien, naked, or defenseless—with compassion. "You go and do the same," says Jesus.

Proper 11: Stop and Listen
Luke 10:38–42

But Martha was distracted by her many tasks; so she came to him and asked, "Lord, do you not care that my sister has left me to do all the work by myself? Tell her then to help me." But the Lord answered her, "Martha, Martha, you are worried and distracted by many things; there is need of only one thing. Mary has chosen the better part, which will not be taken away from her." (Luke 10:40–42)

This story of two sisters' hospitality to Jesus illuminates our understanding of what it means to be hospitable. Jesus' response to Martha makes clear that the "one thing necessary" for hospitality is attention to the guest rather than a domestic performance. If the guest is a prophet, the appropriate response is listening to God's word. Mary positions herself at the feet of the Lord, where she attentively listens to his words. To be seated at the feet, especially to hear someone's word, is to act as a pupil. Martha's preoccupation with work and her resentment of her sister who sat at the feet of Jesus causes her to break the rules of hospitality more radically than does her sister, for she asks a stranger to intervene in a family rivalry.

Both women act; Martha acts to prepare for dinner, while Mary acts to sit and learn at the feet of the Master. Martha is making elaborate preparations for the honored guest. She is secretly vexed with her sister Mary because the latter enjoys the privilege of hearing Jesus, whereas she cannot bring herself to do the same, for fear the meal she intends to serve Jesus will not be good enough. Jesus does not chide Martha for preparing a good meal but for allowing her mind to be distracted and drawn away to things that, for the moment, are unimportant.

Many of us, like Martha, have a thousand things to attend to, but no quiet hour for the Scriptures, for prayer, or for public worship. On the other hand, the action on the part of Mary—sitting at the feet of Jesus to hear his word—is all that we hear about her in this narrative. Yet it is the chief thing for which the narrative is told. By her attentive hearing Mary helps to make the seat of Jesus a pulpit, her own humble place at his feet a pew, and the whole room a chapel in which the mercy of God is proclaimed and a sanctuary where God himself draws nigh to the sinful heart with grace. It's not that Martha's actions are unnecessary, but in terms of priorities, Mary's desire to spend time with Jesus is the more fitting choice between the two women that day. Mary's meditative act is declared by Jesus to be a fitting use of her time.

The challenge for both women is a matter of priorities. Which is more important? The busyness of the mundane, or time spent in the presence of the Master? Time spent in matters of the heart deepen and enrich our understanding of the ways of God and God's will for the created order. The moment Jesus indicates that he has something to impart to Mary, she turns from everything else to sit and to be absorbed in what he says.

To receive the words of Jesus with a humble heart is better than any work, labor, sacrifice, or suffering. To close the ear, to turn the heart away, no matter what the cause, is bound to be fatal, for it shuts off the life stream on which our faith depends. Far too many people operate under the illusion that mere busyness means substantial gains are being made from our endeavors. Mary is applauded for her simple act of devotion and love to the Lord.

Proper 12: Be Persistent in Prayer
Luke 11:1–13

And he said to them, "Suppose one of you has a friend, and you go to him at midnight and say to him, 'Friend, lend me three loaves of bread; for a friend of mine has arrived, and I have nothing to set before him.' And he answers from within, 'Do not bother me; the door has already been locked, and my children are with me in bed; I cannot get up and give you anything.' I tell you, even though he will not get up and give him anything because he is his friend, at least because of his persistence he will get up and give him whatever he needs." (Luke 11:5–8)

In today's reading, Jesus teaches us to pray simply and directly to God as Father. After teaching what has come to be known as the Lord's Prayer, Jesus instructs that we are to pray not in fear and doubt but rather in confident trust that God delights to answer our prayers, just as human parents take delight in answering the requests of their children.

The brief parable of the Persistent Friend makes this concise point: God is approachable and should be approached often and with confidence. Confident assurance in what? That God will act and answer the prayers of those who approach him. The importunate friend approaches a friend at midnight and asks a favor. Jesus in effect is asking, "Which of you has the nerve to wake up a neighbor—and his family—at midnight to ask for bread for a visiting friend?" In our approach to God, Jesus is encouraging us to have the kind of shamelessness in the friend's request. The friend who has the guest on his hands will not take no for an answer; implied is the awakened neighbor's realization that he and his family will not get sleep until he acts on the persistent request of the friend.

Jesus bolsters the faith we should have in approaching God in prayer with the following commands and promises: "Ask, and it will be given you; search, and you will find; knock, and the door will be opened for you. For everyone who asks receives, and everyone who searches finds, and for everyone who knocks, the door will be opened" (Luke 11:9). These verses appear to be addressed to people who are fearful, because they see themselves as unworthy, or who are passively resigned, because they believe that nothing can change. The claims made here by Jesus are extravagant and broad. They fling open God's wide door of mercy. The promises are lavish and assertive, and they encourage everyone to come with confidence and assurance to the throne of grace, hesitating not for a moment to ask of God the desires of our hearts.

While we know that many requests we make of one another (especially when they involve waking someone in the middle of the night!) are not answered positively, and that this seems to be equally true of God, Jesus insists that God is ready to respond; therefore people must not be shy in presenting their requests. No matter how many times we have petitioned God, we must trust that God hears and is in fact eager to give us what we need. Jesus promises that God will act, in love, on behalf of those who come to him in prayer. The action is binary. We have a part to play in approaching God with confidence; God, according to Jesus, takes delight in answering our prayers. Therefore our approach should be frequent and filled with confidence that God will act.

Proper 13: Look beyond Yourself
Luke 12:13–21

Then [Jesus] told them a parable: "The land of a rich man produced abundantly. And he thought to himself, 'what should I do, for I have no place to store my crops?' Then he said, 'I will do this: I will pull down my barns and build larger ones, and there I will store all my grain and my goods. And I will say to my soul, 'Soul, you have ample goods laid up for many years; Relax, eat, drink, be merry.' But God said to him, 'You fool! This very night your life is being demanded of you. And the things you have prepared, whose will they be?' So it is with those who store up treasures for themselves but are not rich toward God." (Luke 12:16b–21)

In the parable of the Rich Fool, Jesus is asked to resolve a family dispute over an inheritance, but he refuses to be put in the middle of the dispute. Though the rich man appeals to Jesus for advice, his personal affairs, not the teaching of Jesus, are the supreme thing for him. Even though Jesus refuses to intervene into this dispute between two brothers, he does warn against covetousness—the greedy desire to have and to hold earthly possessions for ourselves. A person's life—the actual life within them—says Jesus, is not determined by earthly possessions. Jesus then tells this parable about a rich man, in order to help the disciples fully to grasp his warning about greed and self-absorption in its fullness.

Jesus does not denigrate the rich man's wealth, as it is no crime to be rich. There is no hint of wrongful, ill-gotten riches. He is not pictured as an extortionist or an oppressor of poor laborers. He is apparently an honest man of standing in his community, admired by many. His land has produced so well that he cannot accommodate his crop. His problem is that he is filled with covetousness; he lives for earthly things. They and they alone fill his life and his soul. In his abundance he thinks he has *space* trouble, but Jesus points out that he really has *soul* trouble. He thinks his problem is merely that he has no place to store his tremendous harvest. In his mind, the "action required" is not the sharing of his abundance but the building of new barns to store it all!

In the man's trite conversation with himself and his soul, he does not thank God for this gift. He does not consider what God would have him do with this blessing. Moreover, his complaint of a lack of space is really hollow, for secretly he is full of elation at the increase of his wealth. His actions are all directed toward himself. "I" and "my" run through his short conversation no less than eleven times. Such language suggests exclusive self-interest.

While we may not talk aloud to our souls, the silent language of our acts may be the same as the rich man's. We come too much to rely on our many possessions and overlook the fact that our lives are ultimately dependent on the will of God. The rich man seems unmindful of the fact that he is not the only actor in the game of life. The rich man's actions based on self-love run counter to the actions of God. The contrast is striking. The rich man acts out of the belief that he has "ample goods laid up for many years." But God's actions are based on his sovereign will that "this night" the man's soul will be required of him. The years of ease this rich man eagerly anticipates are cut short by the one who has authority over his life. Our actions and ways of being in the world are but a part of life's calculations.

In the end, God requires of us not just loving action but our very souls. When we stand before God, will our record show acts of love and mercy or acts of self-interest? Here a rich man acts out of love for himself, but God acts out of love for the entire created order. In our free will, we can act in nearly any way we choose. Will we choose the way of God?

Summer Series 3: Pillars of Faith

Four Parts: Proper 14 through Proper 17

What does it mean to have faith, to trust in things not seen?

CLEOPHUS J. LaRUE

Series Overview Hebrews 11:1 describes faith as "the assurance of things hoped for, the conviction of things not seen." This series begins with the Heroes Hall of Fame in Hebrews 11 as an introduction to the "pillars of faith" we can all follow—not just those individuals but the markers of faith we can follow as we strive to live with such utter trust in God. In Hebrews and in Jesus' teachings in the Gospel of Luke, we learn how faith empowers us to see the unseen, boldly seek God in the face of opposition, and trust God to accomplish things we can only imagine.

Tips and Ideas for This Series The title of this series refers to pillars of faith not just as people but as principles. Invite "pillar" members of your congregation to share a bit about their own faith each week. Display four small pedestals across the front of your worship space, adding each week an object symbolic of the message—eyeglasses for Proper 15 and a china place setting for Proper 17, for example.

	Sermon Title	Focus Scripture	Theme
Proper 14	How Faith Acts	Heb. 11:1–3, 8–16	Faith lets us lay hold of the promises of God.
Proper 15	The Eyes of Faith	Heb. 11:29–12:2; Luke 12:49–56	Faith helps us to discern the will of God and see what lies ahead.
Proper 16	Faith in the Face of Opposition	Luke 13:10–17	Faith enables God to accomplish great things through us.
Proper 17	Faith Enough to Wait	Luke 14:1, 7–14	Faith trusts that we have not been overlooked by God.

Now faith is the assurance of things hoped for, the conviction of things not seen. Indeed, by faith our ancestors received approval. By faith we understand that the worlds were prepared by the word of God, so that what is seen was made from things that are not visible. (Hebrews 11:1–3)

This eleventh chapter of Hebrews has often been described as one of the grand chapters of the Bible. Others have characterized it as the Heroes Hall of Fame. All the names listed in this chapter had one thing in common: great faith. They all believed the unseen, they all trusted a promise, and they all held out and held on to things for which they had to wait and hope. The word "faith," quite common throughout Scripture, can and does have many meanings. Consequently, the verses we read today do not by any means exhaust what can be said about faith, but they do provide in a highly focused way the essential *characteristics* of faith that inform the understanding of the writer of Hebrews.

The first part of the author's definition relates to the aiming at and attainment of hoped for goals. Those goals are constantly repeated in different settings: divine favor, salvation, inheritance, a promised blessing, and so forth. The manifestation of each person's faith is lifted before us as testimony to their endurance and stamina: Enoch attains immortality (v. 5); Noah, salvation (v. 7); Abraham, a place of inheritance (vv. 8–9); Sarah, a promised offspring (v. 12); Joseph, burial in Israel (v. 22); and Moses, a reward (v. 26). By their faith they aimed at and attained hoped-for goals.

The second part of the definition—the conviction of things not seen—relates to the perception of imperceptible realities. Here the author continually highlights instances where individuals perceived through faith a reality not apparent to the senses. Those unseen realities were so clearly laid before them that they held on to them until the end. Such things are the fact of creation (v. 3), the existence and providence of God (v. 6), impending disaster (v. 7), the transcendent and future city (v. 10), and God's power to raise the dead (v. 15). The author argues in the first part of the definition that it takes faith for hopes to come true, and in the second part that it takes faith to put the believer in touch with what is most real, though it is unseen.

Moreover, the writer argues that faith involves both feelings and the will to choose (decisive behavior) and conscious intellectual activity (trusting belief). It involves doing and believing; both components are essential to faith. In contemporary times the believer is called on to trust in the promises of God. That unyielding faith allows those promises to come true. It involves an act of the will, in terms of a heartfelt choice to trust and a cognitive assent that God is faithful. We must take care not to trivialize the faith of which this writer speaks. The ancients had faith that God could be trusted and that God's promises concerning the ultimates of their lives would be realized. Their trust was not in the fleeting, transitory things of this world but in the long-hoped-for redemptive purposes of God. The trust that they exhibited concerned itself with salvation, promises, and rewards put before them by none other than God. Their faith in God allowed them to believe some things to be true where the evidence was not sufficient to establish such knowledge. That faith is ours to claim here and now.

Proper 15: The Eyes of Faith
Hebrews 11:29–12:2; Luke 12:49–56

He also said to the crowds, "When you see a cloud rising in the west, you immediately say, 'It is going to rain'; and so it happens. And when you see the south wind blowing, you say, 'There will be scorching heat'; and it happens. You hypocrites! You know how to interpret the appearance of earth and sky, but why do you not know how to interpret the present time?" (Luke 12:54–56)

Today we consider two texts that are admittedly a bit frightening. In Hebrews, we read the conclusion of the Heroes Hall of Fame section in which more ancient figures—judges, kings, and prophets—are hailed for their faith in the face of persecution, even to the point of flogging, imprisonment, stoning, and being sawn in half. The "world was not worthy" of those saints who endured so much. By contrast, Jesus finds the people to whom he speaks far too lackadaisical, unprepared for the trials that are to come.

Jesus warns that the times to come will not be peaceful or easy. It is to inaugurate judgment that he has come, Jesus says, claiming that the necessary signs of the judgment are already present, if only people will open their eyes to them. One way this judgment can be clearly seen is in the motif of division. Jesus applies this image of the division of loyalties within families to the context of his ministry. One of the consequences of his ministry will be the destruction of conventional family bonds. Even in the close-knit family people will divide over the question of their relationship to Jesus. Jesus then proceeds to rebuke the crowds because they can read the weather signs but cannot read the spiritual signs to see what is ahead of him, of them, and of the nation of Israel. All the signs point to him being the Redeemer and to the crisis that is coming in Jerusalem with Israel's rejection of him—a crisis that in the days ahead will catch them all up in a fiery judgment ripe with division and struggle.

To Jesus it is all very clear, yet they are blind to it. The present time is a time of critical decision that they cannot escape. To side with him is to side with God. To see with him, however, can happen only through the eyes of faith. As the writer of Hebrews attests, even those who are commended for their faith haven't yet received what was promised, for it comes when we follow Jesus. Like that "great cloud of witnesses," who modeled faith in what was not yet seen, Jesus admonishes his followers not to open their physical eyes but rather to open the eyes of faith, which will allow them to see and attest to the unseen things of the Spirit. It takes the eyes of faith to see in Jesus God's redemptive work for humankind. It takes utter trust in God to become actively involved in that work as witnesses to the rule and reign of God upon the earth and the consequences that flow from that inbreaking activity of God.

Proper 16: Faith in the Face of Opposition
Luke 13:10–17

Now he was teaching in one of the synagogues on the sabbath. And just then there appeared a woman with a spirit that had crippled her for eighteen years. She was bent over and was quite unable to stand up straight. When Jesus saw her, he called her over and said, "Woman, you are set free from your ailment." When he laid his hands on her, immediately she stood up straight and began praising God. (Luke 13:10–13)

What kind of courage does it take to step forward in faith before a disapproving crowd? The woman in today's text found it within her to step forward at the invitation of Jesus to be healed, even though she knew her healing would meet with the disapproval of the authorities who represented organized religion in her day. This miracle story of a bent-over woman, crippled for eighteen years, appears only in Luke. No setting is given other than a synagogue on a Sabbath.

The woman was bent over and quite unable to stand up straight, says Luke. This expression described a condition in which the woman's spine was curved so that she could not straighten up. She no doubt was a familiar figure to the synagogue attendants, since she had been in this condition for eighteen years. Jesus "called her over," focusing her attention on the fact that he was going to do something about her spinal condition. In some cases of healing, Jesus spoke only to the person. In other cases, he touched the part of the body that was to be healed, for instance, ears, tongue, eyes, arm. He laid his hands on this woman's curved spine. His touch no doubt added to his words another stimulus to faith. This one through whom God's power was working had actually touched her. Her cure was immediate. The result was that she began to praise God for what Jesus had done.

The religious authorities of her day were not happy with her blessing. According to the traditional laws of the Jews, the practice of medicine or of healing in any way was illegal on the Sabbath. While there is no indication that the ruler of the synagogue was uninterested in a cure for the unfortunate woman, he was indignant that Jesus had healed on the Sabbath. In the presence of the woman who had just been healed, the ruler of the synagogue turned to the crowd, as if to fend off any further requests for healing, and told them that there were six work days out of seven and that if anyone desired healing they should return on one of those days.

Surely this distressed woman must have known the requirements of the law, and perhaps anticipated the disapproval that was to come, but at the request of Jesus she stepped forward to be healed. She moved toward Jesus with utter dependence on almighty God. In defiance of religious law and authorities, she trusted God to be at work in her life in a marvelous way. Jesus honored her faith by touching her and healing her. She had the faith, and God had the power. We must not only expect great things from God but also attempt great things for God. So often, God is willing, but we are reticent. Faith requires we make a bold response to the initiatives of almighty God. There is no telling what God can do if and when we believe!

Proper 17: Faith Enough to Wait
Luke 14:1, 7–14

"When you are invited by someone to a wedding banquet, do not sit down at the place of honor, in case someone more distinguished than you has been invited by your host; and the host who invited both of you may come and say to you, 'Give this person your place,' and then in disgrace you would start to take the lowest place. But when you are invited, go and sit down at the lowest place, so that when your host comes, he may say to you, 'Friend, move up higher'; then you will be honored in the presence of all who sit at the table with you. For all who exalt themselves will be humbled, and those who humble themselves will be exalted." (Luke 14:8–11)

In this parable, recorded only in Luke, Jesus openly rebuked those who sought the best seats at the banquet. He admonished those who apparently believed that they could be honored in a way befitting them only if they were seated higher than anyone else at the banquet. How often do we jostle for positions, reach for telling titles, and run for top places, in order to signal to the rest of the world that we have arrived? Why are we so inclined to believe that unless we take measures to highlight our work, signal our importance, and sit where we can be seen, the people will misunderstand how we rank in the kingdom of God? Time and again we are told that pride goes before destruction and a haughty spirit before a fall. Jesus consistently spoke of how the exalted will be humbled and the humbled will be exalted. Still we lack enough faith to believe that we have not been forgotten by God and that our contributions to the work of God on the earth will be made known in the unfolding purposes of God.

Jesus had been invited to this dinner party at the home of a leader of the Pharisees and had already made a bit of a scene by once again healing on the Sabbath. Then he called out how the guests were choosing to seat themselves in places of honor. The word translated "places of honor" is literally "the first couches" or the "chief couches." Having noticed how they raced to seat themselves in the most prominent positions at the banquet, Jesus instructed the guests to practice humility rather than pride. The path of pride is so tempting because many of us suffer from a desire for immediate gratification in terms of the acknowledgment of our work and worth.

Jesus recognized the realities of such an honor-shame culture and advised against taking the first seats. He then outlined a more prudent strategy when one is entering a banquet room. Because honor was socially determined in that day, if one's claim to honor failed to be reciprocated by one's audience, public humiliation followed. It is better, said Jesus, to have honor bestowed on you by another than to make a bid for honor that may not be granted. Jesus taught that to be invited to a place of greater importance than one had chosen is most gratifying. On the other hand, to be called down and assigned to a place of lesser importance results only in humiliation.

What is clearly being taught here is a paradox, one that can be received only through the eyes of faith: the way down is up, and the way up is down. It takes great faith to believe that appearing to do the opposite is the very thing that will grant, in time, the desired outcome. Scripture is filled with such admonitions: if you want to have, you must give away; if you want to live, you must be willing to die; if you want to be great, you must be willing to become a servant. We've seen such paradoxes throughout this series: in faith, there is conviction without proof; we can see what the eyes cannot; the crippled are made courageous; and finally, greatness comes not through self-elevation but through humility and faith in God

Fall Series: What Disciples Do

Twelve Parts: Proper 18 through Proper 29 (Reign of Christ)

Christ's followers are known not as much by what they believe as what they do.

MARTIN THIELEN

Series Overview

Although Christians are often identified by what they believe, Jesus seemed to care more about what his followers did. Faith practices, along with theological beliefs, are crucial to Christianity. These twelve weeks of Ordinary Time offer an excellent opportunity to explore what disciples do: practice generosity, wrestle with God, and take their faith public, to name a few. The themes for Propers 20 and 21 lend themselves well to a brief stewardship campaign. Although twelve weeks is a lengthy sermon series, this series tackles a wide variety of engaging topics and will not feel repetitive or too long. Instead, church members will be challenged to live out the exciting call of Jesus, "Follow me."

	Sermon Title	Focus Scripture	Theme
Proper 18	Disciples Take Faith Seriously	Luke 14:25–33	Move beyond nominal Christianity.
Proper 19	Disciples Seek People for Christ and Church	Luke 15:1–10	Evangelize with integrity.
Proper 20	Disciples Resist Greed	Luke 16:1–13	Love God more than money.
Proper 21	Disciples Practice Generosity	1 Tim. 6:6–19	Practice generous financial stewardship.
Proper 22	Disciples Take Their Faith Home	2 Tim. 1:1–14	Pass on faith to our family.
Proper 23	Disciples Make the Best of "Babylon"	Jer. 29:1, 4–7	Redeem our current circumstances.
Proper 24	Disciples Wrestle with God	Gen. 32:22–31	Grapple with God and faith.

	Sermon Title	Focus Scripture	Theme
Proper 25	Disciples Don't Judge	Luke 18:9–14	Leave judgment to God.
All Saints *(observed in place of Proper 26)*	Disciples Affirm Resurrection Hope	Eph. 1:11–23	Celebrate All Saints' Day.
Proper 27	Disciples Live by Faith	Job 19:23–27a	Practice faith in difficult times.
Proper 28	Disciples Take Their Faith Public	Isa. 65:17–25	Faith impacts both the personal realm and the public realm.
Proper 29 (Reign of Christ)	Disciples Give Ultimate Allegiance to Christ	Col. 1:11–20	Make Christ the center of everything.

Tips and Ideas for This Series

The weeks following Labor Day are a prime time for those whose church attendance has grown lax to recommit to regular attendance, and this series on practical, relatable faith practices is a perfect way to engage Christians new and old. Consider a design for promotion and worship visuals with the words "What Disciples Believe," with "Believe" crossed out and "DO" boldly stamped over it, emphasizing that faith is about more than intellectual assent to certain ideas. The order of worship for each week could use the following outline as a thematic structure:

- Disciples Gather to Worship God
- Disciples Listen to the Word of God
- Disciples Respond to the Call of God
- Disciples Celebrate at the Table of God
- Disciples Depart to Serve God

Proper 18: Disciples Take Faith Seriously
Luke 14:25–33

Now large crowds were traveling with him; and he turned and said to them, . . . "Whoever does not carry the cross and follow me cannot be my disciple." (Luke 14:25, 27)

The biggest threat to the Christian faith in America is not secularism or the growing number of "nones" and "dones." Rather, the biggest threat to vibrant faith is nominal Christianity. Shallow and noncommittal faith does not breed vital believers and congregations. Who would be attracted to such a lame faith? As one young man said, "If all my religion is going to change is my Sunday schedule, then I'm not interested. I want something that is going to change my finances, my sex life, the way I work, the way I treat my family, the way I treat others, and the way I use my time."

This young man understands something important. Authentic faith impacts every part of our lives: how we spend our money; how we work; how we treat our family, friends, neighbors, and coworkers; how we use our time. Authentic faith impacts how we treat the environment and how we treat the poor. Authentic faith impacts our character, ethics, and values. In short, Christian disciples are called to take their faith extremely seriously.

Jesus makes this clear in today's text. In this passage, Jesus tells his followers to count the cost of discipleship. He clearly tells us that we need to be "all in," or it's not worth the effort. According to Jesus, our commitment to him is more important than our possessions and even more important than our family. There is a serious cost to discipleship. But there are also incredible rewards, including a life of meaning, purpose, service, and vitality.

I once heard a story about a seventh-grade girl in Texas. She ran on the junior-high girls' track team at her school. Due to bad weather an important Saturday track meet got postponed to the next Saturday. However, this girl had already committed to be on a church mission trip on that Saturday. She went to her track coach and told him about the conflict. He told her, "Your teammates are counting on you, and you can't let them down. You are either here for the meet, or you turn in your uniform." After many tears and much deliberation, she went to her coach, handed him her uniform, and walked away. That evening she explained her decision to her family. She said, "This is about God. And God is more important than sports."

This seventh-grade girl gets the point of discipleship. She understands that faith is primary and that our commitment to God outweighs every other priority in our life. In short, she counted the cost. She decided to be "all in." As we explore these next few months how disciples live out their faith, I hope we'll decide to be "all in" too.

Proper 19: Disciples Seek People for Christ and Church
Luke 15:1–10

Now all the tax collectors and sinners were coming near to listen to him. And the Pharisees and the scribes were grumbling and saying, "This fellow welcomes sinners and eats with them." So he told them this parable: "Which one of you, having a hundred sheep and losing one of them, does not leave the ninety-nine in the wilderness and go after the one that is lost until he finds it? When he has found it, he lays it on top of his shoulders and rejoices. And when he comes home, he calls together his friends and neighbors, saying to them, 'Rejoice with me, for I have found my sheep that was lost.'" (Luke 15:1–6)

Many mainline Christians are suspicious of evangelism. A lot of us have been turned off by inappropriate and obnoxious forms of evangelism, so we neglect it all together. However, reaching lost people was a huge priority for Jesus. He once said, "For the Son of Man came to seek out and to save the lost" (Luke 19:10). This is a crucial passage of Scripture. Jesus said his primary mission in life was to reach lost people.

We see that clearly in today's text. In this passage, Jesus tells the story about a shepherd with one hundred sheep. One got lost, so he left the other ninety-nine to find the lost one and rejoiced when he found it. The story is followed by a similar parable about a lost coin. Seeking the lost is a central theme of the gospel.

Unfortunately, most churches focus almost all their attention, time, and money on the ninety-nine sheep and the nine coins. But in today's text and other passages, Jesus challenges us to seek the lost sheep and the lost coin. The fact is that Christians and churches *can* do evangelism with integrity in at least three ways.

First, Christians and churches can engage in *lifestyle evangelism.* One of the best ways we can witness to our faith is to live it. When we live like Christ—when we live lives of love, grace, compassion, integrity, service, and social justice—we testify that we are people of faith. People see our lives and think, *If this is what Christianity looks like, I'm interested.* Francis of Assisi once said, "Preach the gospel at all times; use words if necessary."

Second, Christians and churches can engage in *relational evangelism.* I'm not talking about a sales pitch or pressuring people or annoying them. But all of us, in our network of relationships, can find opportunities to share our faith naturally with people we know. It can be as simple as letting folks know that our faith is important to us, grounds us, gives us meaning and purpose, helps us through hard times, and motivates us to serve others. This kind of relational evangelism can be done naturally in our conversations with others and can make a huge impact on people.

Third, Christians and churches can engage in *invitational evangelism.* In short, this is a "come and see" method of evangelism. The most common form of invitational witness is to invite people to church for worship or a special event or to a small group. This is a simple and easy way to share faith. And it's exceptionally effective. Studies constantly show that about 90 percent of people first visit a church because somebody they know invited them to come.

I once heard about a man who was asked, "Is Jesus Christ your personal Savior?" He replied, "No, I prefer to share him." This news is too good to keep to ourselves.[1]

Proper 20: Disciples Resist Greed
Luke 16:1–13

"No slave can serve two masters; for a slave will either hate the one and love the other, or be devoted to the one and despise the other. You cannot serve God and wealth." (Luke 16:13)

Mark Twain once said, "It ain't the parts of the Bible that I can't understand that bother me, it is the parts that I do understand."

I thought about that quote while reading this text. Luke 16:1–12 is extraordinarily difficult to understand. Various interpretations exist, and you can read about them in almost any commentary. Some interpreters believe the manager cheated his master by discounting the debts. Others say the manager simply reduced interest payments that were not allowed by Jewish law; therefore he did nothing inappropriate. The text is not clear. However, the parable's conclusion in verse 13 is *not* difficult to understand. Jesus says we cannot love God and money at the same time.

Why does Jesus condemn materialism so harshly? Many reasons can be given. For example, when money is given first place in our lives, we are guilty of practicing idolatry, placing things above God. When we prioritize material possessions, we also do great damage to God's creation. And when we love money more than God, ultimately we waste our lives in a worthless pursuit to accumulate more and more stuff—stuff we think we need but that ultimately becomes a burden and is thrown away.

I once heard an old Indian parable about a guru who had a star disciple. He was so pleased with the man's spiritual progress that he left him on his own. The disciple lived in a little mud hut. His only clothing was a loincloth, a small covering around his midsection. He lived simply, begging for his food. Each week, the disciple washed his loincloth and hung it out to dry. One day he came back to discover the loincloth torn and eaten by rats. He begged the villagers for

---

1. For two stories about evangelism (one negative example and one positive one) from this author, visit www.GettingReady ForSunday.com, click on "Stories," and find "The Restaurant" and "Welcome to Our Church." Additional stories can also be found to illustrate most of the sermons in this series.

another loincloth, and they gave it to him. But the rats ate that one too. So he got himself a cat.

That took care of the rats, but now when he begged for his food, he had to beg for milk for his cat. So he got a cow to feed his cat, but now he had to beg for hay to feed his cow. So, in order to feed his cow, he decided to till and plant the ground around his hut. But soon he found no time for contemplation, so he hired servants to tend his farm.

Overseeing the laborers became a chore, so he got married to have a wife to help him with the farm. His wife didn't like the mud hut he lived in and demanded a real house. So the man had to grow even more crops and hire more servants to keep his wife happy. In time, the disciple became the wealthiest man in the village.

Years later this man's guru was traveling nearby, so he stopped in to see his old student. He was shocked at what he saw. Where once stood a simple mud hut, there now loomed a palace surrounded by a vast estate worked by many servants. "What is the meaning of this?" he asked his disciple. "You won't believe this, sir," the disciple replied. "But there was no other way I could keep my loincloth."[2]

It's easy to get sucked into a materialistic lifestyle of accumulation. But making the accumulation of stuff the center of our life is cancer to our soul. As Jesus said, "You cannot serve God and wealth." Obviously, all of us need at least some possessions. But we must never make them the focus of our lives.

Proper 21: Disciples Practice Generosity
1 Timothy 6:6–19

As for those who in the present age are rich, command them not to be haughty, or to set their hopes on the uncertainty of riches, but rather on God who richly provides us with everything for our enjoyment. They are to do good, to be rich in good works, generous, and ready to share, thus storing up for themselves the treasure of a good foundation for the future, so that they may take hold of the life that really is life. (1 Timothy 6:17–19)

In recent years we've heard a lot about the "1 percent." These are the richest of the rich. Recent research shows that by the year 2016 the 1 percent will own more than half of the world's assets. This growing inequality of wealth is extremely troubling and threatens to cause global turmoil in the future.

2. This story is shared in my recent book: Martin Thielen, *Searching for Happiness: How Generosity, Faith, and Other Spiritual Habits Can Lead to a Full Life* (Louisville, KY: Westminster John Knox Press, 2016).

So in today's text, when Paul refers to "those who in the present age are rich," is he speaking about the 1 percent? Yes and no. The 1 percent would certainly be included in this statement. However, compared to conditions in the ancient world and compared to today's global financial landscape, any American in the middle class is clearly "rich." So when Paul talks about the rich, he's talking about most American clergy and most members of U.S. congregations. And Paul's words to us are clear: God expects us to be generous with our financial assets.

Unfortunately, most American Christians are not particularly generous. Last year I read a book titled *Passing the Plate: Why American Christians Don't Give Away More Money.*[3] After extensive research in giving patterns, the authors come to the sad conclusion that most American Christians are "remarkably ungenerous." For example, 20 percent of U.S. Christians give absolutely nothing to charity. They spend every dime on themselves. Of the 80 percent who do give to charity, most give very little, usually only 1 to 2 percent of their total income. In the author's opinion, the primary reason Christians give so little is because we live in a radically consumerist culture, one intentionally designed to create permanent discontentment so that we'll buy more and more stuff. In short, we spend so much money on ourselves that we have little left for God and for people in need.

In this kind of hyperconsumerist context, the words of 1 Timothy are especially relevant. In the text, Paul says:

> There is great gain in godliness combined with contentment; for we brought nothing into the world, so that we can take nothing out of it; but if we have food and clothing, we will be content with these. But those who want to be rich fall into temptation and are trapped by many senseless and harmful desires that plunge people into ruin and destruction. For the love of money is a root of all kinds of evil, and in their eagerness to be rich some have wandered away from the faith and pierced themselves with many pains. (1 Tim. 6:6–10)

By resisting greed, living simply, and being content with the basics, Christian disciples can afford to be generous. When we do practice generosity, our text tells us we will store up true "treasure" that leads to "life that really is life" (1 Tim. 6:19). So, in the end, generosity is not a burden but a blessing. Generosity is a life-giving practice. As Proverbs 11:25 puts it, "A generous person will be enriched, and one who gives water will get water."

---

3. Christian Smith and Michael O. Emerson, *Passing the Plate: Why American Christians Don't Give Away More Money* (New York: Oxford University Press, 2008).

Proper 22: Disciples Take Their Faith Home
2 Timothy 1:1–14

I am reminded of your sincere faith, a faith that lived first in your grandmother Lois and your mother Eunice and now, I am sure, lives in you. (2 Timothy 1:5)

We are currently exploring "What Disciples Do." One thing disciples do is take their faith home. In other words, they live out their faith in their family life. It's impossible to deal with the subject of the Christian family in one sermon. So in this particular message, we'll focus on the important topic of passing on our faith to our children.

Someone once said, "The church is always one generation away from extinction." Given that reality, it's crucial that parents successfully pass on their faith to their children. Of course, it's not the job only of parents to pass on faith. It's also the job of other family members, family friends, and our church family. When we baptize a child in the church, the entire congregation takes a vow to help raise and nurture that child in Christian faith. So passing on our faith to our children is relevant not only for parents—but for all believers. Virtually every follower of Christ has at least some opportunity to influence the faith of children.

A good example of a family that passed on their faith to their children can be found in this text from 2 Timothy. Although a young man, Timothy played a key leadership role in the life of the early church. In today's text we learn that Timothy had a strong and "sincere" faith. Where did that faith come from? As we see in verse 5, it came from his family, especially his mother Eunice and his grandmother Lois. Timothy's family was a family that successfully passed on their faith. How did they do it?

First, they lived it. As Paul said to Timothy, "I am reminded of your sincere faith, a faith that lived first in your grandmother Lois and your mother Eunice and now, I am sure, lives in you." Timothy's mother and grandmother lived out sincere faith in front of Timothy, and that deeply impacted his faith. The fact is that faith is caught more than it is taught. When parents live out Christian faith, values, and standards in front of their children, their children soak it up.

If you read further in 2 Timothy, you discover that Timothy's family not only lived their faith in front of Timothy but also directly taught him their faith. In 3:15 Paul says, "From childhood you have known the sacred writings that are able to instruct you for salvation through faith in Christ Jesus." Although it's critical that we live out our faith in front of our children, we must also teach them about the Christian faith, which can be done both at home and in the church. Praying together, reading the Bible together, and talking about how

Jesus would have us live and respond to certain situations are all valuable ways to pass on your faith to others in your family.

I once heard about a teenage boy from a devout Christian home. The young man, like his parents, took his faith extremely seriously. One day his youth minister asked him, "Why is faith so important to you?" The teenage boy replied, "I don't know. I guess it just runs in the family."

Proper 23: Disciples Make the Best of "Babylon"
Jeremiah 29:1, 4–7

Thus says the LORD of hosts, the God of Israel, to all the exiles whom I have sent into exile from Jerusalem to Babylon: Build houses and live in them; plant gardens and eat what they produce. Take wives and have sons and daughters; take wives for your sons, and give your daughters in marriage, that they may bear sons and daughters; multiply there, and do not decrease. But seek the welfare of the city where I have sent you into exile, and pray to the LORD on its behalf, for in its welfare you will find your welfare. (Jeremiah 29:4–7)

In today's text we find the people of Israel in exile in a foreign land called Babylon. They felt unhappy, discouraged, and restless. So they constantly fantasized about returning to Israel. If only we could go home again, they thought, then they would be happy. If only we could leave Babylon and return to Israel, then life would be good. In that context God sent them some advice through a letter written by the prophet Jeremiah.

God's message to these restless exiles is clear. God said to the people, "Quit fantasizing about returning to Israel. Instead, make the best of what you have. Put down roots. Build homes. Plant crops. Have children and grandchildren. Enjoy life in Babylon and seek its welfare." It's interesting advice. The people of Israel want to go somewhere else, but God says to live life fully where you are. In short, God is saying, "Redeem the circumstances you find yourself in."

God knows that external circumstances such as geographical location play a very small role in our overall contentment. Contentment isn't about having a perfect job, a perfect spouse, belonging to a perfect church, living in the perfect house, or attending a perfect school. Such things don't exist. They never have, and they never will. In one way or another, we always live in Babylon. External circumstances are never perfect. Therefore, one of the secrets of a good life is learning to make the best out of the circumstances we have.

We would do well to listen to God's advice to these restless exiles in Babylon. Perhaps a few of us need to make a change—get a new job, move to a new city. That's not necessarily a bad thing. But very few of us need those kinds of changes in order to be happy. Most of us need to follow God's advice and flourish in Babylon. We need to make the best of our job, make the best of our marriage and family, make the best of our church, and make the best of our life, not just tolerating the imperfect but investing ourselves in it. In other words, most of us need to quit fantasizing about living a perfect life somewhere else and start living fully right where we are—in spite of the imperfections. Only then will we overcome our restlessness and find contentment.

You may have seen the classic old movie *City Slickers*. It tells the story of a restless middle-aged man who is considering changing jobs. Near the end of the film his wife says to him, "Honey, if you really want to change jobs, it's OK with me." With great insight he replies, "I don't need a new job. I just need to do my current job better." Sometimes all that needs to change is your perspective.

Proper 24: Disciples Wrestle with God
Genesis 32:22–31

Jacob was left alone; and a man wrestled with him until daybreak. . . . Then the man said, "You shall no longer be called Jacob, but Israel, for you have striven with God and with humans, and have prevailed. . . . So Jacob called the place Peniel, saying, "For I have seen God face to face, and yet my life is preserved." (Genesis 32:24, 28, 30)

It's hard to know what to make of this text. In this strange story, Jacob wrestled with a stranger all night long. Eventually the wrestling partner blessed Jacob. But he also gave him a limp. We don't know the identity of this unnamed stranger. At one point the text says that Jacob wrestled with a "man." However, that's not Jacob's understanding at all. Jacob believed his wrestling partner was God. Indeed, at the end of the long night of wrestling, Jacob said, "For I have seen God face to face."

Rather than attempt a factual or rational explanation of this story, it's best to allow the mystery and ambiguity to remain. Whatever actually happened that night with Jacob, the image of wrestling with God is a powerful metaphor, one that proves true for all authentic disciples.

I once went to a worship service where the congregation recognized their graduating seniors. The pastor read from today's text, spoke eloquently about wrestling with God, and then gave the final blessing. On behalf of the congregation he said to the seniors, "Our hope and prayer for you today is that you will spend the rest of your life wrestling with God."

True disciples are not satisfied with simplistic answers and pious religious platitudes, so they spend their lives wrestling with God, especially during times of struggle. For example, after years of praying for a child with no results, Abraham and Sarah wrestled with God. Frustrated with leading the people of Israel through the wilderness, Moses wrestled with God. Sick in mind, body, and spirit, Job wrestled with God. Hiding for his life in a desert cave, his enemies in hot pursuit, David wrestled with God. Crying out to God in anger and anguish, the prophet Jeremiah wrestled with God. Believing God had abandoned him, the psalmist wrestled with God. After repeatedly praying for healing but not receiving it, the apostle Paul wrestled with God. In anguish over his inability to believe Jesus was alive, Thomas wrestled with God.

Wrestling with God is a crucial activity for true disciples. Sometimes we need to wrestle with God about our theological beliefs, both personally and as a church. At other times we need to wrestle with God concerning our relationships at home, work, and church. Faithful disciples must constantly wrestle with God about the implications of the gospel on our personal lives, the life of our church, and society as a whole. Discipleship can sometimes be hard and complex work. Therefore, our wrestling match with the Almighty is never done.

So don't be afraid to wrestle with God. Instead, join Jacob in the match. Jacob's wrestling match did result in a limp. But it also brought a great blessing. And in the struggle, Jacob saw God "face to face." Such is the mystery, the pain, and the beauty of wrestling with God.

Proper 25: Disciples Don't Judge
Luke 18:9–14

He also told this parable to some who trusted in themselves that they were righteous and regarded others with contempt: "Two men went up to the temple to pray, one a Pharisee and the other a tax collector. The Pharisee, standing by himself, was praying thus, 'God, I thank you that I am not like other people—thieves, rogues, adulterers, or even like this tax collector.'" (Luke 18:9–11)

In this text, Jesus points out two characteristics of toxic faith that true disciples attempt to avoid. Unfortunately these two traits of unhealthy religion still exist today, and disciples are called to resist them.

The first attribute is self-righteousness. As we see in the opening words of the text, Jesus' parable was addressed to those "who were confident of their own righteousness" (Luke 18:9 NIV). The Pharisee in this story clearly felt superior to other people, especially the sinners whom he mentioned—robbers, adulterers, and tax collectors. When he went into the temple, he essentially prayed, "Lord, I thank you that I'm better than everyone else." His prayer reeked of arrogance and self-righteousness. Unfortunately arrogant religion is still alive and well. A lot of religious people in today's world believe they alone have pure religion, and that makes them feel superior to others. In this text Jesus warns his followers to resist that kind of superior and arrogant religion.

The second characteristic of toxic religion that we see in this text is a judgmental spirit. In the opening words of the text, Luke speaks of people who "looked down on everybody else" (Luke 18:9 NIV). The Pharisee in this story exhibited severe judgment of others, including his fellow worshiper in the temple, a tax collector praying for mercy. Sadly, this kind of condemning and judgmental spirit can still be found among many Christians and churches today. Tragically, this judgmental attitude is one of the main reasons unchurched people cite for avoiding church.

In short, this text teaches us that authentic disciples avoid self-righteous judging of other people. Instead, they leave judgment to God. This is a major theme of Jesus in the New Testament. Jesus constantly told his disciples to avoid judging others. A good example can be found in the Sermon on the Mount:

> "Do not judge, so that you may not be judged. For with the judgment you make you will be judged, and the measure you give will be the measure you get. Why do you see the speck in your neighbor's eye, but do not notice the log in your own eye? Or how can you say to your neighbor, 'Let me take the speck out of your eye,' while the log is in your own eye? You hypocrite, first take the log out of your own eye, and then you will see clearly to take the speck out of your neighbor's eye." (Matt. 7:1–5)

Instead of practicing arrogant self-righteous judgment like the Pharisee in this parable, Jesus calls us to exhibit humility, like the tax collector in the story. In the parable the tax collector beat his chest in repentance and prayed, "God, be merciful to me, a sinner!" In the end, said Jesus, the tax collector "went down to his home justified rather than the other; for all who exalt themselves will be humbled, but all who humble themselves will be exalted."[4]

4. For numerous sermon illustrations from this author about judging others, visit www.GettingReadyForSunday.com, click on "Stories," and look for "Casting the First Stone," "Destructive Religion," "Getting the Ballast Right," and "Kick Him Out."

All Saints' Sunday: Disciples Affirm Resurrection Hope
Ephesians 1:11–23

I pray that the God of our Lord Jesus Christ, the Father of glory, may give you a spirit of wisdom and revelation as you come to know him, so that, with the eyes of your heart enlightened, you may know what is the hope to which he has called you, what are the riches of his glorious inheritance among the saints, and what is the immeasurable greatness of his power for us who believe, according to the working of his great power. (Ephesians 1:17–19)

Today's text lifts up the glorious resurrection hope that belongs to the saints of God. On this special day of the Christian year, disciples affirm their belief in "the communion of saints," including our hope for "the resurrection of the body, and the life everlasting." This hope is essential to our identity as disciples of Jesus Christ, who was resurrected and promises us the same. On this day when we remember the departed saints of the congregation, we celebrate the example of discipleship they provided us in life and the promise of resurrection we hope for in death.

Celebrating Holy Communion on All Saints' Day—especially when we utilize the All Saints' Day liturgy of the Great Thanksgiving found in our various denominational books of worship—helps affirm our hope that one day all the saints will gather around the great banquet table in the final kingdom of God. After all, while we mourn those who have passed on in the past year, we celebrate the life they and all of us will enjoy in the heavenly kingdom—a life of joy not sorrow, laughter instead of tears.

Susan was in the hospital, near death. Susan's sister was talking to another member of their family on a cell phone. The sister whispered softly into the phone, "You better come soon. She might not last much longer." Susan, who overheard this conversation, said, "I'm not ready to go yet." This made everyone feel uncomfortable, so they quickly changed the subject. But Susan stubbornly said again, much louder, "I'm not ready to go yet!" With that she sat up in the bed and said to the hospital chaplain, "Let's dance. How about Patsy Cline's 'Crazy'?" The chaplain left the room and managed to roust up a boom box and a Patsy Cline CD. When he returned to the room, Susan gave orders to push the furniture back. With a frail body, yet a strong resolve, Susan stood up, and she and the chaplain began to dance to Patsy Cline's "Crazy." At first, all the family members stared in disbelief. But then all of them found a partner and joined the dance. When the dancing was over, Susan went back to bed, and she died a few days later. At her funeral they both laughed and cried as they remembered the dance and how it illustrated her great love for life, even in death.

What an image! Dancing at death's door! But as Christian believers, we can do exactly that. We can—in spite of fear and pain and grief—face death with hope and promise. We, like Susan, can go out dancing. So, as we call the names of those who have died this past year, it's OK to shed tears and feel grief as we acknowledge the reality of our mortality. But let us remember that death is only half the story. The other half of the story is resurrection and eternal life. So, even in death, let us remember to dance.

Proper 27: Disciples Live by Faith
Job 19:23–27a

For I know that my Redeemer lives, and that at the last he will stand upon the earth; and after my skin has been thus destroyed, then in my flesh I shall see God. (Job 19:25–26)

Most of us are familiar with the story of Job. In spite of Job's faithfulness, he lost his health, his financial assets, and even his children. At first, Job exhibited remarkable faith (see Job 1:20–21 and 2:9–10). However, in the chapters that follow, we see a different story. We learn that Job's faith, like ours, questioned, struggled, and vacillated between belief and disbelief. At times Job even expressed anger toward God (see Job 10). However, in spite of his ordeal, Job continued to have faith. Even in his pain and anger, Job held on to his faith. Even when he was in agony and wanted to die, he affirmed faith in God. Even when he hurt at the core of his soul, he worshiped God. Even when he was deeply disappointed in God, Job cried out in today's text, "I know that my Redeemer lives" (Job 19:25). We find a similar expression of faith in the midst of suffering in chapter 13 when Job said, "Though he slay me, yet will I hope in him" (Job 13:15 NIV).

Disciples, even in difficult circumstances, live by faith. Their faith, like Job's, may struggle. But in the end they say, along with Job, "I know that my Redeemer lives." That kind of authentic faith, even in tough times, is enough to carry disciples through whatever circumstances come their way.

Job's faith in spite of his doubts, questions, and struggles reminds me of the following story from Elie Wiesel, a survivor of the Holocaust. Wiesel was just fourteen years old when he and his family were taken to a Nazi concentration camp. His story of the Holocaust is an awful story—a nightmare beyond belief. In a public television interview some years ago, Wiesel recalled a vivid experience at the concentration camp. A group of men in his barracks decided to have a trial—a trial unlike any trial you've ever heard of before. These men decided to try God for the horrors of the Holocaust. They had been men of faith, but their faith had profoundly disappointed them. So they decided to put God on trial for abandoning the Jewish people. Young Wiesel was asked to witness the proceedings. The charges were brought; the prosecutor listed them one by one: God's people had been torn from their homes, separated from their families, beaten, abused, murdered, and burned in incinerators. A defense was attempted. But in the end God was found guilty of abandoning his people, maybe even guilty of not existing.

When the trial was over, a dark and profound silence fell on the room. A few moments later the men realized it was time for the sacred ritual of evening prayer. At this point in the story, Wiesel recounted a remarkable fact. These men who had just found God guilty of abandoning them—these same men began to pray their evening prayer.

Proper 28: Disciples Take Their Faith Public
Isaiah 65:17–25

For I am about to create new heavens and a new earth. . . . No more shall there be in it an infant that lives but a few days, or an old person who does not live out a lifetime. . . . They shall build houses and inhabit them; they shall plant vineyards and eat their fruit. . . . They shall not labor in vain, or bear children for calamity. . . . The wolf and the lamb shall feed together. (Isaiah 65:17a, 20a, 23a, 25a)

When people think about discipleship, they usually think of it on a personal level. And there is much truth in that. Following Christ impacts our personal lives in profound ways, including our beliefs, values, relationships, ethics, and the way we spend our time and money. However, Christian discipleship also has profound social ramifications. In short, authentic disciples take their faith public, trying to make the world more like the kingdom of God. Isaiah 65 offers a powerful glimpse of this kingdom, God's dream for the world.

In this passage Isaiah says, "No more shall there be in it an infant that lives but a few days." In God's kingdom infant mortality does not exist. Therefore, issues like health insurance and prenatal care are kingdom issues. Isaiah then says, "No more shall there be . . . an old person who does not live out a lifetime." In God's kingdom, senior adults live long, productive, and healthy lives. Therefore, issues like Medicare and Social Security are kingdom issues. Isaiah adds, "They will build houses and inhabit them." In God's kingdom every person lives in a decent house. Therefore, issues like fair mortgage rates and affordable housing are kingdom issues.

Isaiah continues, "They shall plant vineyards and eat their fruit."

In God's kingdom food is plentiful. Therefore, healthy, accessible, and affordable food are kingdom issues. Isaiah goes on to say that people "shall long enjoy the works of their hands. They shall not labor in vain." In God's kingdom people get fairly compensated for their work. Therefore, issues like minimum wage and employee benefits are kingdom issues. People will not "bear children for calamity." In God's kingdom children thrive. Therefore, issues like child nutrition and early education are kingdom issues.

Finally, Isaiah dreams of the day when "the wolf and the lamb shall feed together, the lion shall eat straw like the ox. . . . They shall not hurt or destroy on all my holy mountain." In God's kingdom violence and warfare are contraband. Therefore, peacemaking between peoples and nations is a major kingdom issue.

Because these kinds of social issues matter to God, they should also matter to the people of God. Individual Christians, local churches, denominations, and the entire worldwide church must constantly seek ways to advance God's dream as found in Isaiah 65, both locally and around the world. This is not forcing Christian values on other people; it is letting your personal values inform how you interact with other people and work for the good of all people, regardless of their personal faith.

Christian leader and activist Jim Wallis often says that "faith should be personal but never private." While we cherish our beliefs and our relationship with Christ, disciples must also live their faith publicly, working to make God's kingdom a reality "on earth as it is in heaven."

Proper 29 (Reign of Christ): Disciples Give Ultimate Allegiance to Christ
Colossians 1:11–20

May you be made strong with all the strength that comes from his glorious power, and may you be prepared to endure everything with patience, while joyfully giving thanks to the Father, who has enabled you to share in the inheritance of the saints in the light. . . . He is the head of the body, the church; he is the beginning, the firstborn from the dead, so that he might come to have first place in everything. (Colossians 1:11–12, 18)

As we conclude our series on "What Disciples Do," we return to the very heart of what it means to be a disciple: to follow. "Following," by definition, means not being first, not being the leader, not being in charge. This can be a very uncomfortable thought for many of us. Americans value independence and self-sufficiency. We like feeling we are in complete control of our lives and destiny. However, as we see in today's text, disciples willingly give their ultimate allegiance to Jesus Christ, king and ruler over all creation.

Colossians 1 affirms an extremely high Christology. The text speaks of Christ's "glorious power" and speaks of "the kingdom of God's beloved Son." Jesus is the "image of the invisible God, the firstborn of all creation." Jesus is the "head of the body, the church." Finally, Christ is to "have first place in everything." In short, Jesus is the king of all creation, reigning over the universe, the church, and individual believers. Although this is ultimately an eschatological hope, disciples still attempt to make Christ their king here and now. Therefore, disciples of Jesus Christ boldly and willingly profess their ultimate allegiance not to self, family, or country—but to Jesus Christ the King.

I once heard about a teacher who, while cleaning out her attic, came upon a cross she purchased years earlier. It was a crucifix—a wooden cross with a silver image of Jesus hanging on it. She put the cross on her home office desk and left it there for several days. However, she needed some space to work, so she laid the cross on top of her checkbook and her bills. It made her think about how her faith should impact her finances. If her money were really under the cross of Jesus, what would she buy? What would she not buy? How much would she give away? How much would she keep?

A few days later, more papers accumulated on her desk, so she put the crucifix on top of some papers she was grading for her students. It made her think about how her faith should impact her work. If her job were really under the cross of Jesus, how would she treat her students? How would she treat her colleagues? How would she prepare for her classes?

A few days later the cross ended up on top of some recent photographs of her family and friends. It made her think about how her faith should impact her relationships. If her relationships were really under the cross of Jesus, what kind of wife would she be? What kind of mother? What kind of grandmother? What kind of friend?

For several weeks that cross lay on her desk, and it seemed to ask her, on a daily basis: "What difference does my faith make in my life? What impact does my religion have on my finances, my job, and my relationships?" In short it asked, "What would it mean for me to truly make Christ the King of my life?

Calendar of Sundays

This nine-year calendar enables you to plan for up to three lectionary cycles, as well as to observe some of the variation in the liturgical seasons. Due to the varying dates in Lent, Easter, and Pentecost, the seasons of Epiphany before and Ordinary Time after can vary in length. Therefore, you may see blanks in this calendar, denoting Sundays that are not observed in a particular year. For those Sundays that are observed only one or two of the three cycles included in this calendar, you may see "stand-alone sermon" in place of a series sermon. Stand-alone sermons are also suggested for certain weeks between series to allow for special services or a preacher's vacation or to address a topic independent of a longer series.

YEAR A

SUNDAY	SERIES	2016–17	2019–20	2022–23
First Sunday of Advent	A Geography of Salvation (Part 1)	Nov. 27	Dec. 1	Nov. 27
Second Sunday of Advent	A Geography of Salvation (Part 2)	Dec. 4	Dec. 8	Dec. 4
Third Sunday of Advent	A Geography of Salvation (Part 3)	Dec. 11	Dec. 15	Dec. 11
Fourth Sunday of Advent	A Geography of Salvation (Part 4)	Dec. 18	Dec. 22	Dec. 18
Christmas Eve	A Geography of Salvation (Part 5)	Dec. 24	Dec. 24	Dec. 24
First Sunday of Christmas	A Geography of Salvation (Part 6)	Dec. 25	Dec. 29	Dec. 25
Second Sunday of Christmas	*Stand-alone sermon*	Jan. 1	Jan. 5	Jan. 1
First Sunday after Epiphany	New Year, Same Promises (Part 1)	Jan. 8	Jan. 12	Jan. 8
Second Sunday after Epiphany	New Year, Same Promises (Part 2)	Jan. 15	Jan. 19	Jan. 15
Third Sunday after Epiphany	New Year, Same Promises (Part 3)	Jan. 22	Jan. 26	Jan. 22
Fourth Sunday after Epiphany	New Year, Same Promises (Part 4)	Jan. 29	Feb. 2	Jan. 29
Fifth Sunday after Epiphany	New Year, Same Promises (Part 5)	Feb. 5	Feb. 9	Feb. 5
Sixth Sunday after Epiphany	New Year, Same Promises (Part 6)	Feb. 12	Feb. 16	Feb. 12
Seventh Sunday after Epiphany	*Stand-alone sermon in 2017*	Feb. 19		
Transfiguration Sunday (last Sunday before Lent)	*Stand-alone sermon*	Feb. 26	Feb. 23	Feb. 19
First Sunday in Lent	Boot Camp for the Soul (Part 1)	Mar. 5	Mar. 1	Feb. 26
Second Sunday in Lent	Boot Camp for the Soul (Part 2)	Mar. 12	Mar. 8	Mar. 5
Third Sunday in Lent	Boot Camp for the Soul (Part 3)	Mar. 19	Mar. 15	Mar. 12
Fourth Sunday in Lent	Boot Camp for the Soul (Part 4)	Mar. 26	Mar. 22	Mar. 19
Fifth Sunday in Lent	Boot Camp for the Soul (Part 5)	Apr. 2	Mar. 29	Mar. 26
Sixth Sunday in Lent (Palm Sunday)	Boot Camp for the Soul (Part 6)	Apr. 9	Apr. 5	Apr. 2
Easter Sunday	Closer and Closer (Part 1)	Apr. 16	Apr. 12	Apr. 9
Second Sunday of Easter	Closer and Closer (Part 2)	Apr. 23	Apr. 19	Apr. 16
Third Sunday of Easter	Closer and Closer (Part 3)	Apr. 30	Apr. 26	Apr. 23
Fourth Sunday of Easter	Closer and Closer (Part 4)	May 7	May 3	Apr. 30
Fifth Sunday of Easter	Closer and Closer (Part 5)	May 14	May 10	May 7
Sixth Sunday of Easter	Closer and Closer (Part 6)	May 21	May 17	May 14
Seventh Sunday of Easter	Closer and Closer (Part 7)	May 28	May 24	May 21

SUNDAY	SERIES	2016–17	2019–20	2022–23
Pentecost Sunday	God's Creative Connection (Part 1)	June 4	May 31	May 28
Proper 4 or Trinity Sunday[1]	*Stand-alone sermon in 2023*			June 4
Proper 5	God's Creative Connection (Part 2)	June 11	June 7	June 11
Proper 6	God's Creative Connection (Part 3)	June 18	June 14	June 18
Proper 7	God's Creative Connection (Part 4)	June 25	June 21	June 25
Proper 8	God's Creative Connection (Part 5)	July 2	June 28	July 2
Proper 9	God's Creative Connection (Part 6)	July 9	July 5	July 9
Proper 10	Broken (Part 1)	July 16	July 12	July 16
Proper 11	Broken (Part 2)	July 23	July 19	July 23
Proper 12	Broken (Part 3)	July 30	July 26	July 30
Proper 13	Broken (Part 4)	Aug. 6	Aug. 2	Aug. 6
Proper 14	Broken (Part 5)	Aug. 13	Aug. 9	Aug. 13
Proper 15	Broken (Part 6)	Aug. 20	Aug. 16	Aug. 20
Proper 16	*Stand-alone sermon*	Aug. 27	Aug. 23	Aug. 27
Proper 17	*Stand-alone sermon*	Sept. 3	Aug. 30	Sept. 3
Proper 18	No Fair! (Part 1)	Sept. 10	Sept. 6	Sept. 10
Proper 19	No Fair! (Part 2)	Sept. 17	Sept. 13	Sept. 17
Proper 20	No Fair! (Part 3)	Sept. 24	Sept. 20	Sept. 24
Proper 21	The Enemies of Gratitude (Part 1)	Oct. 1	Sept. 27	Oct. 1
Proper 22	The Enemies of Gratitude (Part 2)	Oct. 8	Oct. 4	Oct. 8
Proper 23	The Enemies of Gratitude (Part 3)	Oct. 15	Oct. 11	Oct. 15
Proper 24	The Enemies of Gratitude (Part 4)	Oct. 22	Oct. 18	Oct. 22
Proper 25	The Enemies of Gratitude (Part 5)	Oct. 29	Oct. 25	Oct. 29
Proper 26 / All Saints' Observed	The Good News about Death (Part 1)	Nov. 5	Nov. 1	Nov. 5
Proper 27	The Good News about Death (Part 2)	Nov. 12	Nov. 8	Nov. 12
Proper 28	The Good News about Death (Part 3)	Nov. 19	Nov. 15	Nov. 19
Reign of Christ Sunday	The Good News about Death (Part 4)	Nov. 26	Nov. 22	Nov. 26

1. Trinity Sunday is observed the Sunday following Pentecost. Because it takes the place of the Proper that would fall on that Sunday (which could be a Proper 3, 4, 5, or 6), this resource does not include sermons for Trinity Sunday, in order to begin the series for the season after Pentecost on a consistent Proper.

YEAR B

SUNDAY	SERIES	2017–18	2020–21	2023–24
First Sunday of Advent	Coming Soon (Part 1)	Dec. 3	Nov. 29	Dec. 3
Second Sunday of Advent	Coming Soon (Part 2)	Dec. 10	Dec. 6	Dec. 10
Third Sunday of Advent	Coming Soon (Part 3)	Dec. 17	Dec. 13	Dec. 17
Fourth Sunday of Advent[2]	Coming Soon (Part 4)	Dec. 24	Dec. 20	Dec. 24
Christmas Eve	Coming Soon (Part 5)	Dec. 24	Dec. 24	Dec. 24
First Sunday of Christmas	Coming Soon (Part 6)	Dec. 31	Dec. 27	Dec. 31
Second Sunday of Christmas	*Stand-alone sermon in 2021*		Jan. 3	
First Sunday after Epiphany	Jesus, Man of Mystery (Part 1)	Jan. 7	Jan. 10	Jan. 7
Second Sunday after Epiphany	Jesus, Man of Mystery (Part 2)	Jan. 14	Jan. 17	Jan. 14
Third Sunday after Epiphany	Jesus, Man of Mystery (Part 3)	Jan. 21	Jan. 24	Jan. 21
Fourth Sunday after Epiphany	Jesus, Man of Mystery (Part 4)	Jan. 28	Jan. 31	Jan. 28
Fifth Sunday after Epiphany	Jesus, Man of Mystery (Part 5)	Feb. 4	Feb. 7	Feb. 4
Transfiguration Sunday (last Sunday before Lent)	Jesus, Man of Mystery (Part 6)	Feb. 11	Feb. 14	Feb. 11
First Sunday in Lent	Covenant (Part 1)	Feb. 18	Feb. 21	Feb. 18
Second Sunday in Lent	Covenant (Part 2)	Feb. 25	Feb. 28	Feb. 25
Third Sunday in Lent	Covenant (Part 3)	Mar. 4	Mar. 7	Mar. 3
Fourth Sunday in Lent	Covenant (Part 4)	Mar. 11	Mar. 14	Mar. 10
Fifth Sunday in Lent	Covenant (Part 5)	Mar. 18	Mar. 21	Mar. 17
Sixth Sunday in Lent (Palm Sunday)	Covenant (Part 6)	Mar. 25	Mar. 28	Mar. 24
Easter Sunday	Belong, Behave, Believe (Part 1)	Apr. 1	Apr. 4	Mar. 31
Second Sunday of Easter	Belong, Behave, Believe (Part 2)	Apr. 8	Apr. 11	Apr. 7
Third Sunday of Easter	Belong, Behave, Believe (Part 3)	Apr. 15	Apr. 18	Apr. 14
Fourth Sunday of Easter	Belong, Behave, Believe (Part 4)	Apr. 22	Apr. 25	Apr. 21
Fifth Sunday of Easter	Belong, Behave, Believe (Part 5)	Apr. 29	May 2	Apr. 28
Sixth Sunday of Easter	Belong, Behave, Believe (Part 6)	May 6	May 9	May 5
Seventh Sunday of Easter	*Stand-alone sermon*	May 13	May 16	May 12

2. When the Fourth Sunday of Advent falls on Christmas Eve, can use Advent 4 sermon for morning worship and Christmas Eve sermon for evening services, or simply eliminate the Advent 4 sermon.

SUNDAY	SERIES	2017–18	2020–21	2023–24
Pentecost Sunday	*Stand-alone sermon*	May 20	May 23	May 19
Proper 3 or Trinity Sunday	*Stand-alone sermon in 2018 and 2024*	May 27	May 30	May 26
Proper 4	God at Work (Part 1)	June 3	May 30	June 2
Proper 5	God at Work (Part 2)	June 10	June 6	June 9
Proper 6	God at Work (Part 3)	June 17	June 13	June 16
Proper 7	God at Work (Part 4)	June 24	June 20	June 23
Proper 8	God at Work (Part 5)	July 1	June 27	June 30
Proper 9	God at Work (Part 6)	July 8	July 4	July 7
Proper 10	No Longer Strangers (Part 1)	July 15	July 11	July 14
Proper 11	No Longer Strangers (Part 2)	July 22	July 18	July 21
Proper 12	No Longer Strangers (Part 3)	July 29	July 25	July 28
Proper 13	No Longer Strangers (Part 4)	Aug. 5	Aug. 1	Aug. 4
Proper 14	No Longer Strangers (Part 5)	Aug. 12	Aug. 8	Aug. 11
Proper 15	No Longer Strangers (Part 6)	Aug. 19	Aug. 15	Aug. 18
Proper 16	*Stand-alone sermon*	Aug. 26	Aug. 22	Aug. 25
Proper 17	A Faith That Works (Part 1)	Sept. 2	Aug. 29	Sept. 1
Proper 18	A Faith That Works (Part 2)	Sept. 9	Sept. 5	Sept. 8
Proper 19	A Faith That Works (Part 3)	Sept. 16	Sept. 12	Sept. 15
Proper 20	A Faith That Works (Part 4)	Sept. 23	Sept. 19	Sept. 22
Proper 21	A Faith That Works (Part 5)	Sept. 30	Sept. 26	Sept. 29
Proper 22	The Upside-Down Kingdom (Part 1)	Oct. 7	Oct. 3	Oct. 6
Proper 23	The Upside-Down Kingdom (Part 2)	Oct. 14	Oct. 10	Oct. 13
Proper 24	The Upside-Down Kingdom (Part 3)	Oct. 21	Oct. 17	Oct. 20
Proper 25	The Upside-Down Kingdom (Part 4)	Oct. 28	Oct. 24	Oct. 27
Proper 26 / All Saints' Observed	Gifts of Love (Part 1)	Nov. 4	Oct. 31	Nov. 3
Proper 27	Gifts of Love (Part 2)	Nov. 11	Nov. 7	Nov. 10
Proper 28	Gifts of Love (Part 3)	Nov. 18	Nov. 14	Nov. 17
Reign of Christ Sunday	Gifts of Love (Part 4)	Nov. 25	Nov. 21	Nov. 24

YEAR C

SUNDAY	SERIES	2018–19	2021–22	2024–25
First Sunday of Advent	Living "In Between" (Part 1)	Dec. 2	Nov. 28	Dec. 1
Second Sunday of Advent	Living "In Between" (Part 2)	Dec. 9	Dec. 5	Dec. 8
Third Sunday of Advent	Living "In Between" (Part 3)	Dec. 16	Dec. 12	Dec. 15
Fourth Sunday of Advent	Living "In Between" (Part 4)	Dec. 23	Dec. 19	Dec. 22
Christmas Eve	Living "In Between" (Part 5)	Dec. 24	Dec. 24	Dec. 24
First Sunday of Christmas	Living "In Between" (Part 6)	Dec. 30	Dec. 26	Dec. 29
Second Sunday of Christmas (Epiphany Observed)	A Light to Enlighten the Nations (Part 1)	Jan. 6	Jan. 2	Jan. 5
First Sunday after Epiphany	A Light to Enlighten the Nations (Part 2)	Jan. 13	Jan. 9	Jan. 12
Second Sunday after Epiphany	A Light to Enlighten the Nations (Part 3)	Jan. 20	Jan. 16	Jan. 19
Third Sunday after Epiphany	A Light to Enlighten the Nations (Part 4)	Jan. 27	Jan. 23	Jan. 26
Fourth Sunday after Epiphany	A Light to Enlighten the Nations (Part 5)	Feb. 3	Jan. 30	Feb. 2
Fifth Sunday after Epiphany	A Light to Enlighten the Nations (Part 6)	Feb. 10	Feb. 6	Feb. 9
Sixth Sunday after Epiphany	A Light to Enlighten the Nations (Part 7)	Feb. 17	Feb. 13	Feb. 16
Seventh Sunday after Epiphany	A Light to Enlighten the Nations (Part 8)	Feb. 24	Feb. 20	Feb. 23
Transfiguration Sunday (Last Sunday before Lent)	A Light to Enlighten the Nations (Part 9)	Mar. 3	Feb. 27	Mar. 2
First Sunday in Lent	God on the Move (Part 1)	Mar. 10	Mar. 6	Mar. 9
Second Sunday in Lent	God on the Move (Part 2)	Mar. 17	Mar. 13	Mar. 16
Third Sunday in Lent	God on the Move (Part 3)	Mar. 24	Mar. 20	Mar. 23
Fourth Sunday in Lent	God on the Move (Part 4)	Mar. 31	Mar. 27	Mar. 30
Fifth Sunday in Lent	God on the Move (Part 5)	Apr. 7	Apr. 3	Apr. 6
Sixth Sunday in Lent (Palm Sunday)	God on the Move (Part 6)	Apr. 14	Apr. 10	Apr. 13
Easter Sunday	God on the Move (Part 7)	Apr. 21	Apr. 17	Apr. 20
Second Sunday of Easter	Surprise! (Part 1)	Apr. 28	Apr. 24	Apr. 27
Third Sunday of Easter	Surprise! (Part 2)	May 5	May 1	May 4
Fourth Sunday of Easter	Surprise! (Part 3)	May 12	May 8	May 11
Fifth Sunday of Easter	Surprise! (Part 4)	May 19	May 15	May 18

SUNDAY	SERIES	2018–19	2021–22	2024–25
Sixth Sunday of Easter	Surprise! (Part 5)	May 26	May 22	May 25
Seventh Sunday of Easter	Surprise! (Part 6)	June 2	May 29	June 1
Pentecost Sunday	Surprise! (Part 7)	June 9	June 5	June 8
Proper 6	Intervention (Part 1)	June 16	June 12	June 15
Proper 7	Intervention (Part 2)	June 23	June 19	June 22
Proper 8	Intervention (Part 3)	June 30	June 26	June 29
Proper 9	Intervention (Part 4)	July 7	July 3	July 6
Proper 10	Action Required (Part 1)	July 14	July 10	July 13
Proper 11	Action Required (Part 2)	July 21	July 17	July 20
Proper 12	Action Required (Part 3)	July 28	July 24	July 27
Proper 13	Action Required (Part 4)	Aug. 4	July 31	Aug. 3
Proper 14	Pillars of Faith (Part 1)	Aug. 11	Aug. 7	Aug. 10
Proper 15	Pillars of Faith (Part 2)	Aug. 18	Aug. 14	Aug. 17
Proper 16	Pillars of Faith (Part 3)	Aug. 25	Aug. 21	Aug. 24
Proper 17	Pillars of Faith (Part 4)	Sept. 1	Aug. 28	Aug. 31
Proper 18	What Disciples Do (Part 1)	Sept. 8	Sept. 4	Sept. 7
Proper 19	What Disciples Do (Part 2)	Sept. 15	Sept. 11	Sept. 14
Proper 20	What Disciples Do (Part 3)	Sept. 22	Sept. 18	Sept. 21
Proper 21	What Disciples Do (Part 4)	Sept. 29	Sept. 25	Sept. 28
Proper 22	What Disciples Do (Part 5)	Oct. 6	Oct. 2	Oct. 5
Proper 23	What Disciples Do (Part 6)	Oct. 13	Oct. 9	Oct. 12
Proper 24	What Disciples Do (Part 7)	Oct. 20	Oct. 16	Oct. 19
Proper 25	What Disciples Do (Part 8)	Oct. 27	Oct. 23	Oct. 26
Proper 26 / All Saints' Observed	What Disciples Do (Part 9)	Nov. 3	Oct. 30	Nov. 2
Proper 27	What Disciples Do (Part 10)	Nov. 10	Nov. 6	Nov. 9
Proper 28	What Disciples Do (Part 11)	Nov. 17	Nov. 13	Nov. 16
Reign of Christ Sunday	What Disciples Do (Part 12)	Nov. 24	Nov. 20	Nov. 23

Contributors

Amy K. Butler is senior minister of The Riverside Church in New York City. Her sermons and essays appear on her website, www .talkwiththepreacher.org, as well as a column every two weeks on Associated Baptist Press.

Theresa Cho is copastor of St. John's Presbyterian Church in San Francisco. She has been published in *Christian Century, Sojourners, Christians for Biblical Equality,* Ecclesio.com, *The Presbyterian Leader*, and other websites. She blogs at www.theresaecho.com.

Robert S. Dannals is serving as interim rector at St. Bartholomew's Episcopal Church in New York City. Previously serving parishes in Texas, South Carolina, and North Carolina, he has worked to improve access to affordable housing in a variety of communities.

Magrey R. deVega is pastor of Hyde Park United Methodist Church in Tampa, Florida. He is leadership editor for Abingdon Press's Covenant Bible Study and author of *Awaiting the Already: An Advent Journey through the Gospels*.

Brian Erickson is pastor of Trinity United Methodist Church in Birmingham, Alabama, and author of *The Theological Implications of Climate Control: Reflections on the Seasons of Faith*.

Mihee Kim-Kort is an ordained minister in the Presbyterian Church (U.S.A.) and author of three books: *Making Paper Cranes: Toward an Asian American Feminist Theology; Streams Run Uphill: Conversations with Young Clergywomen of Color;* and *Yoked: Stories of a Clergy Couple in Marriage, Family, and Ministry*. She blogs at www.miheekimkort.com.

Jessica LaGrone is dean of the chapel at Asbury Theological Seminary and author of several Bible studies, including *Namesake: When God Rewrites Your Story* and *Broken and Blessed: How God Changed the World through One Imperfect Family.*

Cleophus J. LaRue is Francis Landey Patton Professor of Homiletics at Princeton Theological Seminary in Princeton, New Jersey. He is the author of *The Heart of Black Preaching* and the editor of *Power in the Pulpit: How America's Most Effective Black Preachers Prepare Their Sermons.*

Jacqueline J. Lewis is minister of Middle Collegiate Church in the East Village of Manhattan, New York City, and executive director of The Middle Project, an institute that prepares ethical leaders for a more just society. She is author of *The Power of Stories: A Guide for Leaders in Multi-Racial and Multi-Cultural Congregations* and a contributor to *The Huffington Post.*

Katherine Willis Pershey is an associate minister of the First Congregational Church in Western Springs, Illinois, and author of *Any Day a Beautiful Change: A Story of Faith and Family.* She was one of the founding editorial board members of *Fidelia's Sisters*, a publication of The Young Clergy Women Project, and is a board member and frequent contributor to the *Christian Century.* She blogs at www.katherinewillispershey.com.

Paul Rock is pastor of Second Presbyterian Church in Kansas City, Kansas, and coauthor with Bill Tammeus of *Jesus, Pope Francis, and a Protestant Walk into a Bar: Lessons for the Christian Church.*

Martin Thielen is pastor of First United Methodist Church in Cookeville, Tennessee, and the author of *What's the Least I Can Believe and Still Be a Christian?*; *The Answer to Bad Religion Is Not No Religion*; and *Searching for Happiness: How Generosity, Faith, and Other Spiritual Habits Can Lead to a Full Life.* His preaching and worship website is www.GettingReadyForSunday.com.

Winnie Varghese is a priest and director of community outreach at Trinity Wall Street, an Episcopal church in Manhattan. She has been active in peace and justice work as a board member of the Episcopal Peace Fellowship and a writer for *The Witness* magazine. She blogs at www.huffingtonpost.com/rev-winnie-varghese.

CPSIA information can be obtained
at www.ICGtesting.com
Printed in the USA
BVOW04s0304141017
497609BV00008B/141/P